AF594452

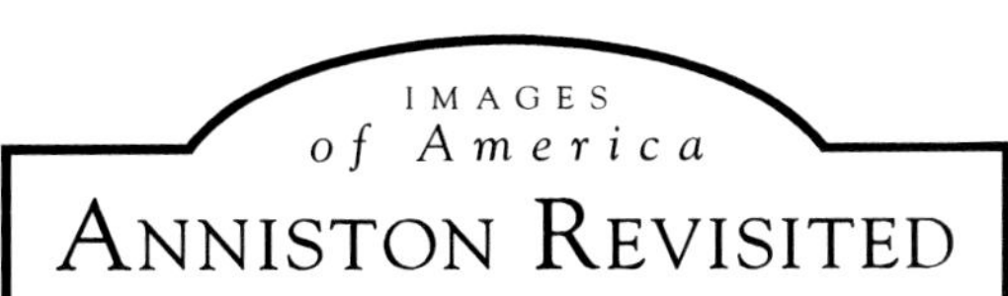
IMAGES
of America
ANNISTON REVISITED

On the Cover: The Silver Moon Hotel & Cafe was located at 1016 Noble Street, next to the Calhoun Barber Shop. The cafe, opened around 1913 by Greek immigrants, was on the first floor, and rooms to rent were on the second floor. By 1930, the Silver Moon was replaced by Lloyd's Sweet Shop. Members of the Calhoun County Demonstration Girl's Career Club, forerunner of the Farmers' Cooperative Extension 4-H Program, pose in front of the building around 1919. (Russell Brothers Collection.)

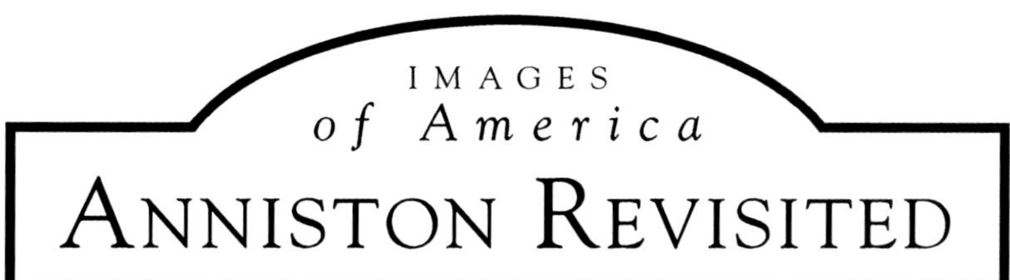

Kimberly O'Dell

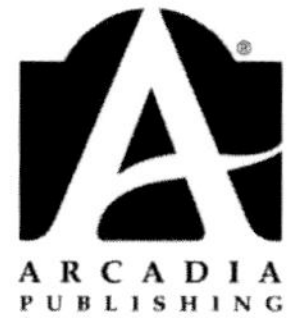

ISBN 978-1-4671-1475-2

Published by Arcadia Publishing
Charleston, South Carolina

Printed in the United States of America

Library of Congress Control Number: 2015936395

For all general information, please contact Arcadia Publishing:
Telephone 843-853-2070
Fax 843-853-0044
E-mail sales@arcadiapublishing.com
For customer service and orders:
Toll-Free 1-888-313-2665

Visit us on the Internet at www.arcadiapublishing.com

This book is dedicated to my two favorite Annistonians—Mom and Dad.

Contents

Acknowledgments		6
Introduction		7
1.	"The Model City"	9
2.	The Business District	31
3.	Life and Arts	81
4.	Outside the City Limits	109
Bibliography		127

ACKNOWLEDGMENTS

It has been over 15 years since *Calhoun County* and *Anniston* were published, but several people who were instrumental in those books also assisted with this volume. I would like to thank the Public Library of Anniston–Calhoun County for sharing its historic photograph collections, with special thanks to Teresa Kisor, Tom Mullins, Linda Dukes, and Shane Spears, whose assistance was invaluable.

I would also like to thank Lance Johnson Studio and Jim Johnson for use of the Russell Brothers Collection.

I am eternally grateful to several Annistonians for the use of their personal archives: Peggy Saxon Wright, Redge and Jeannie Thagard, and Callie Kunkel. In addition, I want to thank Brian McVeigh, Lydia Rollins, and Jesse Darland for their contributions, and Sherry Snider for proofing the manuscript.

Finally, I would like to thank my friends and family for their support, suggestions, and research assistance. I am forever indebted to them for sharing this journey with me.

Unless otherwise specified, all photographs are courtesy of the Russell Brothers Collection. The other photographs in this volume appear courtesy of the Estate of Roy Young (ERY), the Library of Congress (LOC), Public Library of Anniston–Calhoun County (PLACC), Public Library of Anniston–Calhoun County, Banks Collection (PLACC-BC), Redge P. Thagard (RPT), Peggy Saxon Wright (SAX), Noble Street Baptist Church (NSBC), and Callie R. Kunkel (CRK).

Introduction

Industrialists Samuel Noble and Daniel Tyler created the Woodstock Iron Company as a closed town that provided for all the workers' needs, including houses, churches, schools, and a company store. The company operated as a self-sufficient town from 1879 to 1883. When Noble decided to open the town to the public, he originally chose the name Annie's Town, in honor of Annie Tyler Scott, the wife of railroad president Alfred Tyler and daughter-in-law of founder Daniel Tyler. Over time, Annie's Town evolved to Anniston as it rapidly became an iron, steel, and textile town operating around the clock.

As commerce grew, railroads became the lifeline for Anniston. The town was on the route of the Selma, Dalton & Rome Railroad, which eventually was purchased by the East Tennessee, Virginia & Georgia Railroad. Around 1883, the Georgia Pacific Railroad was given land from the Woodstock Iron Company for a right-of-way to come into Anniston, with the agreement that the railroad would build repair shops, roundhouses, and a depot. In 1889, the Louisville & Nashville (L&N) began operating a railroad line in Anniston.

With relatively easy access via railroads, the mountains surrounding the valley were an ideal training location for the military. In 1898, the US Army established Camp Shipp just to the north of Anniston to train and quarter troops who were deployed to Cuba during the Spanish-American War. When a training area for the 1912 US National Guard Training Exercises was needed, Anniston was chosen to host the Southern Maneuvers training at Camp Pettus. In 1917, this area became the site of a training camp for National Guard units. When war broke out, Camp McClellan was constructed to train soldiers during World War I. By 1929, the camp was made into a permanent fort. This new designation led to economic prosperity and population growth for the city of Anniston.

From the 1890s to the 1950s, Anniston was the fifth-largest city in Alabama. In the 1920s, Anniston had five cast-iron foundries, which allowed the "Soil-Pipe Capital of the World" to produce 50 percent of the total cast-iron soil pipes and fittings made globally.

The textile mills expanded production, and the US government decided to locate the Anniston Army Depot, also known as Anniston Ordinance Depot, to the west of the city in 1942. The depot helped pull the city and surrounding county out of the Great Depression and served as one of the largest employers in the area.

The Women's Army Corps was transferred to Fort McClellan nine years after the end of World War II. The military complex continued to expand when the Chemical Corps Training Command was built at Fort McClellan and Anniston Army Depot was enlarged. By 1960, Anniston was at an all-time population high of over 33,000.

Anniston's population began to drop in the 1970s, due in part to economic decline. The soil-pipe industry was no longer viable, due to the increased use of plastic pipes. Textile mills began to close in the 1980s, and Anniston's economy suffered from a lack of diversity. Anniston was dealt another blow when Fort McClellan was selected for closure by the 1995 Base Realignment and Closure Commission. A decommissioning date was set for 1999.

Noble and Tyler had envisioned a "utopian city," but Anniston has faced several difficult issues in her history, including segregation and toxic waste. Like all Southern cities of the time, Anniston had been segregated from its earliest days. There were few racial incidents of note until one involving black soldiers stationed at Camp Shipp in 1899. The main racial strife in the city arose in the 1960s. A bus carrying Freedom Riders was burned a few miles from town on Mother's Day 1961. As a result, the city developed a forum for discussing racial issues, and, in 1963, the biracial Human Relations Council was created. This paved the way for an end to legal segregation. Racial tensions flared again in the early 1970s, leading to the establishment of the Committee of Unified Leadership.

As if racial strife had not already proven toxic for Anniston, the moniker "Toxic Town, USA" has been another difficult feature to overcome. In the 1990s, toxic conditions were discovered from polychlorinated biphenyls (PCBs) manufactured by Monsanto Chemical Company for almost 50 years only a few miles outside the city. Those PCBs were released into the surrounding creeks, contaminating the town's soil and air. Residents faced related health problems, including cancer and respiratory issues. Live chemical agents were also used for training purposes by the Chemical Corps stationed at Fort McClellan, and the Anniston Army Depot's igloos housed thousands of chemical weapons such as mustard gas. With the leaking potential of the igloos, the US government built a chemical-weapons incinerator to destroy the munitions in the 1990s. The incinerator completed destruction of the munitions in 2012. A year later, it was closed and demolished. As a result of various toxic exposures, the cleanup of the Anniston environment has been a long and arduous process. Many people still suffer the consequences of early transgressions.

Even though Anniston was known primarily as an industrial city and a military installation, culture and the arts were always a part of its rich fabric. Anniston has hosted a community theater company since the 1930s, as well as the annual Knox Concert Series. In the 1970s, Anniston took the lead in founding the Alabama Shakespeare Festival, which remained in the city until a state-of-the-art facility was built in Montgomery in 1985. Since 2005, the Monteith Amphitheater at the former military base has hosted Music at McClellan, a free outdoor musical concert series in the summer. The museum complex at LaGarde Park, north of the city, began with Severn Regar's Bird Collection. It, along with John B. LaGarde's African animal collection, formed the nexus of the Anniston Museum of Natural History. Farley and Germaine Berman's weapons and art collections, left to the City of Anniston in 1992, led to the Berman Museum of World History, which opened in 1996. The museum complex expansion also developed the Longleaf Botanical Gardens and Trails in the former Lenlock Community Center.

One

"The Model City"

The Alabama Assembly passed a charter to create the Woodstock Iron Company town in 1879. The charter allowed for an intendant (mayor) and five councilmen, all of whom were employees of the iron company. An amendment to the charter in 1884 allowed for open elections and two councilmen from each of the four wards. The town also had a marshal, but a civil code was not adopted until 1890. The code provided for a hospital, public water, street maintenance, sewage, business licenses, police and fire service, as well as public education to residents.

Anniston grew quickly. After a special election in 1899, the Calhoun County seat was awarded to the city. County offices and courts took up temporary residence in the Anniston City Land Company building until the courthouse was completed in 1900. The courthouse underwent expansion in the 1920s, experienced a fire and rebuilding in the 1930s, and faced several renovations in the latter part of the 20th century.

Over the years, Anniston has had many types of government, including mayor-council, city commission, and council-manager. The 1969 city council election saw Dr. Gordon Rodgers elected as the first black councilman. Gertrude Williams became the first woman elected to the city council seven years later. In 1979, she became the first female mayor of Anniston.

The Georgia Pacific and the L&N Railroads were key to the development of Anniston. Passengers stopped to enjoy the city as a summer resort, and freight from local industries was shipped daily. In addition, the growth of Fort McClellan saw an influx of soldiers arriving on the train.

Establishing a public library was a priority for the founding fathers of Anniston; however, the library struggled to find funding. A city public library was founded in 1895 at Lloyd's Drug Store, and by 1927, a county library was also established. Andrew Carnegie provided funds in 1910 to build the first regular library on Tenth Street. In 1966, with a bequest from the Luther Liles Estate, the Carnegie Library and Calhoun County Library merged into the new Liles Memorial Library building. By the 1950s, the library had branches at Glen Addie, Carver, and North Noble.

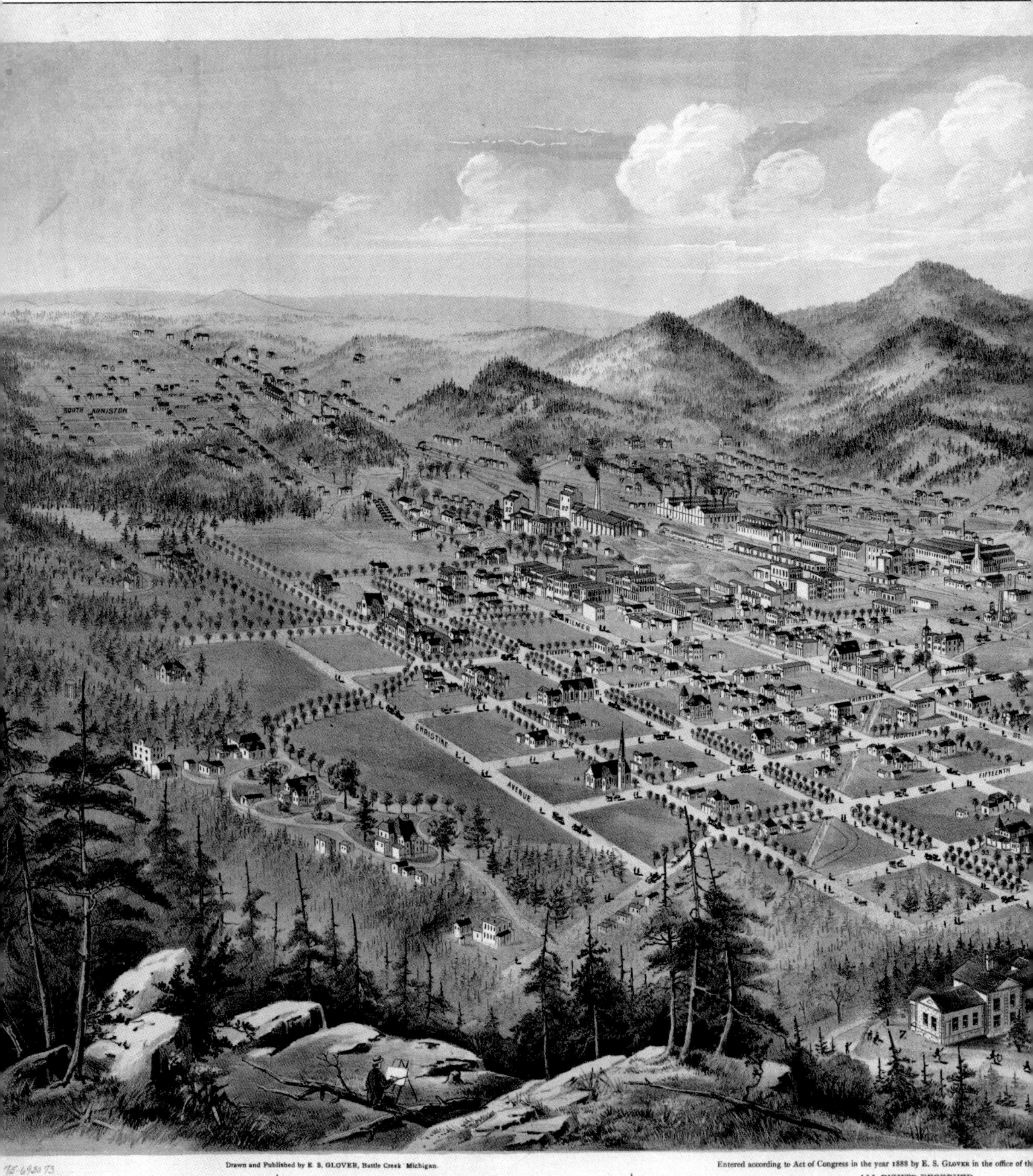
SOUTH ANNISTON
CHRISTINE
AVENUE
FIFTEENTH
75-69073
Drawn and Published by E. S. GLOVER, Battle Creek Michigan.
Entered according to Act of Congress in the year 1888 by E. S. Glover in the office of th
ALL RIGHTS RESERVED.
Choice Business and Residence Lots in this new and thriving
MODEL CITY OF THE SOUTH
on reasonable terms, by the
ANNISTON CITY LAND COMPANY
REFERENCES.
No. 1 Anniston Inn.
No. 2 Union Passenger Depot.
No. 3 City Hall.
No. 4 City Water Works.
No. 5 Reservoir.
No. 6 Noble Institute for Girls.
No. 7 Noble Institute for Boys.
No. 8 Public School.
No. 9 Grace Episcopal Church.
No. 10 Presbyterian Church.
No. 11 Twelfth St. Baptist Church.
No, 12 Christian Church.
No. 13 Noble St. Methodist Church.
No. 14 Leighton Ave. Methodist Church.
No. 15 First Baptist Church.
No. 16 Congregational Church (Colored).
No. 17 Episcopal Church, Glen Addie.
No. 18 Catholic Church, Glen Addie.
No. 19 Methodist Church, Glen Addie.
BIRD'S · EYE · VIEW · OF
ANNISTON,
LOOKING SOUTHWEST
· 1888 ·

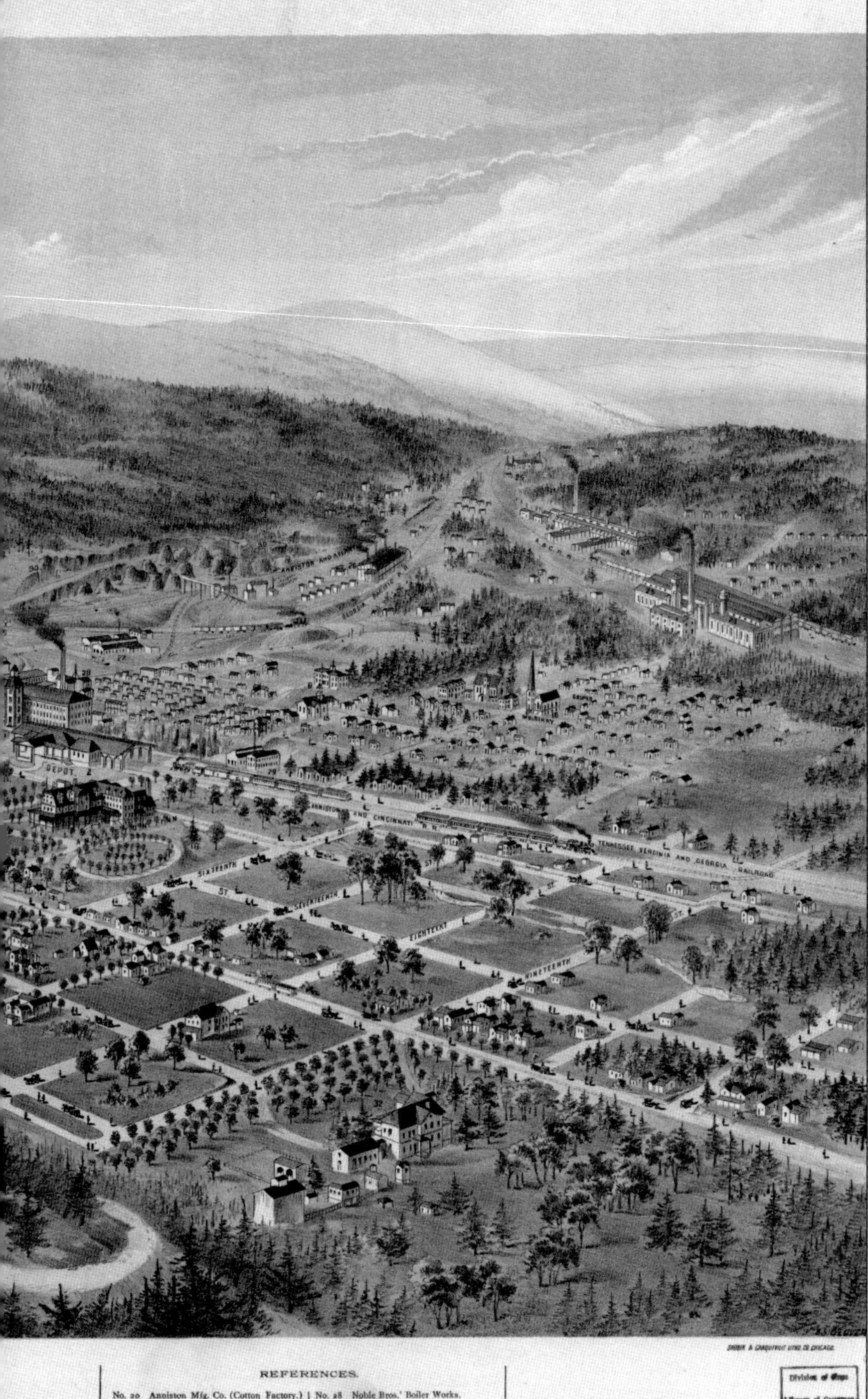

When Samuel Noble decided to open his town to the public, his friend, newspaperman Henry W. Grady, was on hand to dub Annie's Town "The Model City of the New South" on opening day, July 3, 1883. The private company town was designed as a self-sufficient community, with the industrial, residential, and cultural aspects of the late 19th century. The public was invited to join this utopia, but that optimism quickly faded. This map of Anniston dates to around 1888. (LOC.)

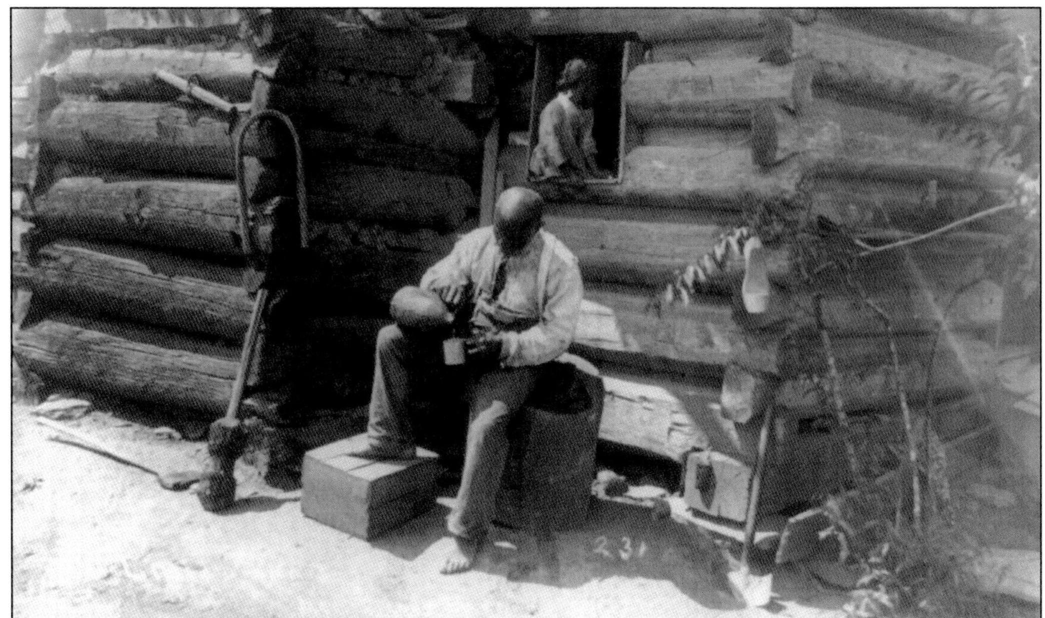

Originally, the land that would become downtown Anniston was inhabited by an African American family's cabin. Prior to 1879, the area called Pine Ankle had Tuttle's Bake Shop, a private drugstore, McKinney's Wheelwright and Blacksmith Shop, and the two-story McCain House. The surrounding area consisted of the Lloyd, Jones, and Maddox farms as well as the Spalding residence, which was used as a boardinghouse in the early days of Anniston.

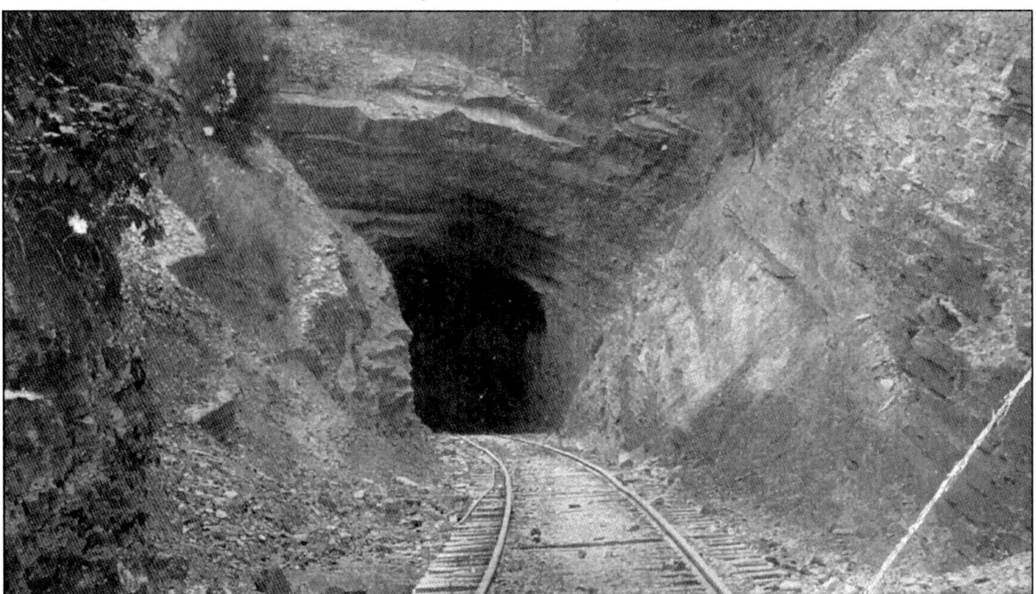

When the Woodstock Iron Company reorganized in 1887, the Anniston & Cincinnati Railroad was created to allow access to the Coosa River and to provide a link to the rich mineral resources north of Anniston. Due to a conflict over the route, the line was built through the mountain near Laney, a few miles northeast of Wellington. The tunnel, the south portal of which is shown here around 1910, was completed by October 1888 and eventually became part of the L&N Railroad line. (PLACC.)

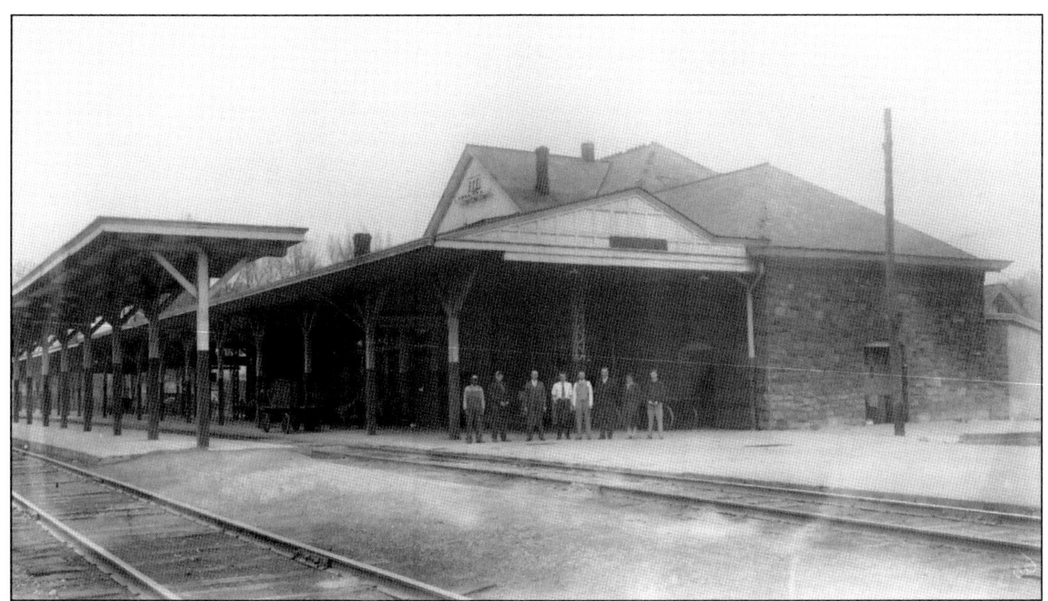

The L&N Railway built the Union Depot passenger station in 1895 at 1300 Walnut Avenue. The rear of the depot is shown above around 1900. Until 1926, it was shared with the Southern Railway. Adjacent to the passenger station was the Express Depot, shown below around 1928. The Express Depot handled freight service for the railway and employed both office staff and drivers. In 1948, due to a decline in passenger travel and a coal strike, L&N dropped passenger service to Anniston and never resumed it. The railway company leased the lower floor of the depot to Kelly Supply and kept an office on the upper floor of the main passenger depot. The building, under renovation at the time, burned down in 2008.

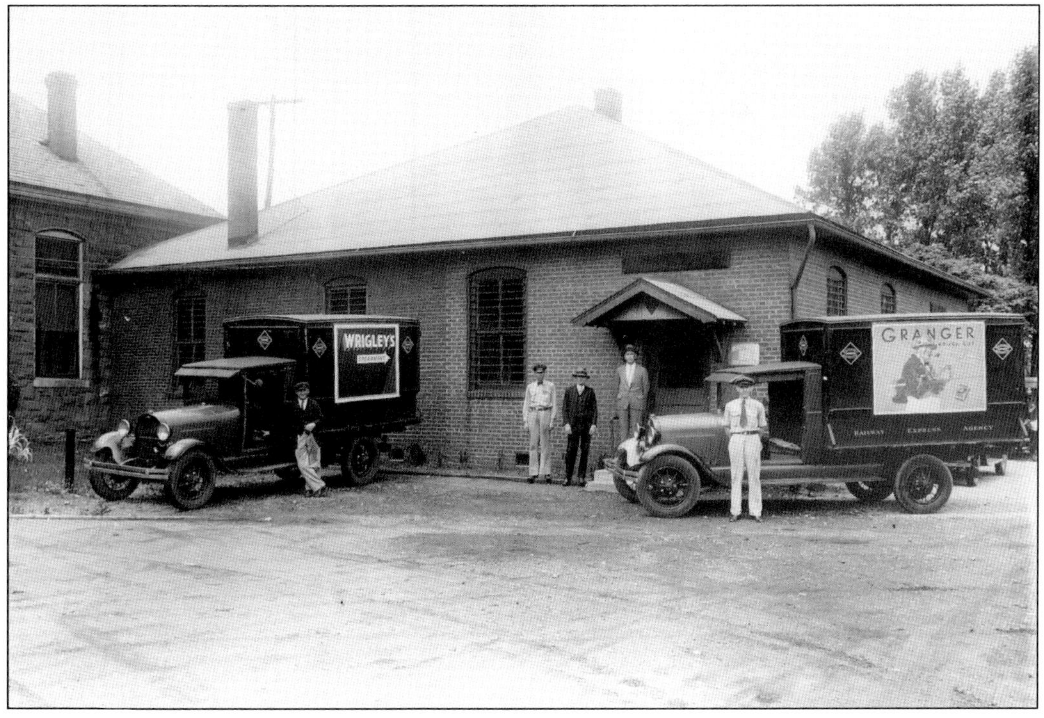

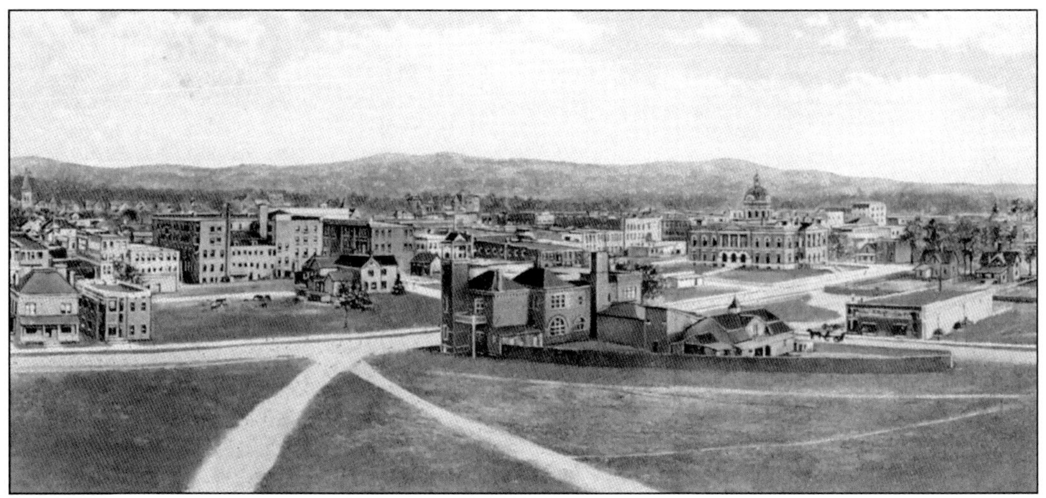

When the county seat was relocated to Anniston in 1899, a two-story brick structure (far left) was built on the east side of Gurnee Avenue between Twelfth and Thirteenth Streets to serve as the jail and residence for the sheriff. The jail was replaced in 1941 by a four-story structure on the north side of the courthouse. The original jail was used for many years as the Calhoun County Department of Pensions and Security office. (PLACC.)

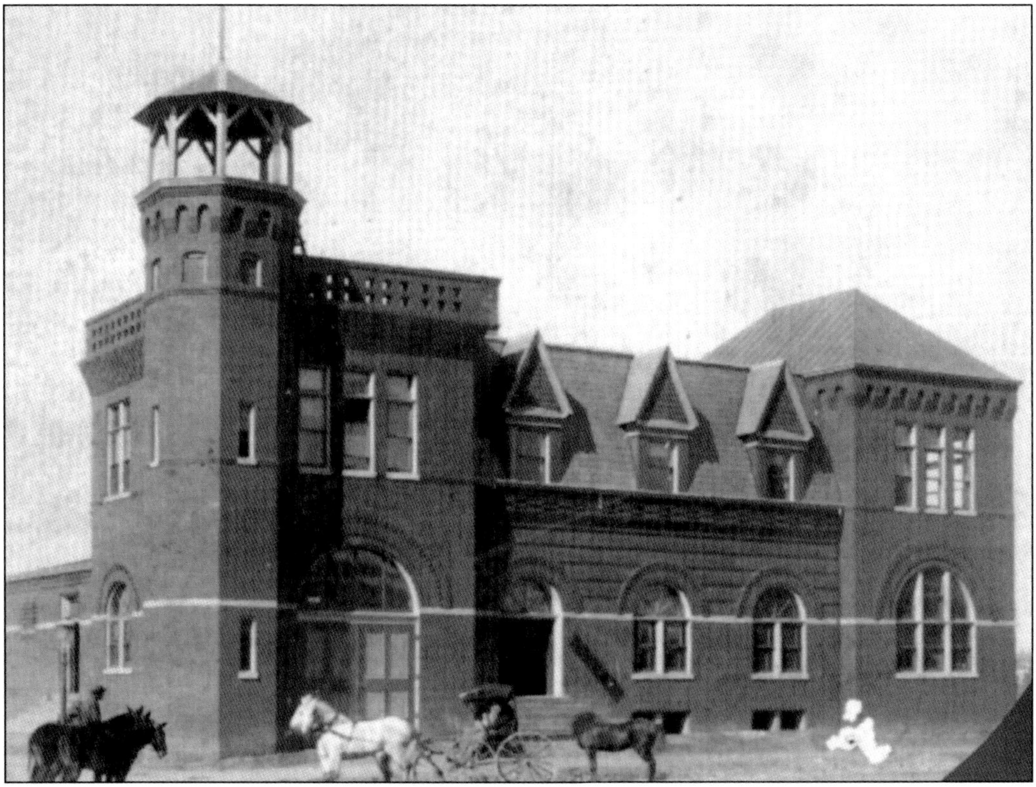

Anniston had no formal city hall, so space at the Noble Theater was obtained in 1885. This remained the site of council meetings until a city hall was constructed at Twelfth Street and Gurnee Avenue. The original structure consisted of the city hall, with police and fire departments added later. The stables were located behind the building.

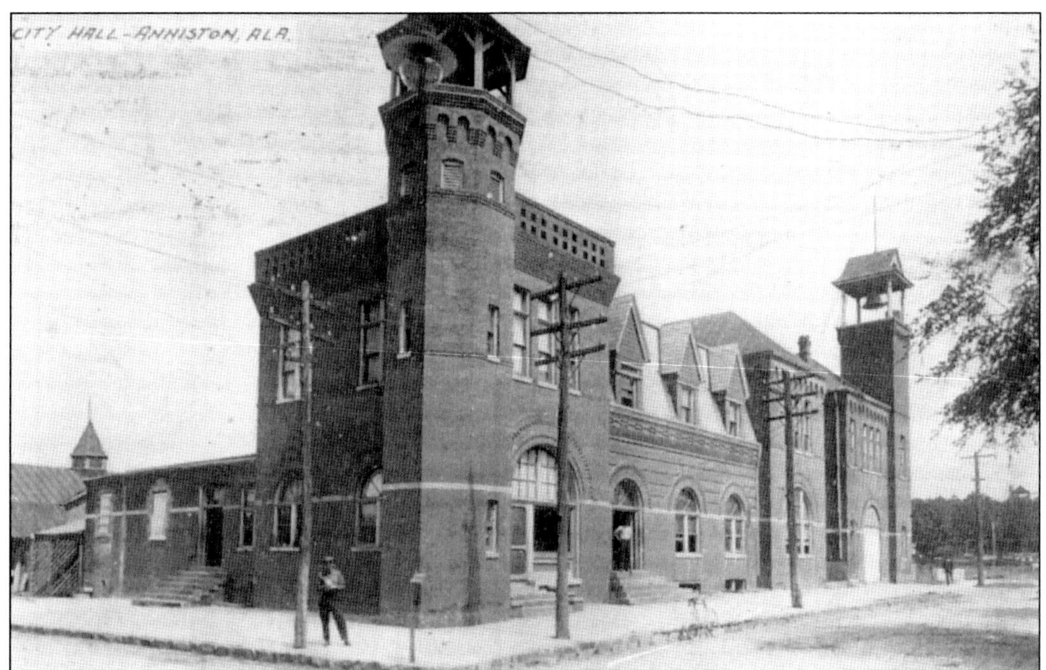

When the city hall offices were moved to the former USO Building in 1951, the police department remained in the old building (pictured) until a new police station was constructed in 1956. The station was replaced in 2013 with the Justin Sollahub Justice Center, built on the site of the 1896 Anniston Land Company Building. Encompassing the 1200 block of Gurnee Avenue, the complex included not only the police station, but also the municipal court, court magistrate's office, and city jail. (ERY.)

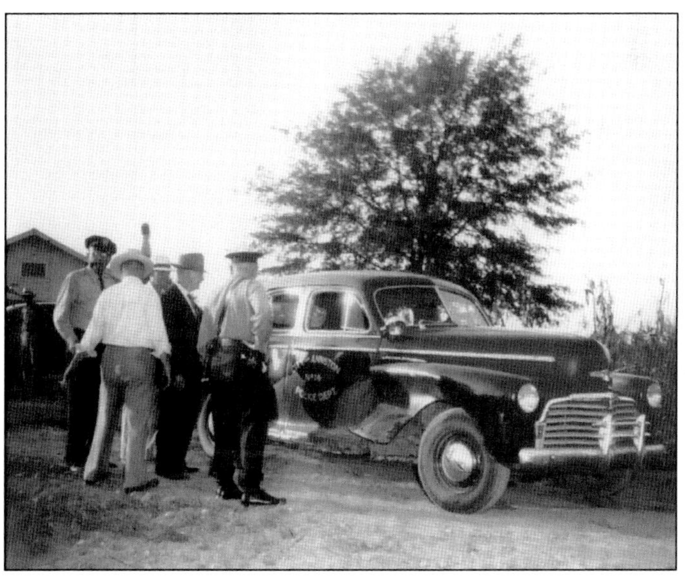

Since Woodstock Iron could dismiss an employee for any infraction, no real police force was needed. The 1890 Civil Code established a small police department that included both foot and mounted patrols. The department remained small until 1939, when Chief J.L. Peek began expanding the 15-man force. A detective division was added in 1943, and by 1945, the department had over 30 officers and 6 detectives. Members of the department are seen here around 1946. (PLACC-BC.)

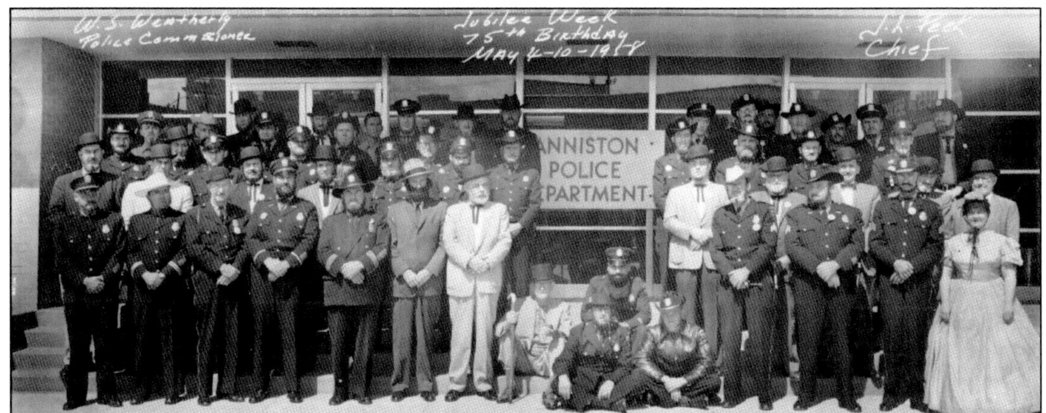

The police department, seen here in 1958, continued to grow. By 1962, the force had 48 officers. The modern police force received firearm training and defense tactics and consisted of a pistol team, 14 patrol cars, and six motorcycles. The department was prepared for any emergency, with an armory that included riot guns, tear gas, and carbines.

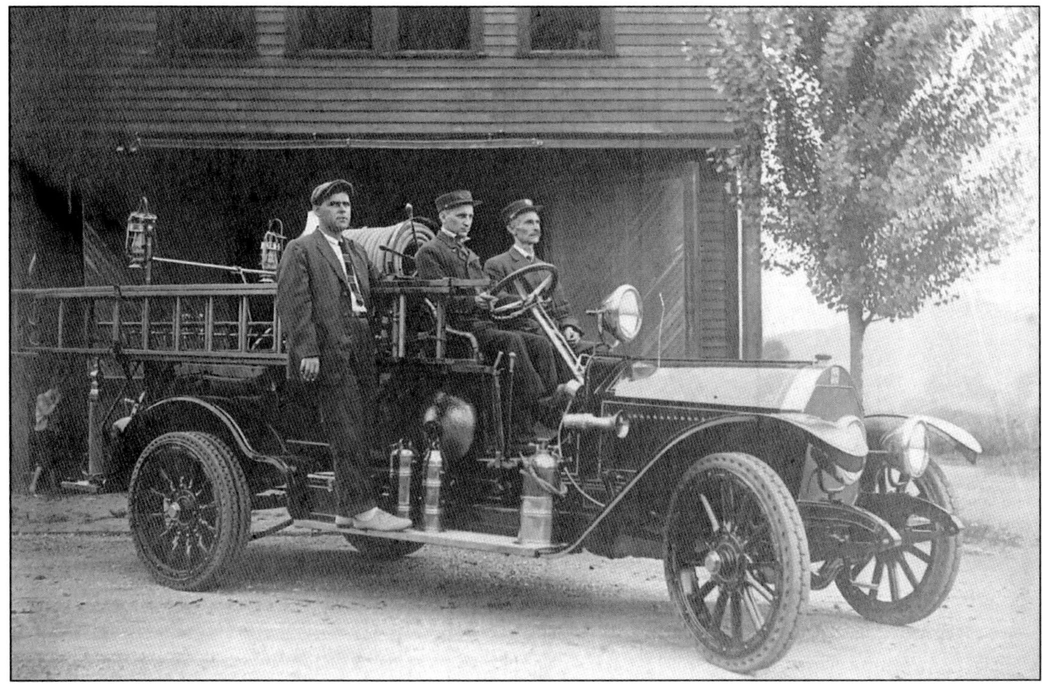

The municipal fire department started as a volunteer unit in the 1880s, in which men paid dues to join the fire companies located near city hall, Glen Addie, and West Fifteenth Street. The early fire department used hand reels, which were replaced by horse-drawn wagons, and each station was given a full-time driver paid for by the city. Every year, the Volunteer Fireman's Association held tournaments to test skills, and the Anniston companies made frequent appearances in the winner's circle. This photograph was taken around 1914. (PLACC.)

Chief D.C. Rainwater is seated in the passenger seat in the car at far left in this c. 1915 photograph at city hall. He joined the regular fire department in 1897 after years as a volunteer at West Fifteenth Street. In 1914, the volunteer companies were disbanded, and the full-time, paid department was instituted. The department had motorized equipment starting in 1912 and continued to purchase the most up-to-date equipment for fighting fires, such as high-powered pumping engines and ladder trucks.

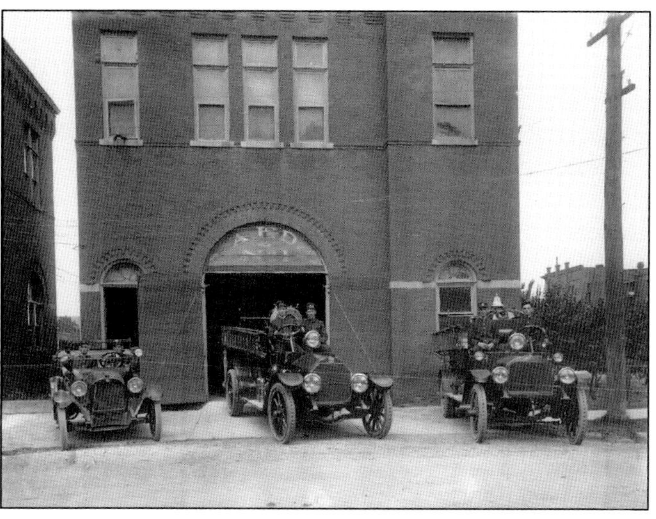

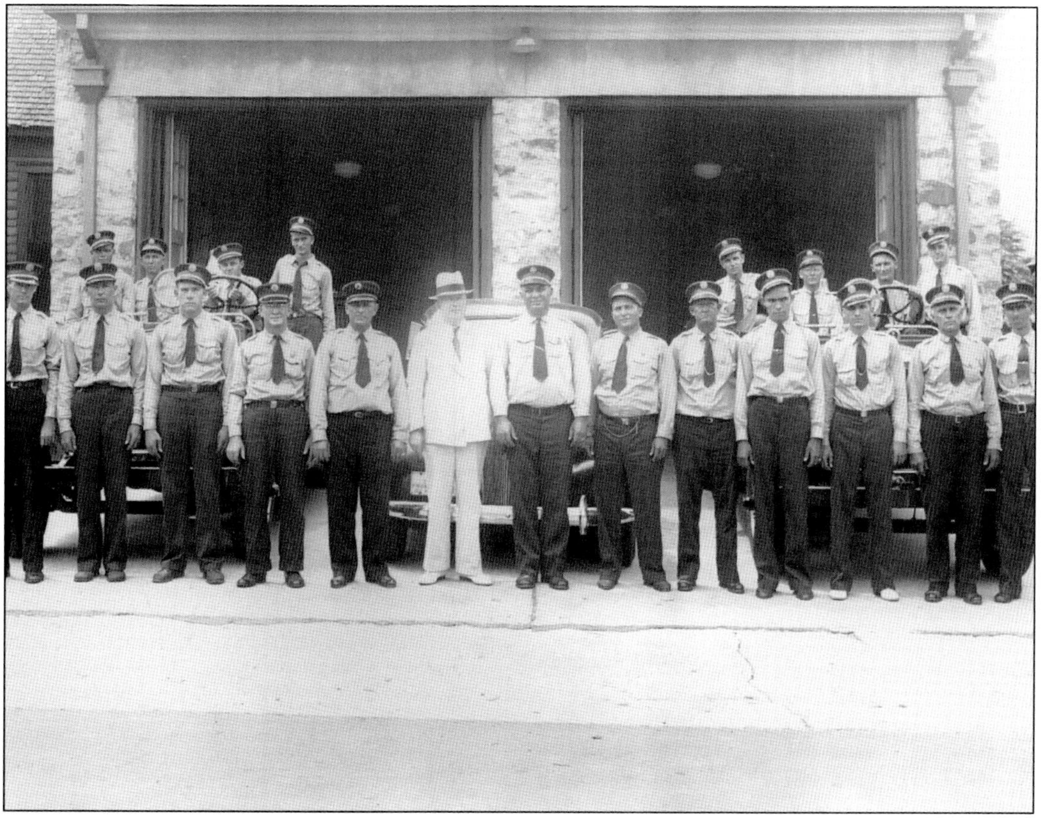

The new West Fifteenth Street Fire Station was built in 1936 using Works Progress Administration (WPA) funds. The station and members of the department pose here on March 5, 1936, with Mayor William Coleman (left of center). By 1943, the department employed 20 firefighters. The manpower to fight fires was increased to 32 full-time employees by 1963. Today, the department has six fire stations throughout the 55 square miles of the city.

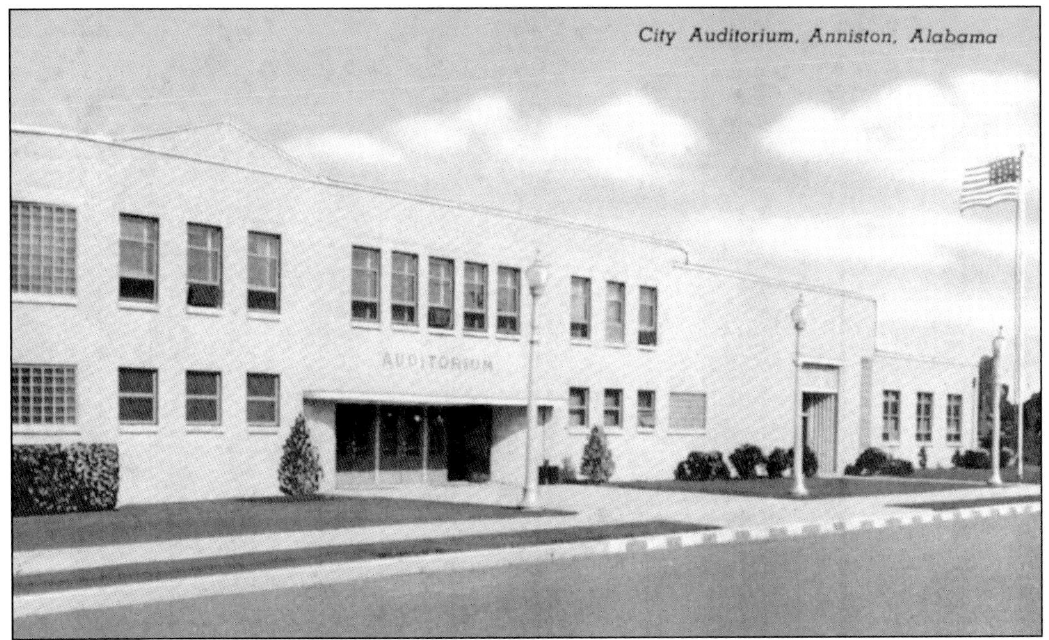

The City Auditorium, located at 1128 Gurnee Avenue, was erected in 1942 as the United Service Organization (USO) building operated by the Jewish Welfare Board. This was one of several USO canteens in Anniston to provide "a touch of home" to members of the armed forces through morale, welfare, and recreation. After World War II, the building became home to the City Auditorium, and eventually, city hall. (PLACC.)

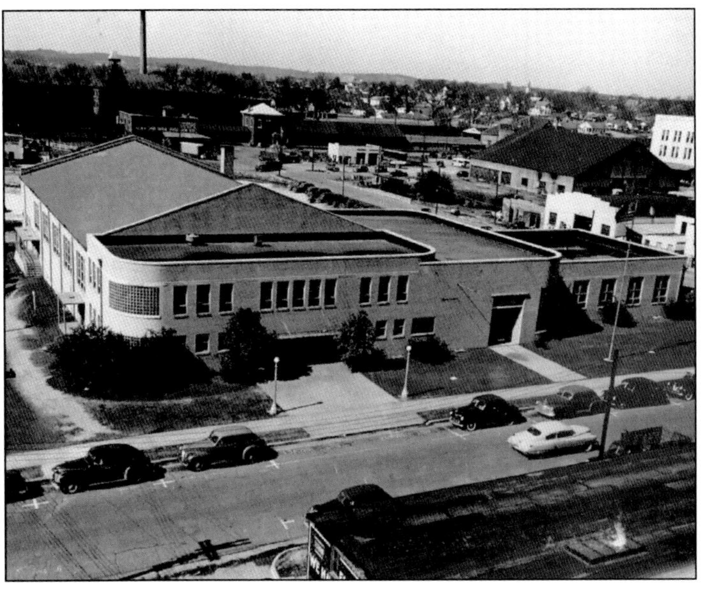

The City Auditorium was used for a variety of purposes, including recitals, civil-service examinations, basketball games, and as a meeting space starting in the late 1940s. When the new Anniston High School was built in 1970, an auditorium was built adjacent to the school. The city hall building, shown here around 1950, was renovated to serve as both a city hall in the main building and to house the municipal courts in the attached building at far right.

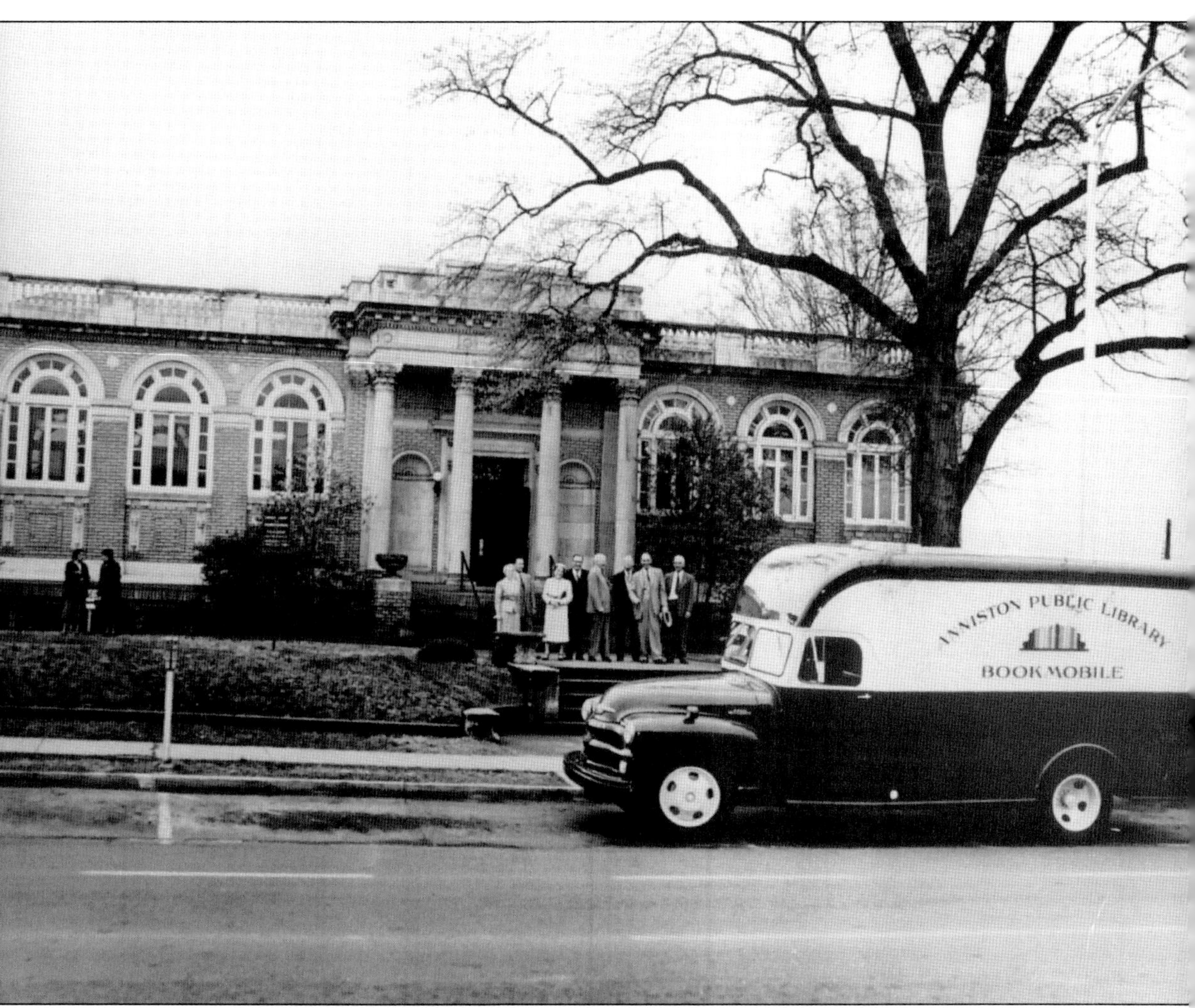

In 1910, R.E. Garner's will bequeathed a tract of land at Tenth Street and Wilmer Avenue to the city. The land was designated as the site for the library. Through funding from philanthropist Andrew Carnegie, the Carnegie Library was constructed and opened in May 1918. It is seen here around 1930. In 1964, the Carnegie and Calhoun County Libraries merged as the Public Library of Anniston–Calhoun County. In October 1966, a new building was dedicated on the site of the Carnegie Library. (PLACC.)

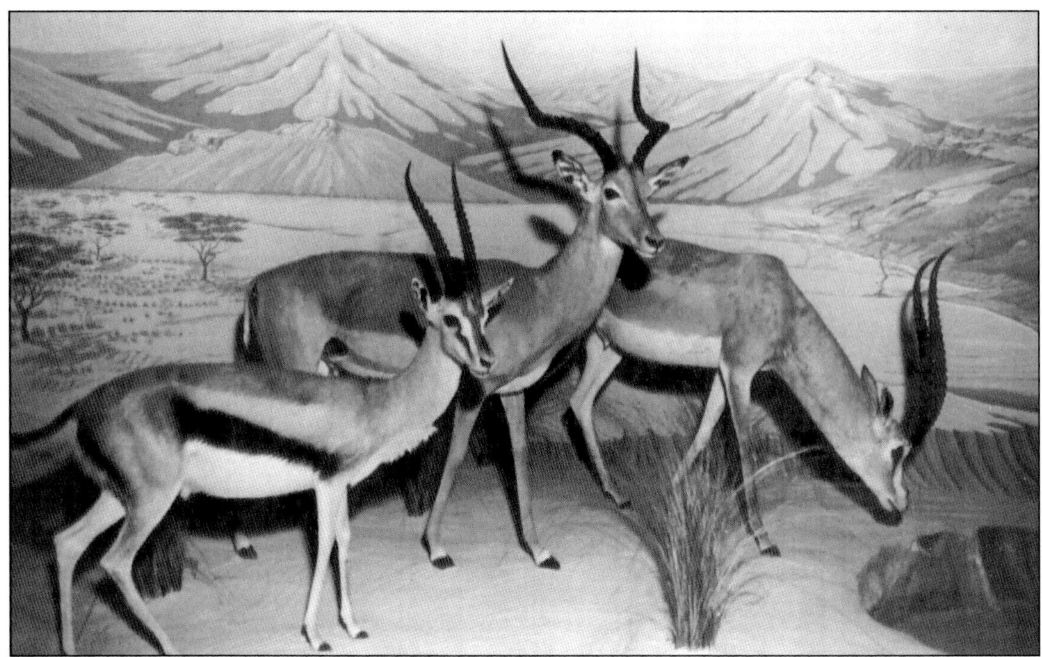

After moving to the city in 1929, H. Severn Regar donated his collection of avian specimens, originally owned by naturalist William H. Werner. The citizens of Anniston collected money to fund the construction of a two-story annex behind the Carnegie Library. The collection, on display from 1930 until 1965 at the Regar Museum, was transferred to the former Calhoun County Library building when a museum board was created. The Anniston Museum of Natural History was constructed near the intersection of Highways 21 and 431 in 1976. John B. LaGarde's African animal collection (shown around 1976) was part of an exhibit in the museum. (ERY.)

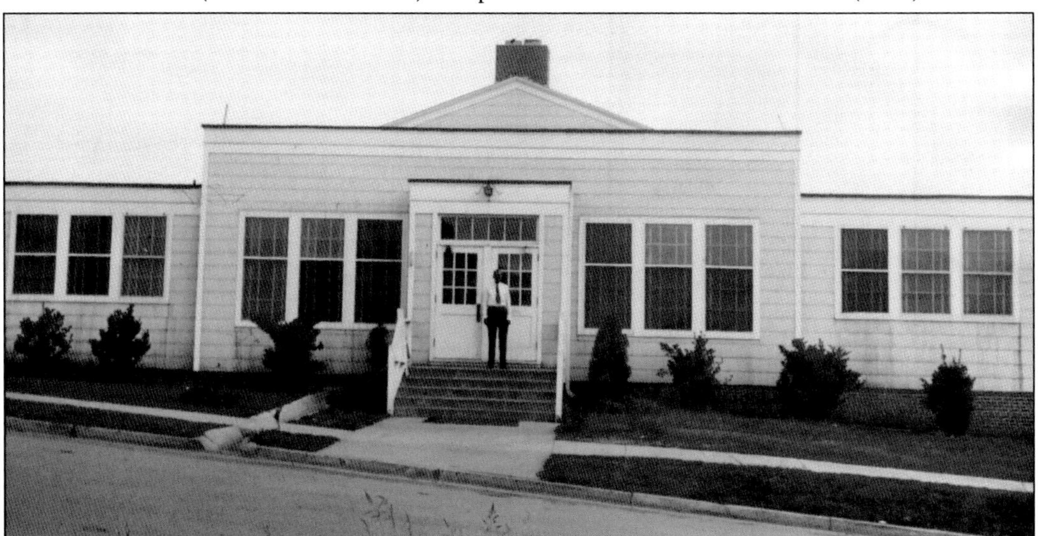

The Carver Branch Library, which served the African American community, opened at the Carver Community Center with Delia B. Leake as the librarian. The library, seen here around 1948, was open from 2:00 p.m. to 6:00 p.m. Monday through Friday. Librarian Lucille Haynes began story hour for young children in 1948. The Carver Branch Library remained in the West Fourteenth Street location, adjacent to the Carver Center. (PLACC.)

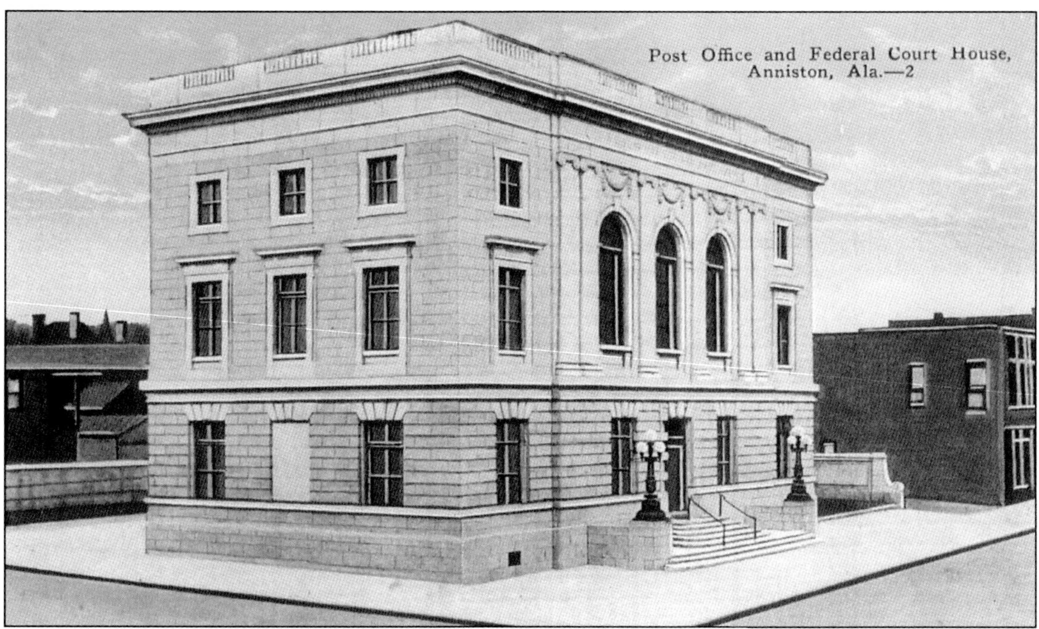

The US Congress authorized the building of a federal post office in 1899 and provided $25,000 for the cost of construction. The tract of land at 1129 Noble Street was deeded to the federal government, and construction took place from 1904 to 1906. In 1935, a two-year renovation to the post office added marble facing to the exterior, a rear wing to the second floor, and an elevator to the third floor. The building, seen here around 1938, housed federal offices. In the early 1960s, a new, larger post office was constructed on Quintard Avenue. (PLACC.)

The Calhoun County Courthouse was originally located in Jacksonville. When Anniston won a special (and contentious) election held in 1899 to relocate the county seat, a new $150,000 courthouse, designed by J. W. Gulucke & Company, was constructed by S.C. Houser and Thomas Wollstonecraft at Eleventh Street and Gurnee Avenue. The cornerstone for the building was laid in November 1900. (PLACC.)

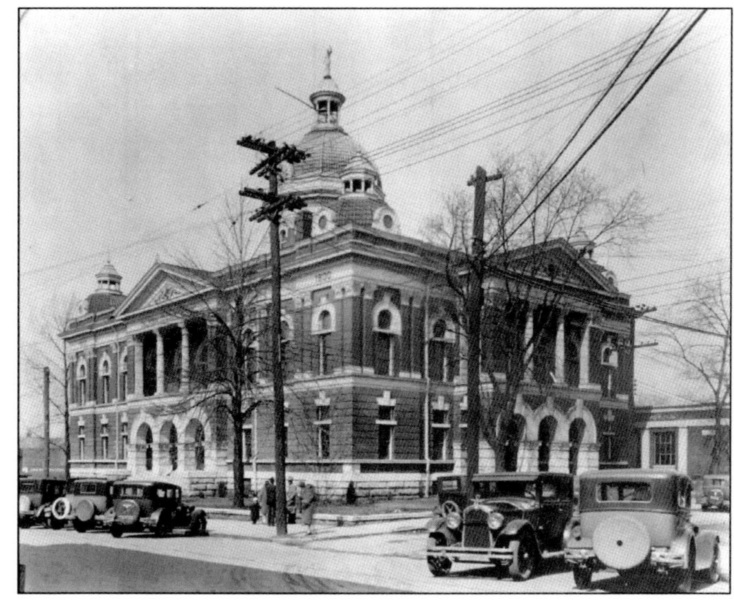

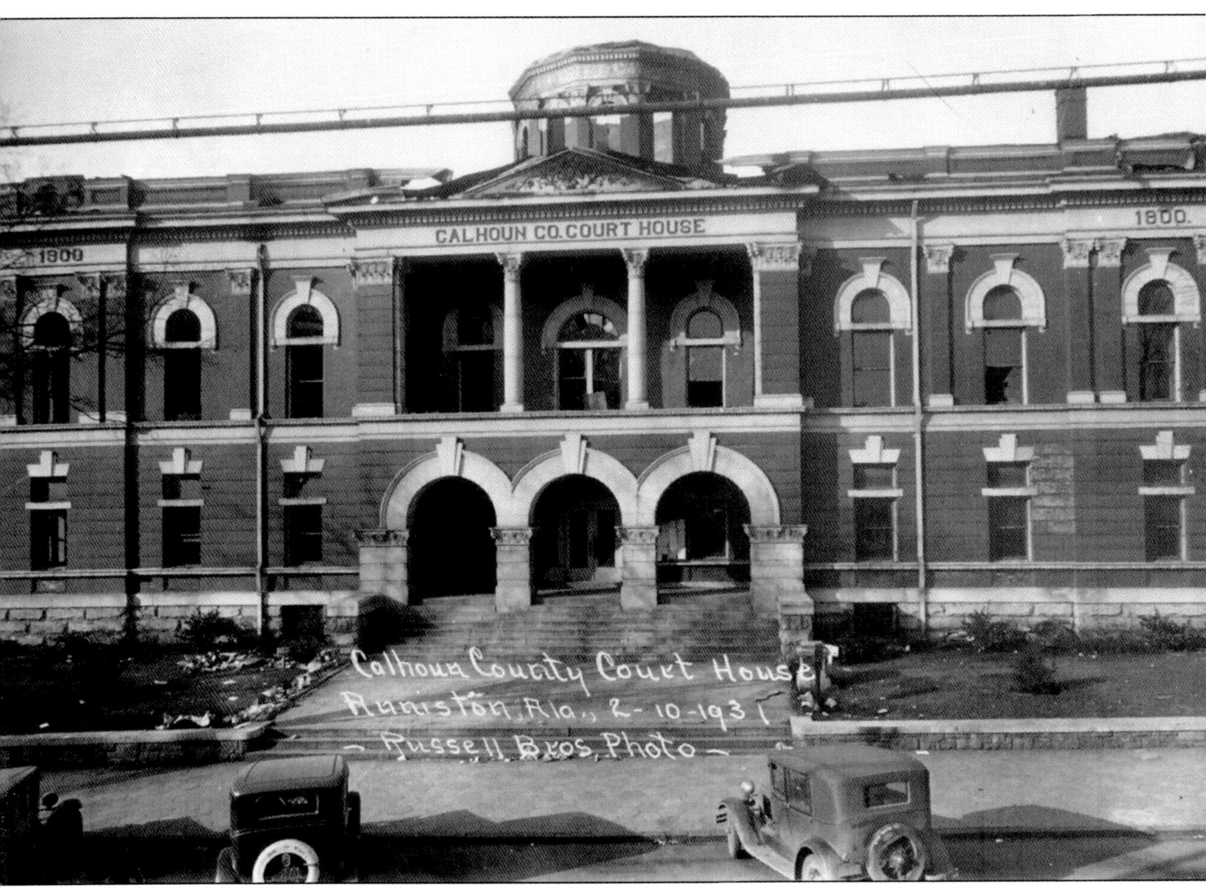

As additional space was needed for the probate office and jail, an annex was added to the north side of the courthouse in 1924. On January 15, 1931, a fire started in the chimney of the courthouse and quickly spread throughout the building, as there were no fire stops in the largely wooden construction. Damages to the courthouse included the loss of two judges' records, court reporters' files, the clock tower, and bell. The annex was saturated with water to protect the probate judge's office. The fire was brought under control by the 13-man fire department along with the assistance of volunteers.

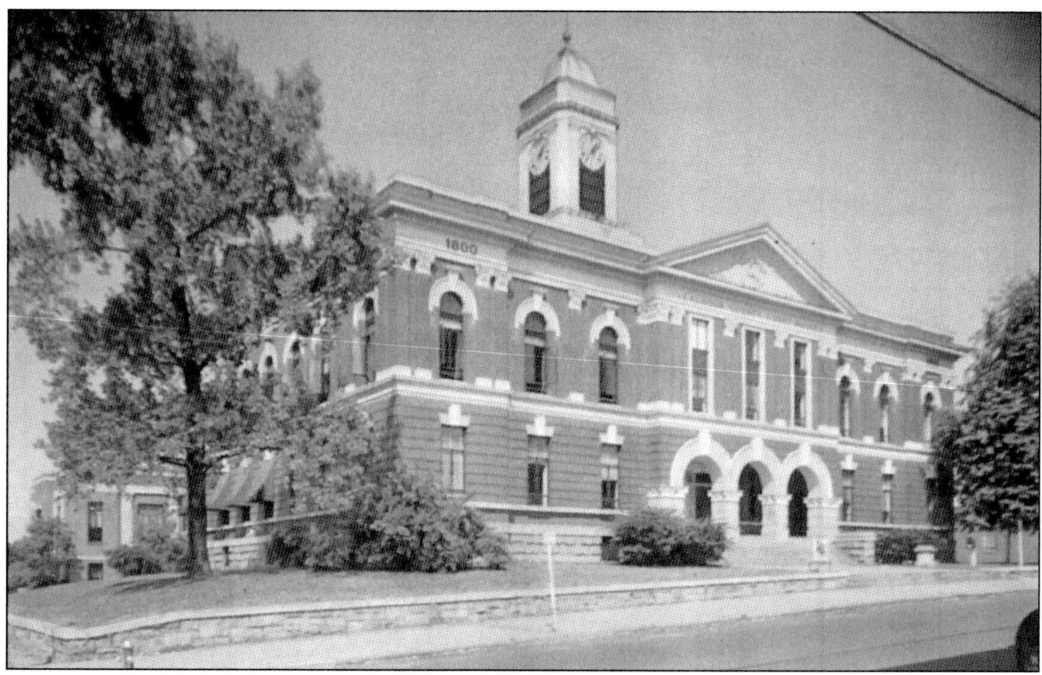

The reconstructed courthouse, completed in 1932, was made as fireproof as possible, with concrete floors, steel partitions, a centralized coal heating system, and an enlarged basement. The 1941 annex included a modern, three-story jail and the county offices. A records room was constructed in the basement under the probate office; the heating system was converted to gas, and air conditioning was added to most offices in 1951. A ground-floor east wing was constructed in the 1960s. In 1990, the building underwent a complete restoration. (ERY.)

The Farmers Market, shown here around 1920, offered produce on the Calhoun County Courthouse lawn at Eleventh Street and Gurnee Avenue. In the late 1940s, a curb market was built between Thirteenth and Fourteenth Streets on Gurnee Avenue. Over the years, the market has relocated to various locations in town, including the renovated Calhoun County Administration Building on Noble Street. In this photograph, the old city hall building can be seen in the distance.

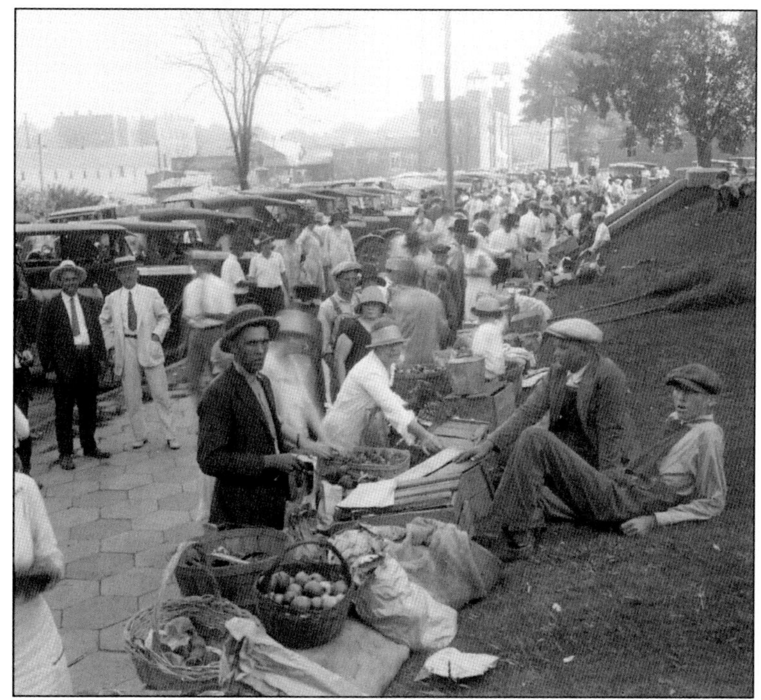

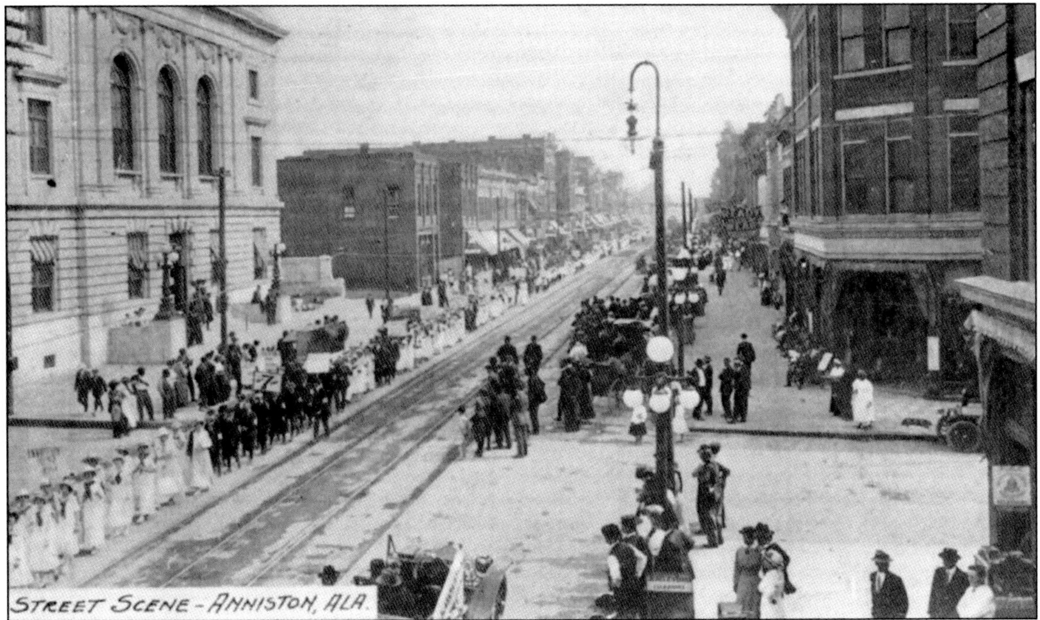

Electricity had been part of Woodstock Iron Company history since 1882, when the company opted for lighting at the furnace operations and streets of the mill community. Alabama Power Company opened for business in the former McIntire Dry Goods Store at the corner of Twelfth and Noble Streets around 1917 (far right corner). This photograph was taken around 1919. Alabama Power Company provided power to the city and was also responsible for the trolley car system.

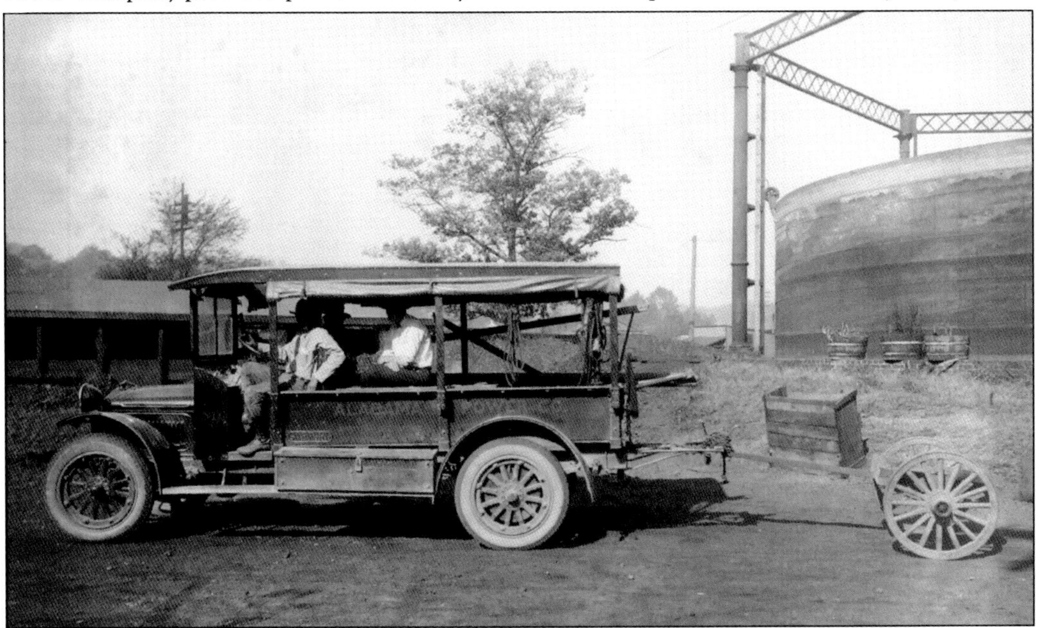

The early power company advertised such services as electric light, power, gas, and appliances. The power plants, such as the one shown here around 1920, were small and isolated. The power company moved to 15–17 East Eleventh Street in the mid-1920s, but its warehouses were maintained at 20 West Third Street. In 1931, the power company turned over gas supplies to Alabama Utilities Service Company, later known as Alabama Gas Company.

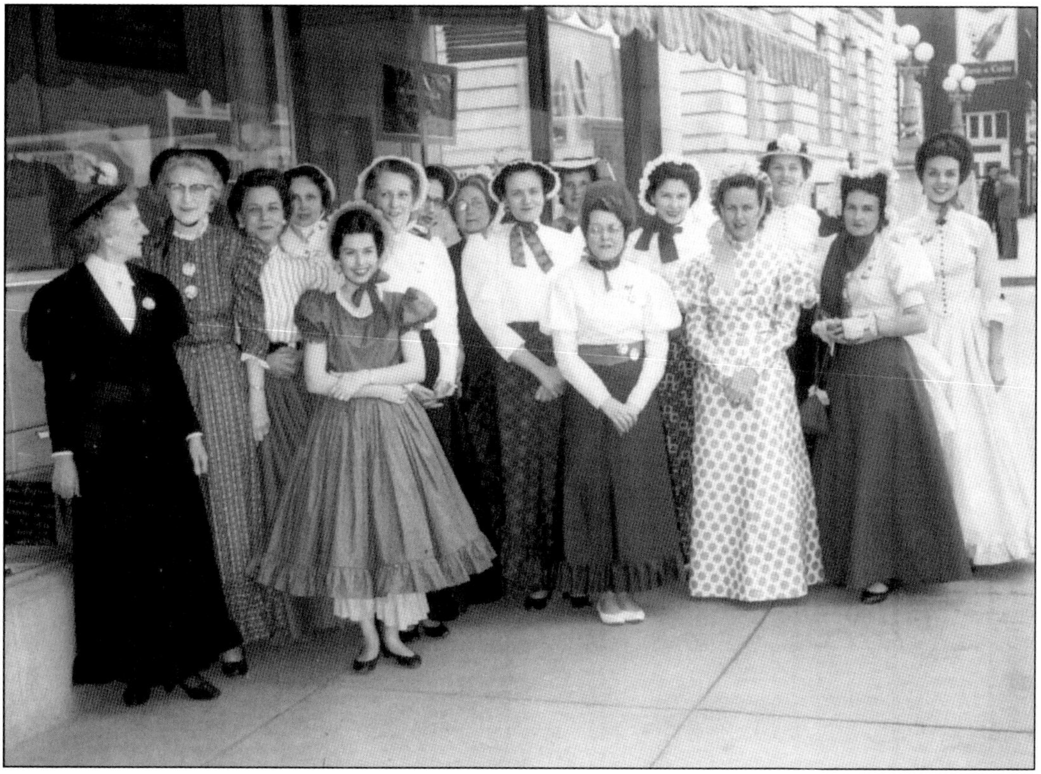

In 1934, Alabama Power Company moved into the former Montgomery Ward Building, in the 1200 block of Noble Street. The building is seen here in 1958 with power company employees dressed for Jubilee Week. After a 1931 fire, the building was completely remodeled for Alabama Power. By 1960, the company employed 155 people in the Anniston office. The company moved to the corner of Tenth Street and Quintard Avenue in June 1964. (ERY.)

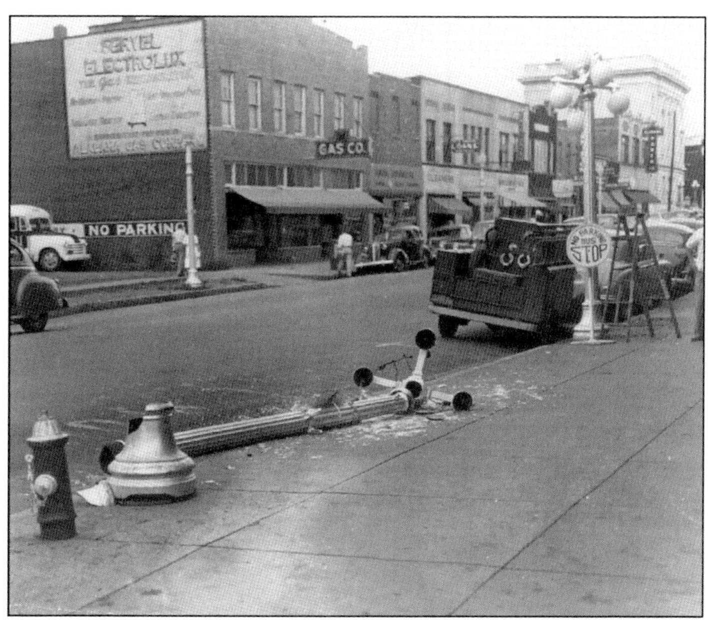

The Alabama Gas Company office in Anniston, incorporated in December 1899, was originally located between Third and Noble Streets. In September 1906, a franchise was granted to Anniston Electric & Gas Company. By 1914, the gas utility was purchased from the company, but in 1929, the utility was sold to Alabama Utilities Service Company. At that time, natural gas became available through Southern Natural Gas Company at 1221 Noble Street, seen here around 1950.

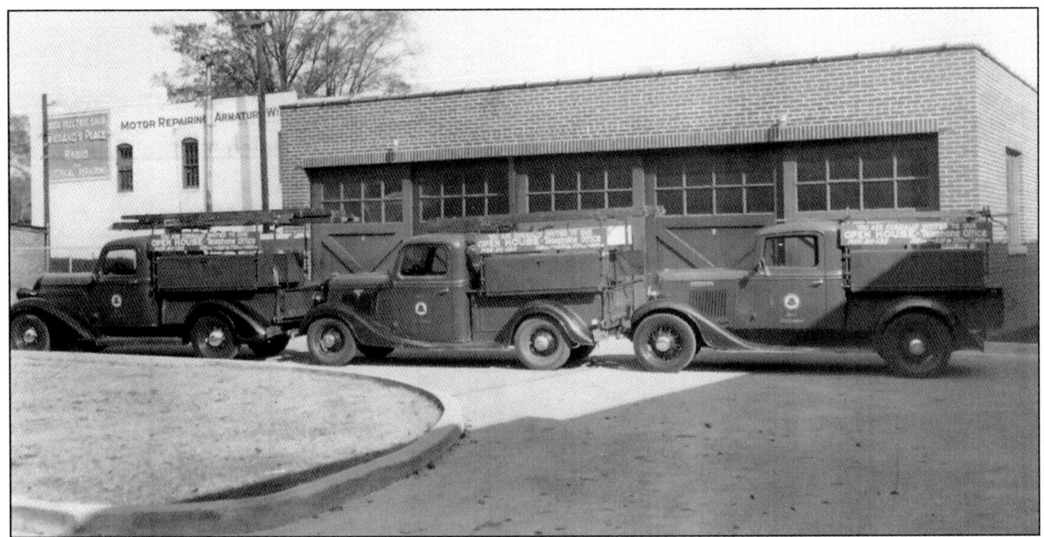

Telephones came to Anniston around 1884, when the Noble–Pan Electric Telephone Company was incorporated. Southern Bell Telephone Company, founded in 1879, came to Anniston in 1888. Originally located in the offices above First National Bank at 909 Noble Street, the company operated at 24 East Twelfth Street from 1908 until 1953. When the phone company moved to the 1300 block of Noble Street, service was converted to dial operation. This c. 1953 photograph shows the rear of the phone company building.

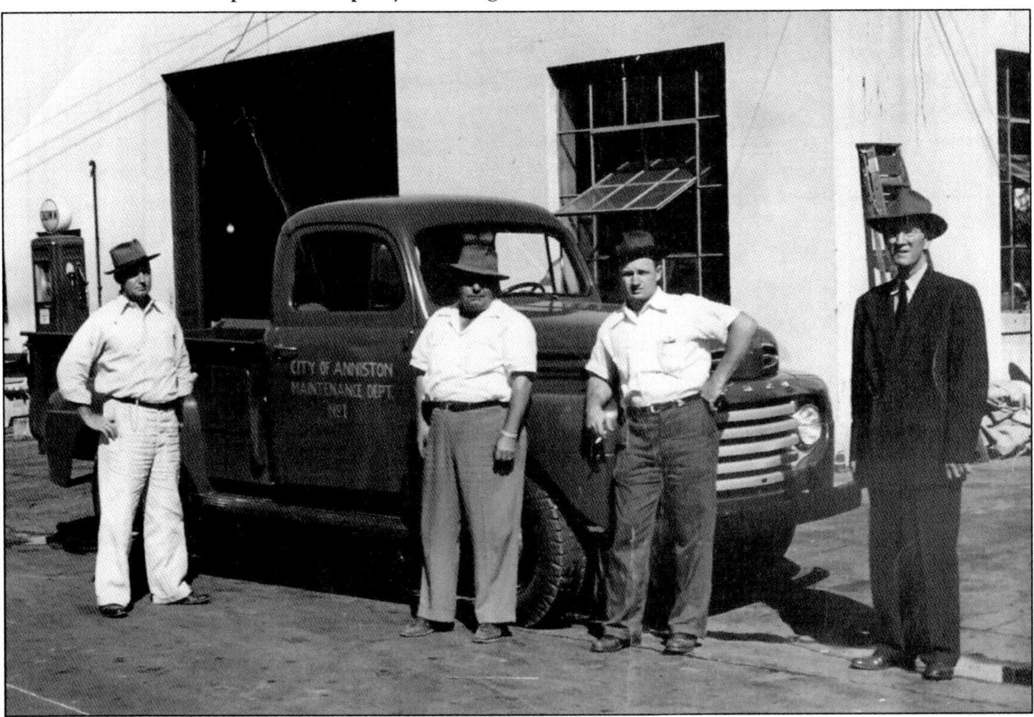

During Mayor E.D. Banks's administration in the late 1940s, a city program for cleanliness and beautification was created. Banks's program consisted of daily sweeping and washing of the streets and sidewalks in the main shopping districts. The administration also secured new vehicles for the Street and Sanitary Departments. Here, Banks stands at far right around 1949. (PLACC-BC.)

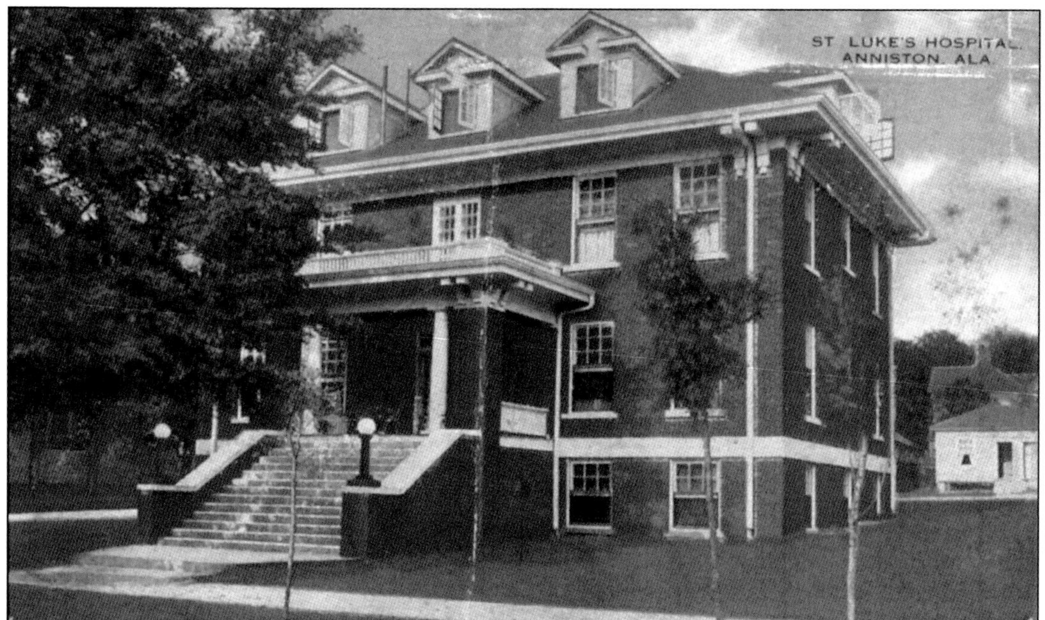

Medical care in the city of Anniston was provided through private clinics until 1908, when the Anniston Hospital was established by Oma Dickert. Several doctors who practiced at the hospital formed the St. Luke's Company in 1911. By 1914, a three-story, 40-bed hospital was built at 1129 Quintard Avenue (seen here around 1914) to operate as a nonprofit civic project. St. Luke's Hospital was sold to the city in 1929, along with St. Michael's Clinic and the Sellers Hospital, to form Garner Hospital. (ERY.)

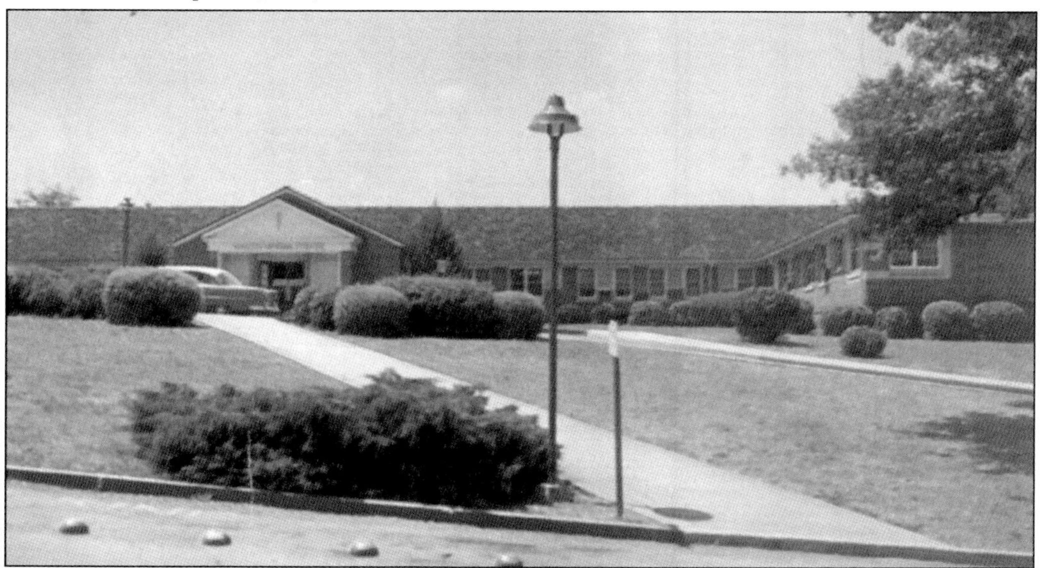

Anniston had plans to build a general hospital as early as 1940, but World War II and the rationing of steel stalled plans. By July 1943, the Federal Works Agency provided $530,000 to construct and furnish the hospital. The Anniston Memorial Hospital, seen here around 1950, was built on the site of A.L. Tyler's residence at Tenth Street and Leighton Avenue. The hospital, completed in October 1944, was sold to the city for $180,000. In the 1980s, the one-story hospital was replaced with a multistory medical complex. (PLACC.)

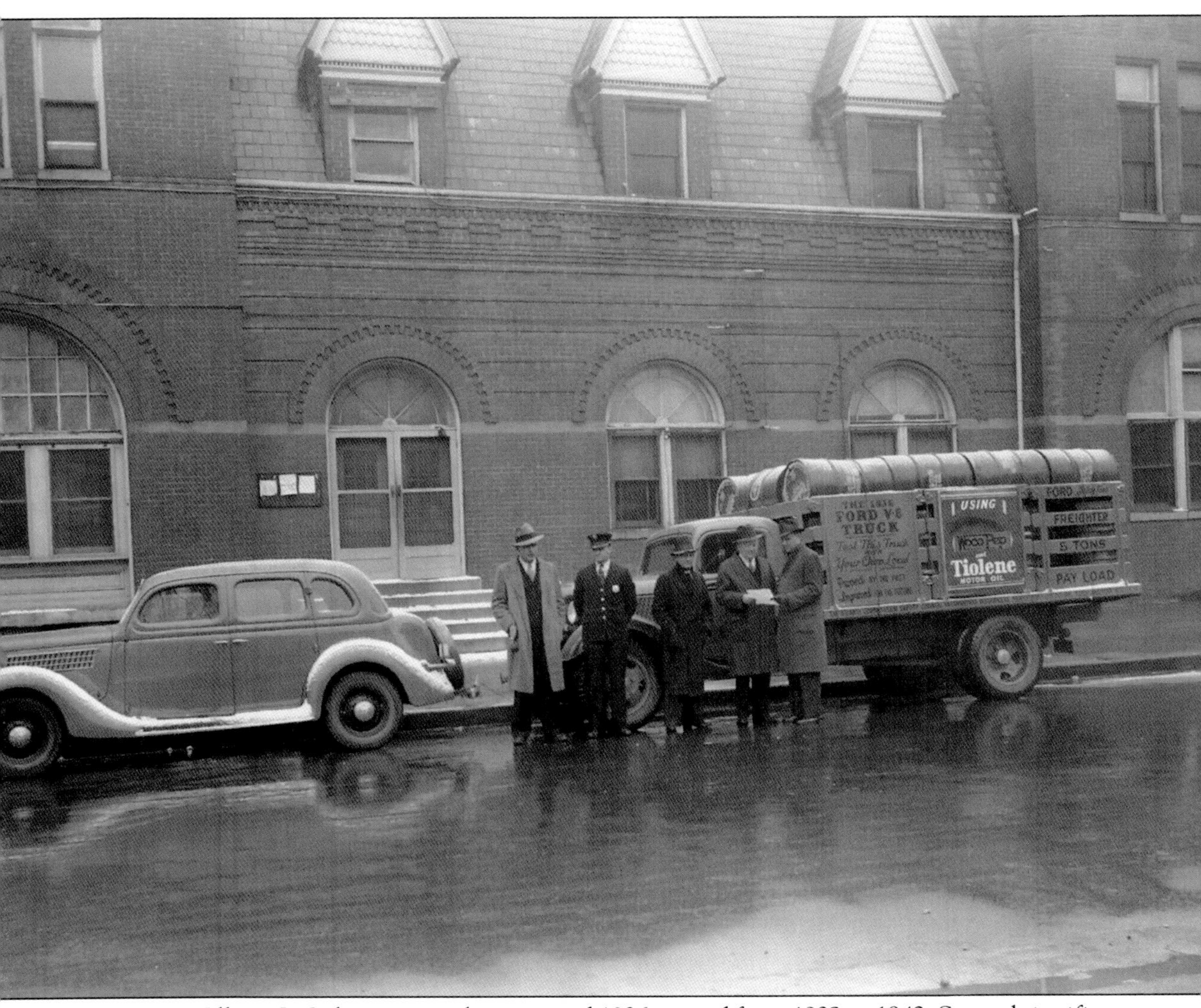

Mayor William S. Coleman, seen here around 1936, served from 1932 to 1942. Several significant events marked his term. In 1939, the city changed from a mayor-council form of government to a city commission system. Around the same time, the mayor formed a committee to address substandard housing problems. The committee recommended passing a housing ordinance to create a public housing authority. During Coleman's administration, the Housing Authority of the City of Anniston submitted an application to the US government to create Glen Addie Homes (164 public units) and Cooper Homes (101 public units). At the turn of the 21st century, the Anniston Housing Authority managed around 1,000 housing units as well as the nonprofit Housing Development Corporation, established in 2002. (PLACC.)

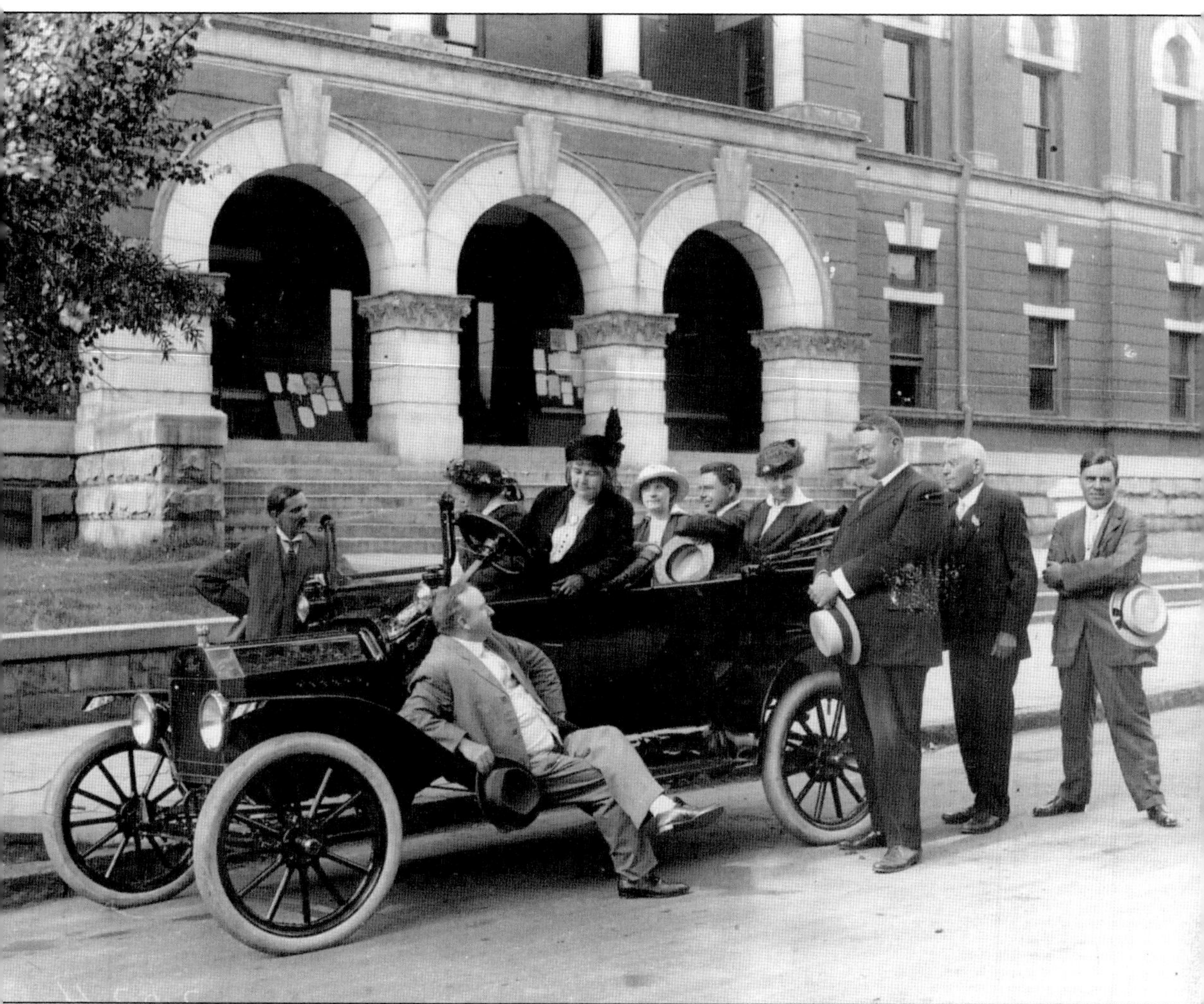

Gov. Thomas Kilby (on running board) was a native of Tennessee who had come to Anniston as an agent for the Georgia Pacific Railroad in 1887. Kilby became a successful businessman when he created the Anniston (Soil) Pipe Company with partners Charles A. Hamilton and William Frances Johnston. Kilby entered politics as a Democratic candidate and served in all facets of state and local government, including as mayor of Anniston (1905–1909), state senator (1911–1915), lieutenant governor (1915–1919), and governor (1919–1923). After leaving politics, he returned to Anniston to run his businesses, including Kilby Steel. When Kilby died in 1943, he was buried in Highland Cemetery, only a few blocks from his home on Woodstock Avenue.

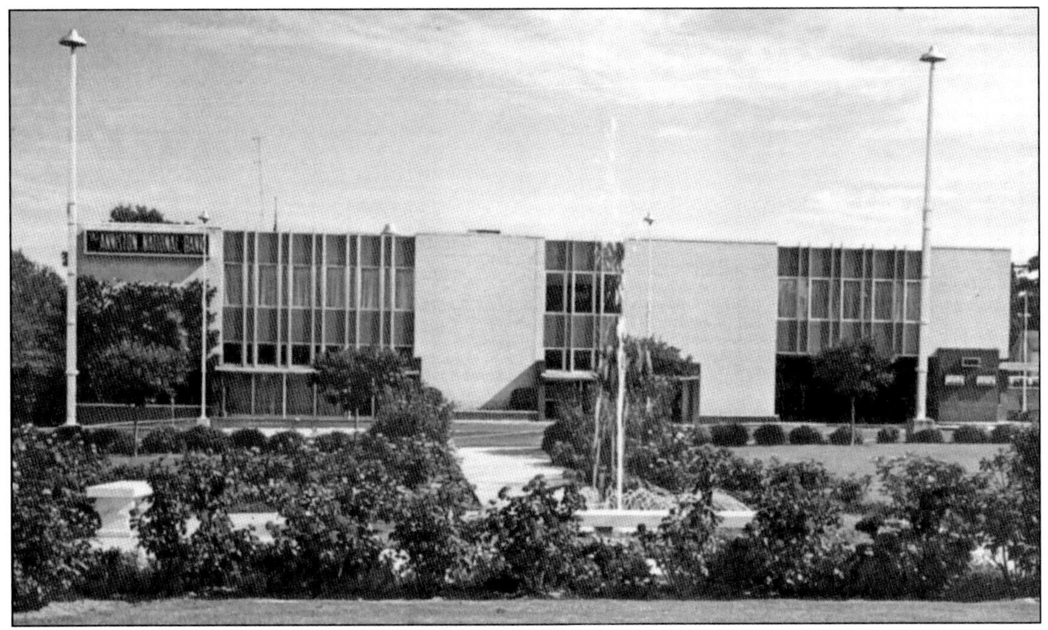

In February 1890, twenty prominent Annistonians joined together to create the Anniston National Bank at Eleventh and Noble Streets. In 1911, Anniston National merged with City National Bank (founded in 1901) to become the Anniston City National Bank. By 1918, the bank was known as Anniston National Bank. In 1954, the bank moved to Twelfth and Noble Streets, then on to Eleventh Street and Quintard Avenue four years later. The latter location is shown here around 1960. After AMSouth and Regions Banks merged in 2007, the building was vacated. (ERY.)

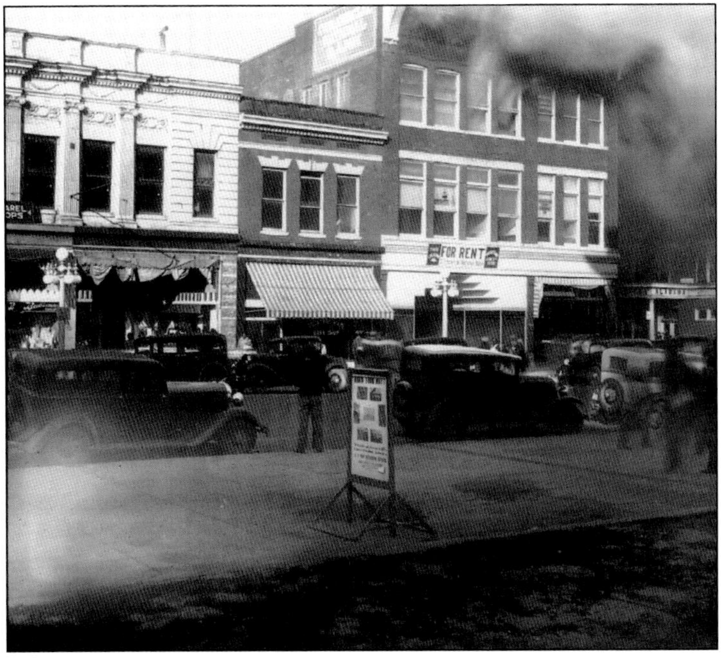

The Commercial National Bank opened for business at 1134 Noble Street in June 1920 with a starting capital of $300,000. The bank suffered two fires while at this location. The first fire (pictured) occurred in 1937, causing minimal damage. The second blaze, in 1945, completely destroyed the bank building. The bank moved to temporary quarters at Twelfth and Court Streets until 1947, when a permanent home was found in the Liles-Wilson Building.

Two

The Business District

The hub of Anniston was the 900 and 1000 blocks of Noble Street. The Woodstock Iron Company was built near Ninth Street, on the site of a burned-out Confederate furnace. The company mill was located at the corner of Tenth Street near the Noble Theatre. The Anniston Manufacturing Company was just across the railroad tracks off Eleventh Street. Quintard, Leighton, and Christine Avenues were residential areas that developed east of downtown. After being surveyed and mapped by Gen. John H. Forney, the Woodstock Iron Company land, except for the area between Noble Street and the East Tennessee Railroad, was purchased by the Anniston City Land Company.

Starting in July 1883, land auctions were held in front of the Noble Theatre for many years. Some of the earliest buildings constructed were the Nonenmacher Bakery, the Caldwell Building, and the Wilmer Hotel. By 1887, Anniston was home to numerous retail stores, including Ullman Brothers, The Famous, and Lippman Brothers. After 1905, Noble Street expanded south of Ninth Street, and the area around Thirteenth and Noble Streets developed by 1917.

During World War I and the postwar boom, pipe foundries located on the west side of Noble Street brought more industry to town. While the pipe industry gave Anniston the title "Soil-Pipe Capital of the World," it was the textile mills that were the largest employers. Anniston Manufacturing, the Adelaide Mills, the Woodstock Mill, and the Blue Mountain Mill employed a large portion of the population.

The town's golden age was the 1950s and 1960s, when pipe shops and textile mills were hiring, and the growing military complex was becoming one of the largest employers in the area. North Noble Street, up to Twenty-second Street, was changing from residential to commercial property. In the 1950s, businesses began rapidly relocating to Quintard Avenue after it was opened to the south as a bypass for US 431. The change from residential area to business district on Quintard Avenue was complete by the early 1980s. Economic decline began in the late 1960s and early 1970s, when the soil-pipe foundries closed, followed by the textile mills in the 1980s and 1990s. When Fort McClellan closed in 1999, the town saw a further decline in both population and businesses.

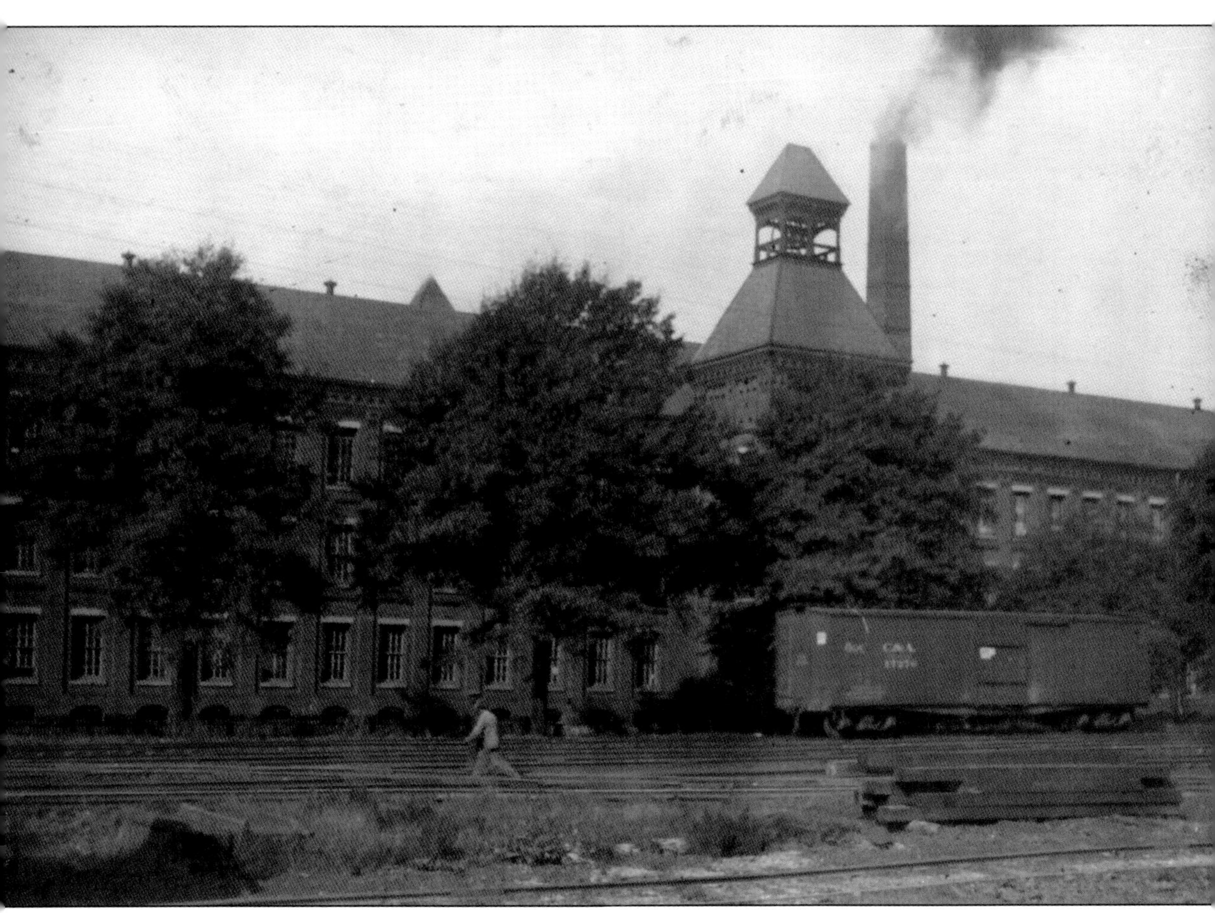

Anniston Manufacturing Company began operation in 1880 as an employer for the wives and children of Woodstock Iron employees. The Italian Renaissance Revival mill building, located at 215 West Eleventh Street, had 5,000 spindles making sheeting. Occupying 14 acres, the original three-story brick structure contained a central Lombardy bell tower. A two-story wing was added in 1928, and two non-adjoining buildings were erected during World War II to accommodate war-production needs. The well-maintained grounds hosted regularly scheduled flower shows. By 1958, Chicopee Mills had acquired the mill from Alfred Tyler's heirs and expanded the production capacity to manufacture cloth. The plant operated until 1977, when it was purchased by Chalk Line to manufacture sports jackets and screening operations. The mill closed in 1994 and was torn down in 2004. In 2012, the Department of Human Resources was built on the site after an industrial cleanup of PCB contamination. (LOC.)

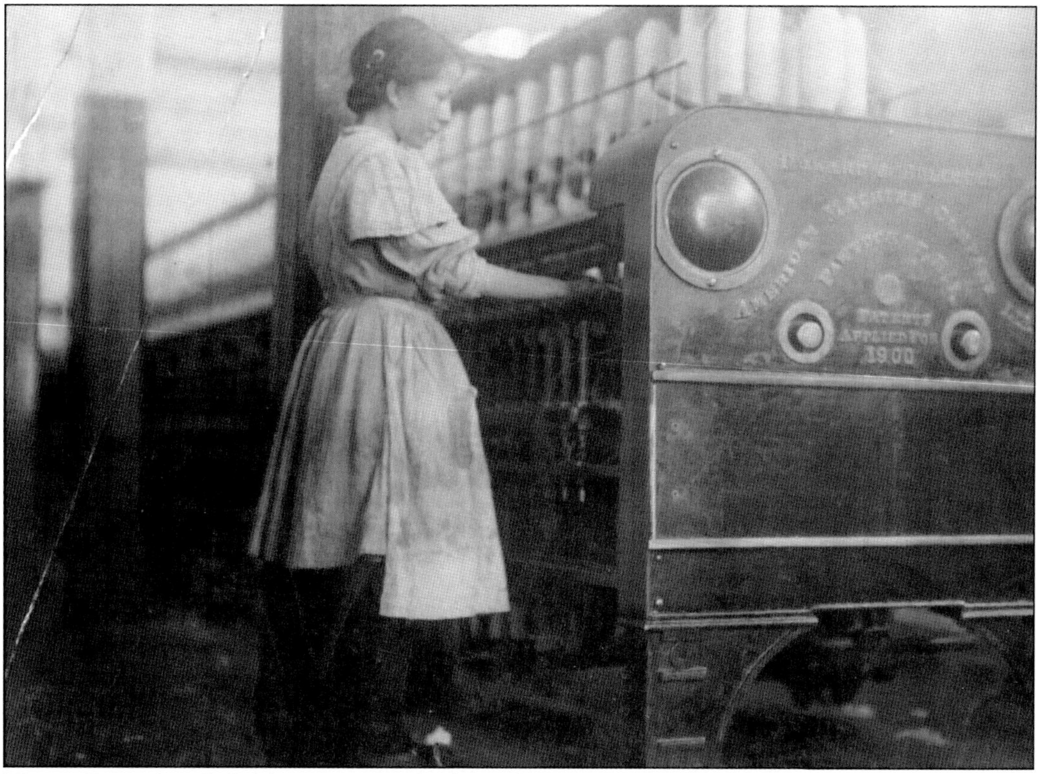

The mill employed children in its early days of operation. Lewis Hine, a noted sociologist and investigator from the National Child Labor Committee, found that the life of a child mill worker in Anniston was not as advertised by the company. Hine noted that the sanitation was bad and that the conditions for children at the Anniston Manufacturing Company were the worst in town. Mill employees included children under the age of 12, some of whom had been there for many years. These 1910 photographs depict the difficult life in the textile mills, which operated six days a week. The Woodstock Mill originally operated hand looms. These were replaced in 1908 by semiautomatic looms, and the facility was fully automatic by 1922. (Both, LOC.)

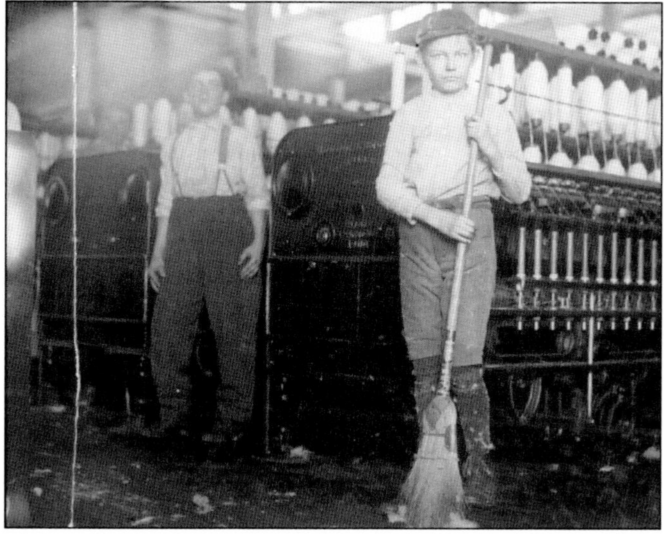

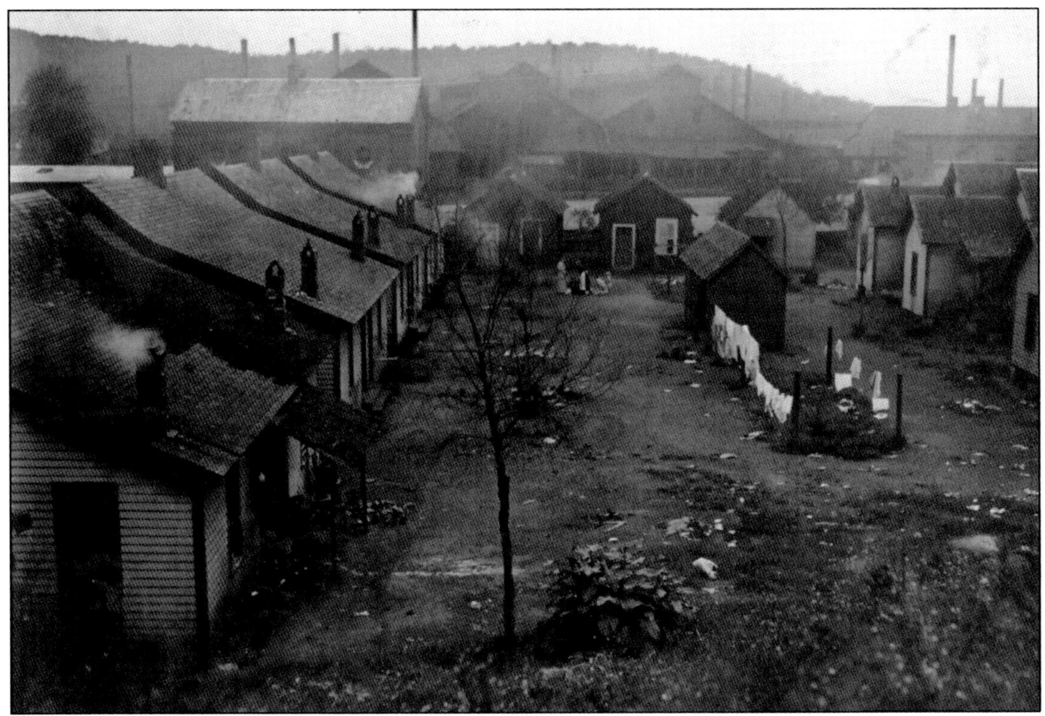

Adelaide Mills, seen in the background of this c. 1914 photograph, was located at 129 West Seventh Street. The facility was owned and operated by the Robinson family, then by the Roberts family, which managed the mill until 1980. Built on the site of the old Woodstock charcoal furnaces, the iron company's blowing engineer room was adapted for use by the mill as a machine shop, and stone from the furnace walls was incorporated into the mill's foundation. The mill, established in 1900, manufactured yarn using cotton grown by local farmers. It operated under the Adelaide Mills name until 1983. (LOC.)

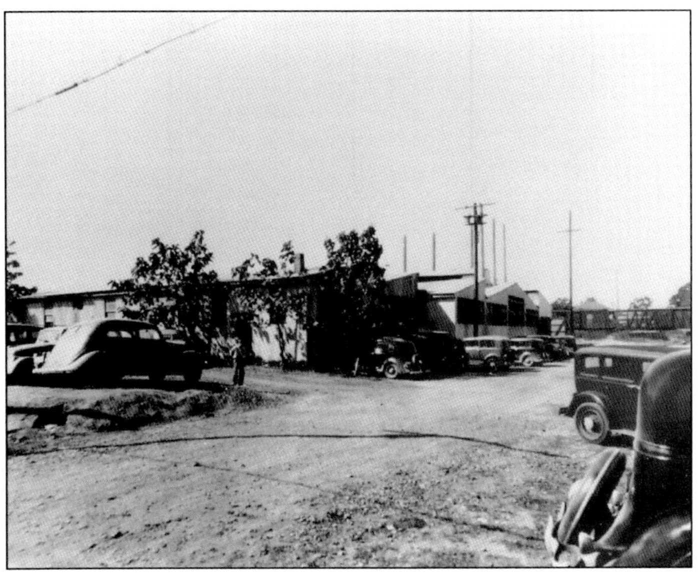

Lee Brothers started in 1917 as Fields & Lee Foundry with three employees. When E.T. Fields died in 1918, his partner, Alfred J. Lee, took over the company in 1919 and renamed it Lee Brothers (shown at Seventeenth Street and Walnut Avenue around 1930). In the early 1950s, the company, then known as Lee Brass, moved to 100 acres of land in Golden Springs and was a leading producer of brass fittings and castings, with commercial and military contracts.

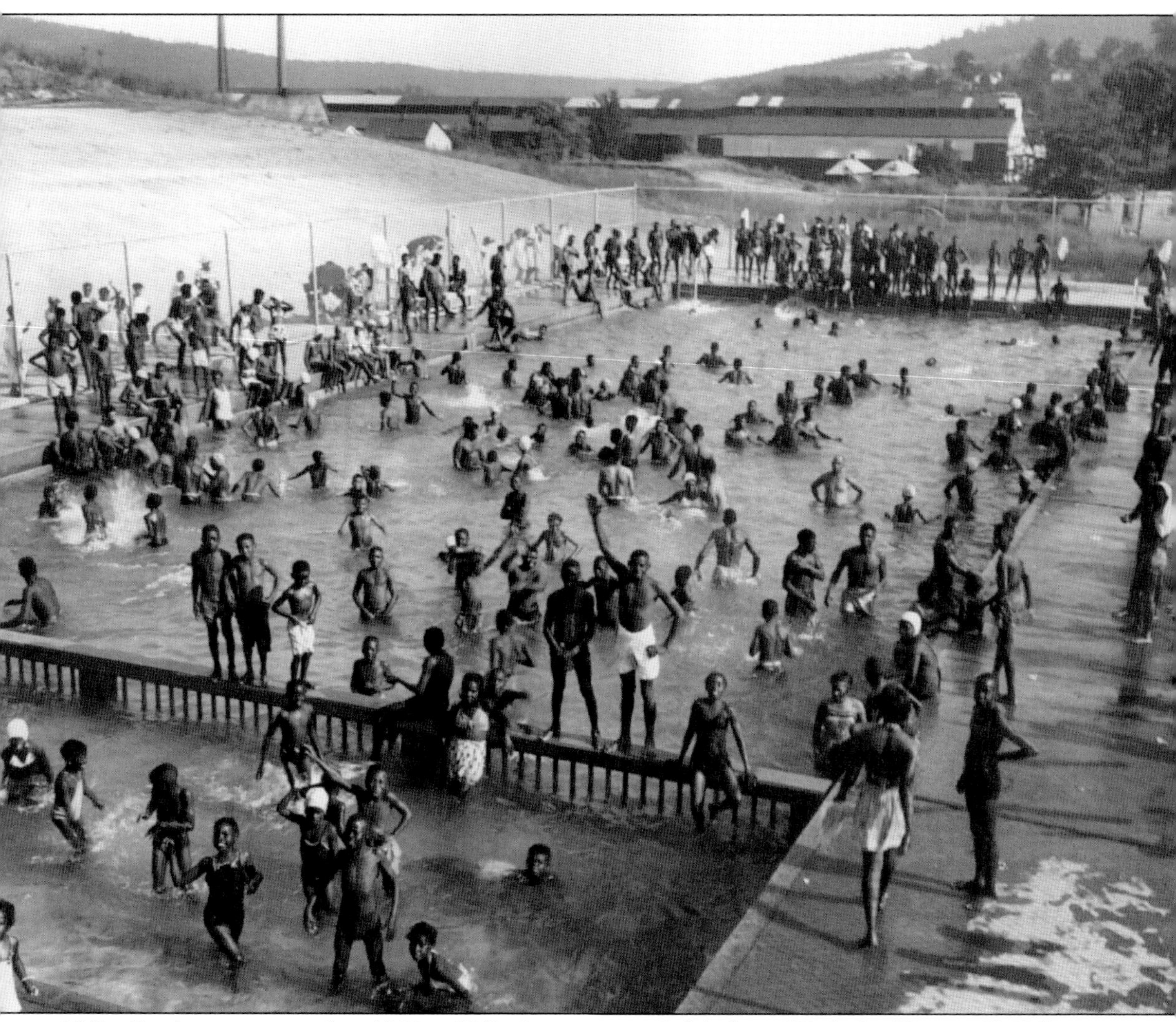

Kilby Steel was organized in 1900 as Kilby Locomotive & Machine Works by Thomas E. Kilby to build steam locomotives and, later, logging cars for use in sawmills. Kilby Steel manufactured artillery shells during World War I, World War II, and the Korean War. In 1948, the company moved from its Tenth Street and Glen Addie Avenue site, seen here in the background around 1948. J.L. Case used the facility until Anchor Metals moved to Anniston in 1959. (PLACC-BC.)

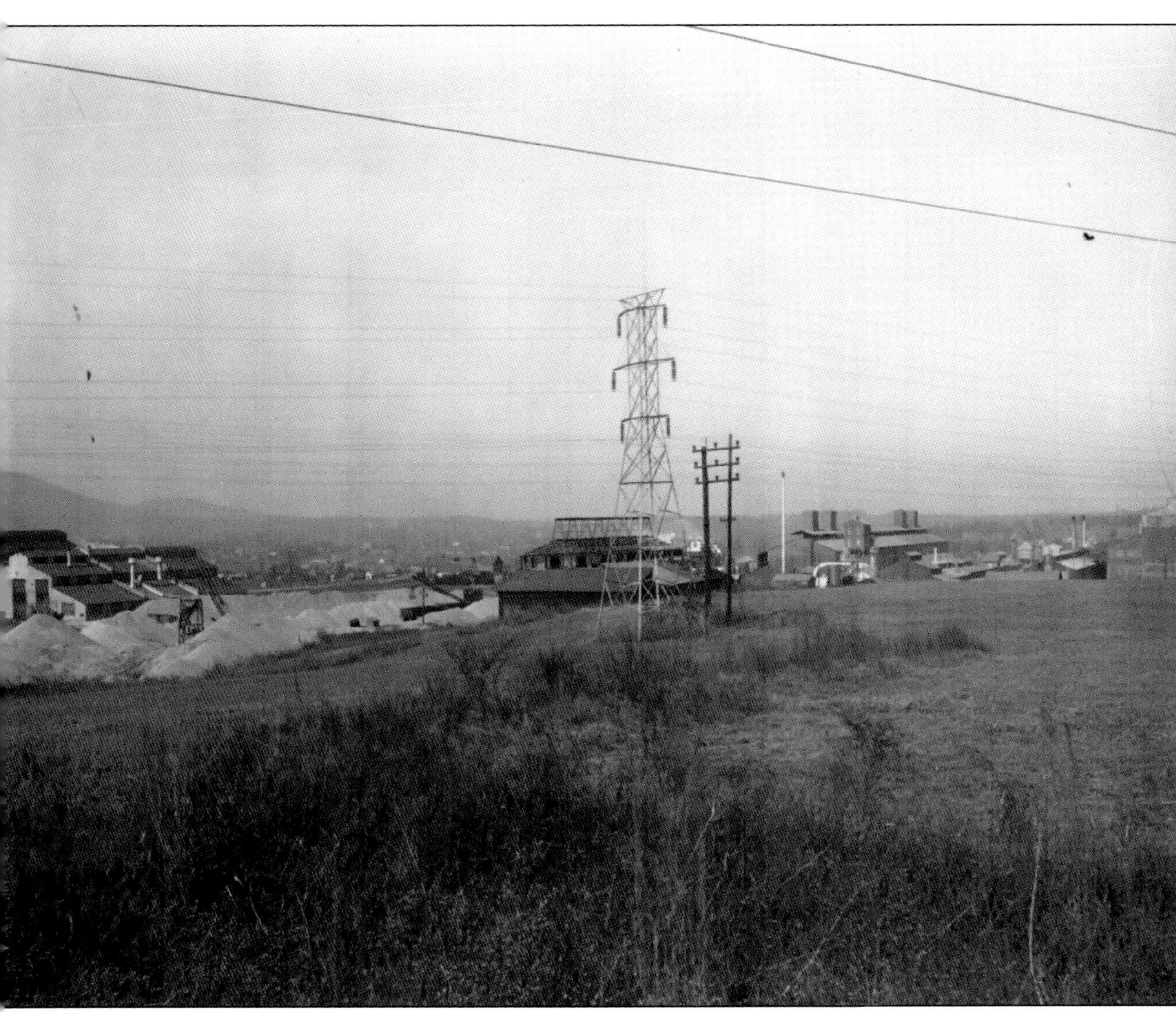

During World War I, Theodore Swann located the Southern Manganese Company near the western city limits of Anniston. Swann built an experimental electrical furnace to make ferromanganese steel, later used to make munitions for the US Army. By 1919, the company had converted from making steel to producing chemicals. This was the beginning of the Anniston Branch of Monsanto Chemical Company, where PCBs were produced from 1935 until 1977. When it was discovered in 1993 that Anniston had been exposed to toxins, the town earned the dubious title of "Toxic Town." In 1997, Monsanto's chemical operations were incorporated into Solutia Inc., which continued to operate at the West Anniston location.

A carriage factory on East Twelfth Street was built around 1890, with George Harrison Brummel's factory locating in the building in 1892. In the early days, carriages and buggies were built, but production gave way to automobiles. The first floor of the building housed a woodworking area, and a paint shop was located on the second floor, accessed by a ramp. During World War II, the second floor was used as a USO. Brummel lived next door to his factory until his death in March 1949. The carriage factory is shown here around 1930.

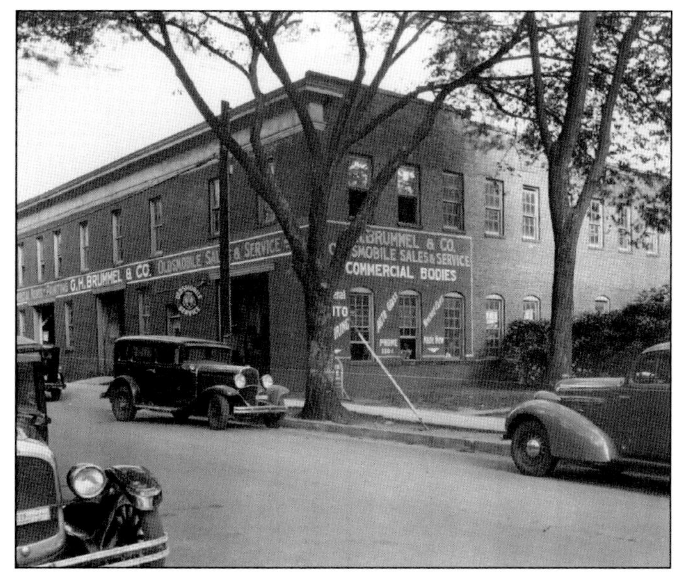

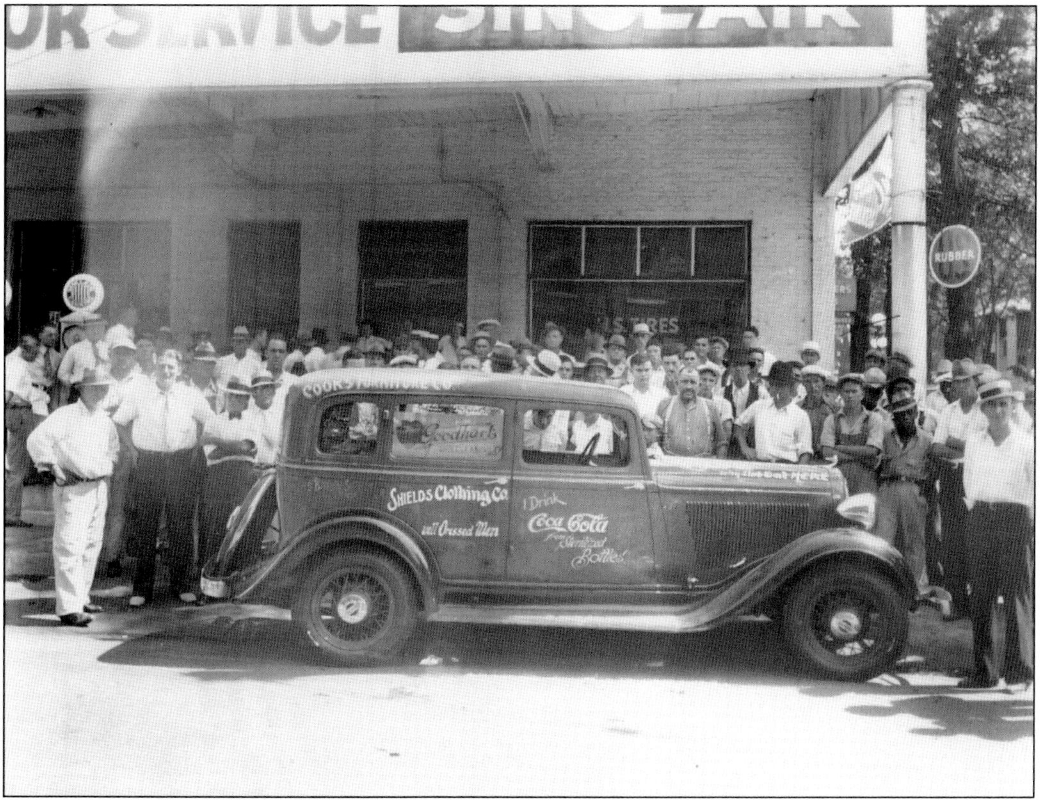

Sinclair Oil stations were affiliates of the Sinclair Refining Company, located at 818 Noble Street, which started in Calhoun County in 1926. Local agent Henry H. Booth started with one truck and one employee. He then built Sinclair's business into three trucks to provision 30 service-station dealers. Around 1942, this Anniston Sinclair station hosts a rolling billboard car while men sign up to fight in World War II.

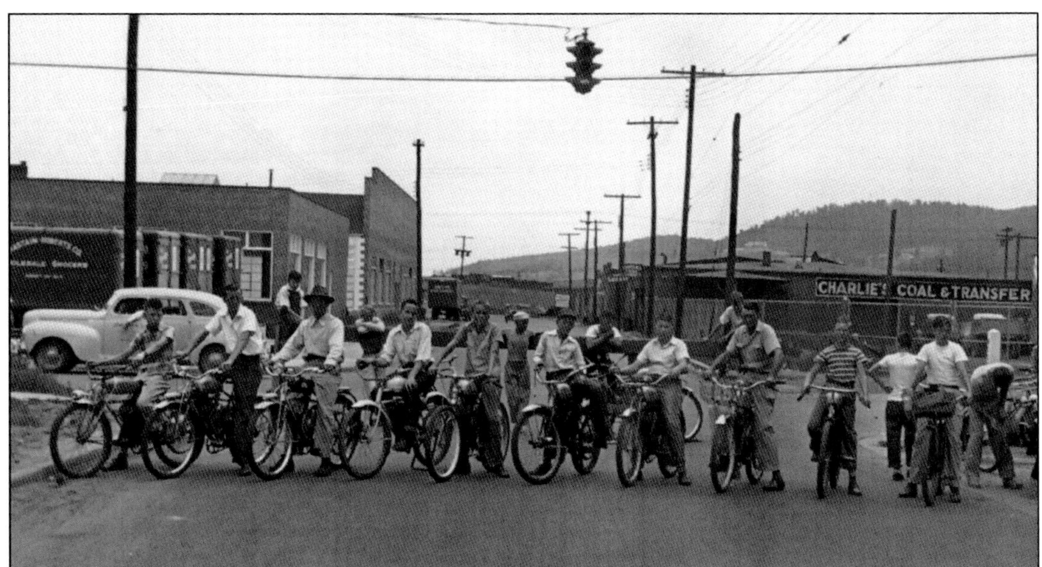

Chastain-Roberts, shown at left behind these Boy Scouts around 1946, was formed in 1933 as a flour and feed wholesaler at 1100 Moore Avenue. In 1939, the firm purchased Alabama Supply Co, a full-line grocery wholesaler. Chastain-Roberts joined the Independent Grocery Alliance (IGA) and received the franchise to serve Northern Alabama in 1959. The company became a subsidiary of SuperValu and relocated to the Anniston Industrial Park in the early 1970s. (PLACC-BC.)

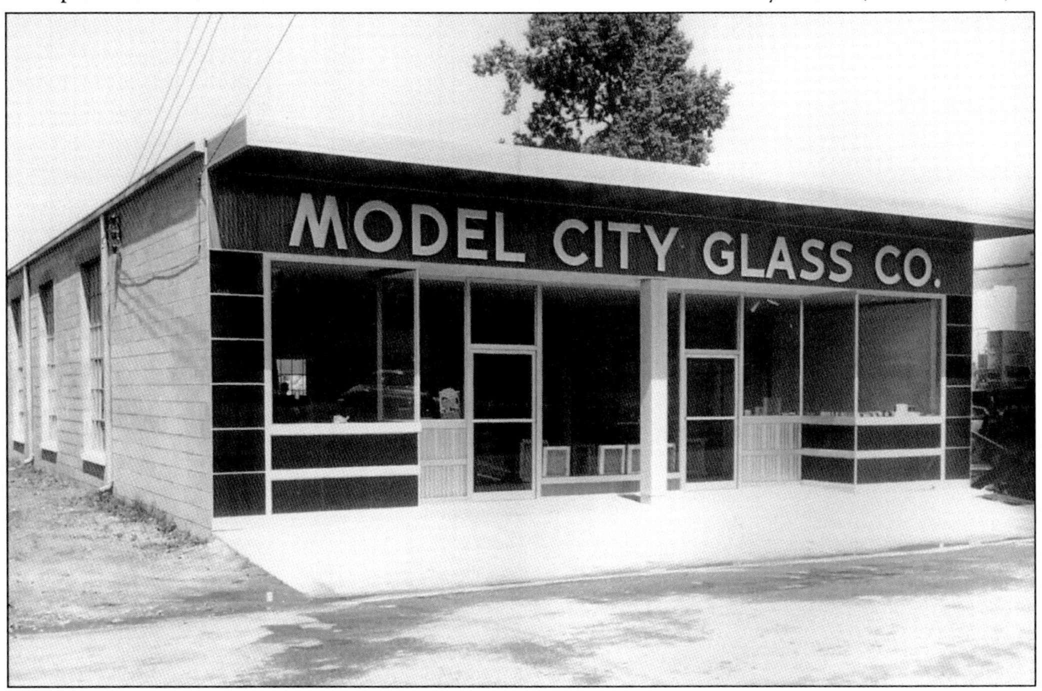

Model City Glass Company was opened by Lowell A. Tyson in 1947. The company, located at 1316 Walnut Avenue, specialized in metal storefront construction, plate glass, doors, and bath essentials. By 1962, the company relocated first to 934 West Tenth Street for three years, then to its permanent location, 100 West Tenth Street. The Walnut Avenue location, seen here around 1958, served as the state ABC Store until 1989.

The Auto Beauty Shoppe, seen here from Atlanta Avenue around 1940, was originally part of the Hale Buggy Company. The shop was located at Fifteenth Street and Walnut Avenue, but by 1958, it had moved to 930 West Tenth Street. In the 1950s, owner Cliff Worsham offered a 24-hour towing service with seven wreckers, body and fender repair, and auto painting.

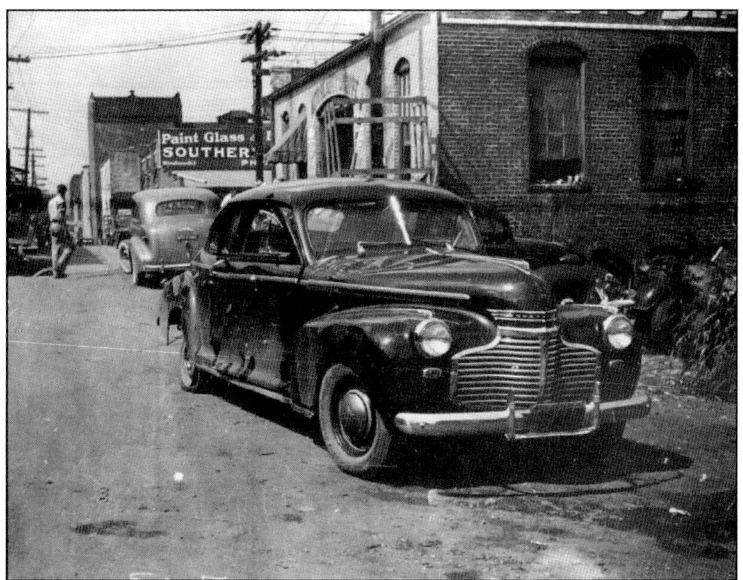

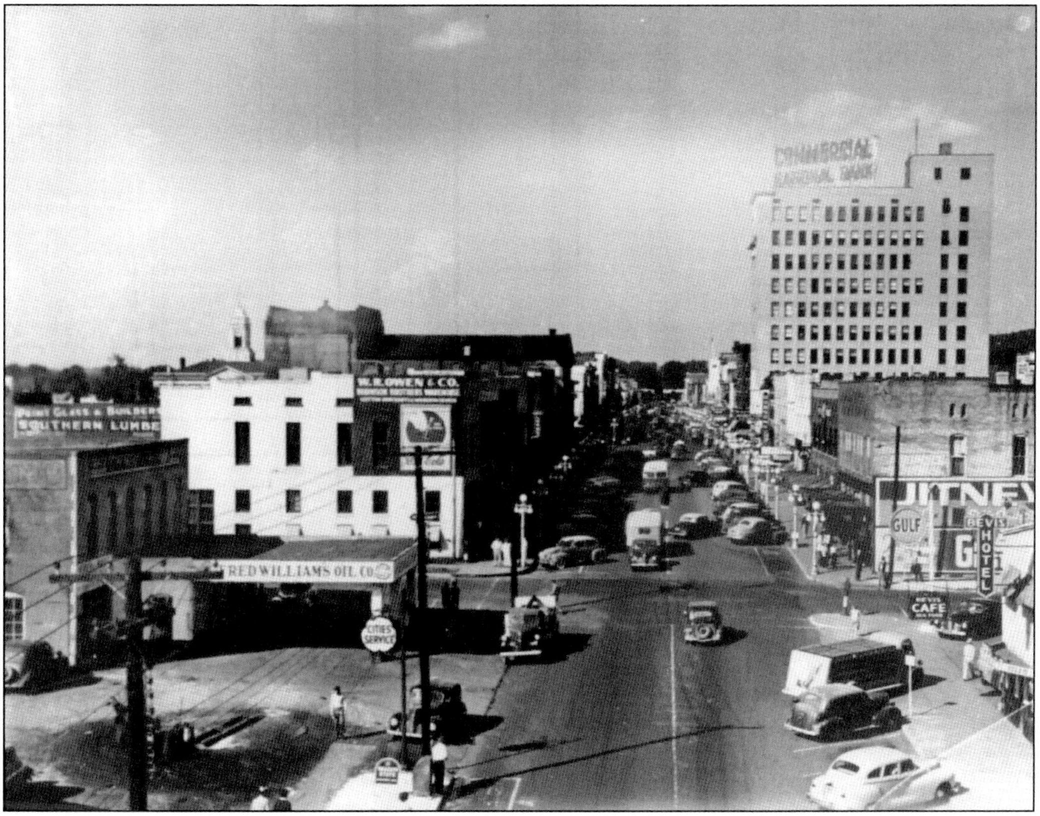

This north-facing photograph, taken around 1948, shows Noble Street, home to numerous chain stores, including Woolworth's, Grant's, and J.C. Penney. The street also featured multiple movie theaters and several locally owned stores. Military personnel would take the bus from Fort McClellan and spend the day enjoying all the offerings on Noble Street, which remained the major downtown district until the 1950s, when business began shifting east to Quintard Avenue.

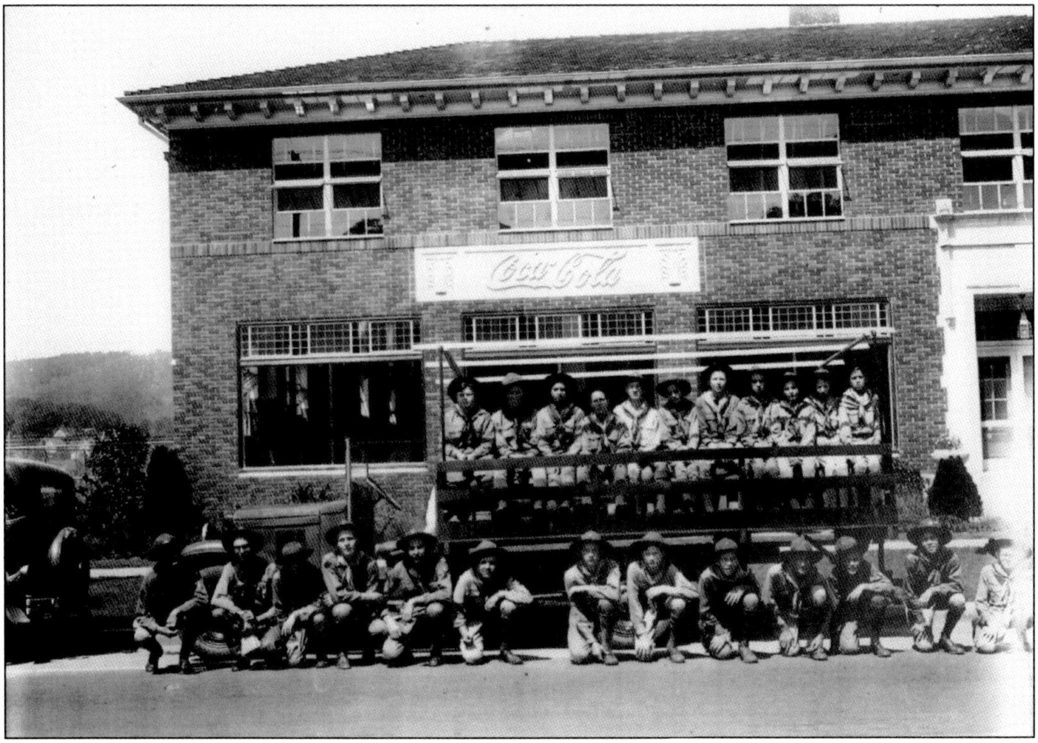

Bottling of Coca-Cola in Anniston started around 1903 on West Thirteenth Street with a foot-powered machine and a one-mule delivery wagon. In 1907, Charles Rainwater and Joseph Edmondson purchased the Anniston plant, along with other plants in northeast Alabama, to create the Alabama Coca-Cola Bottling Company. The Anniston plant, seen here around 1931, was completed in early 1931 at the 420 Noble Street site, where the bottling operation remained until 1976, when a modern plant was constructed in Oxford. The Salvation Army has occupied the building since 1977.

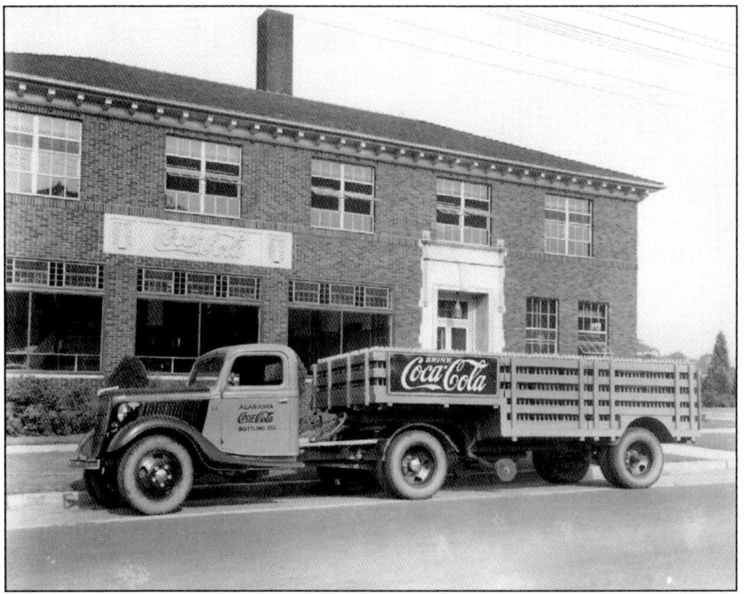

The Coca-Cola Bottling Company expanded in 1956 with the creation of a vending operation called Vendala Inc. to service local industrial plants with snacks and food. By 1966, the business was chartered as a subsidiary of Alabama Coca-Cola Bottling and began a full-service vending operation at 407 Noble Street until 1982. Vendala Inc. then moved to the main bottling plant at Oxford.

In March 1933, the Acme Stores and the Farmers Supply Company merged and operated under the latter name. C.R. Everett (pictured around 1930) and J.M. Peters managed the company. Located at 715 Noble Street, Farmers Supply sold international motor trucks, farm tractors, and farm machines, as well as industrial tractors and equipment until closing in 1977. The building burned down in the 1980s.

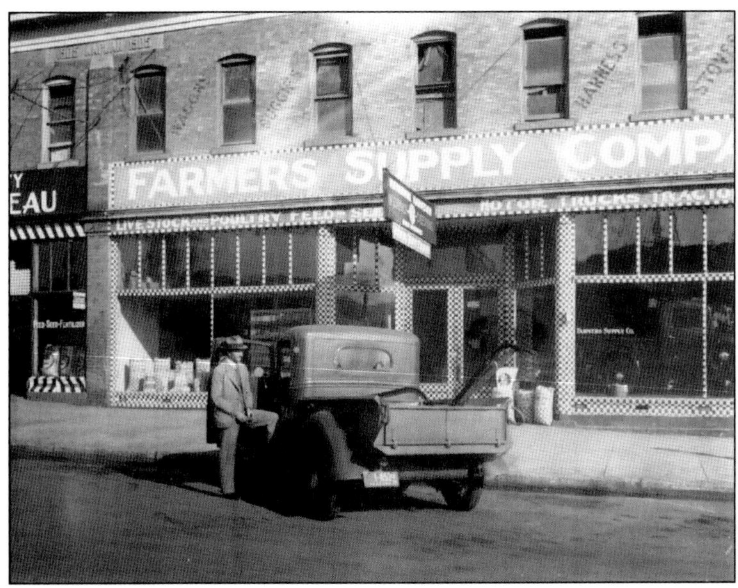

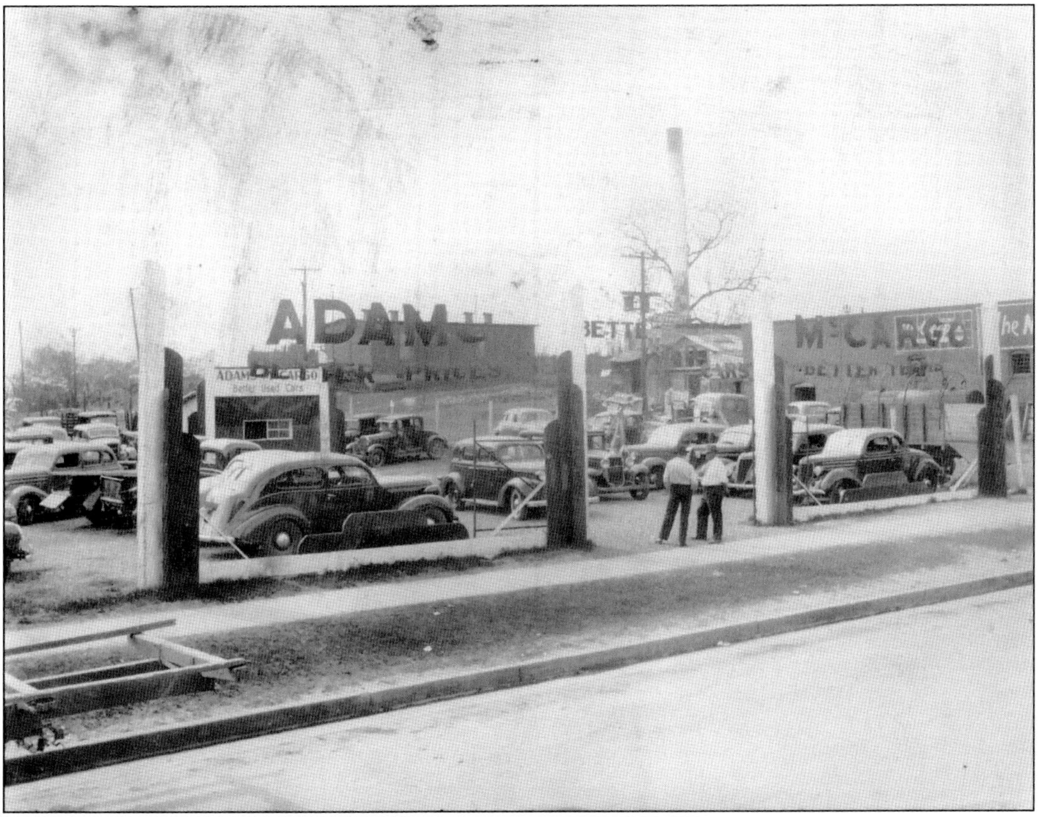

In September 1927, Virgil Adams of Meridian, Mississippi, and Dewitt McCargo of Talladega, Alabama, took over the Fox-Bandy Motor Company at Twelfth Street and Gurnee Avenue. The Adams-McCargo Used Car Lot was located at several sites during its 38 years of operation. Shown here around 1940 is the lot on Seventh and Noble Streets. This was an ideal location for the servicemen stationed at Fort McClellan to browse for a car while on leave.

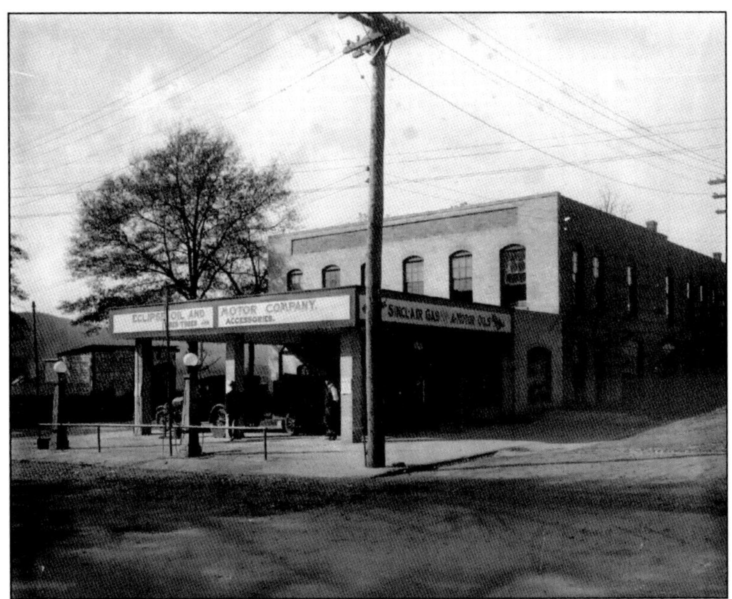

Eclipse Motor Company was built in the early 1920s at 830 Noble Street, on the site of the old American House Hotel. Throughout the 1920s and 1930s, the Eclipse dealership operated a Woco-Pep repair service station next door (seen here around 1922). From 1938 until 1962, the service station operated as Fred Williamson Oil. The site has served as a Goodyear Tire store in the 1960s, a flower shop in the 1970s, and Goodson Funeral Home in the 21st century.

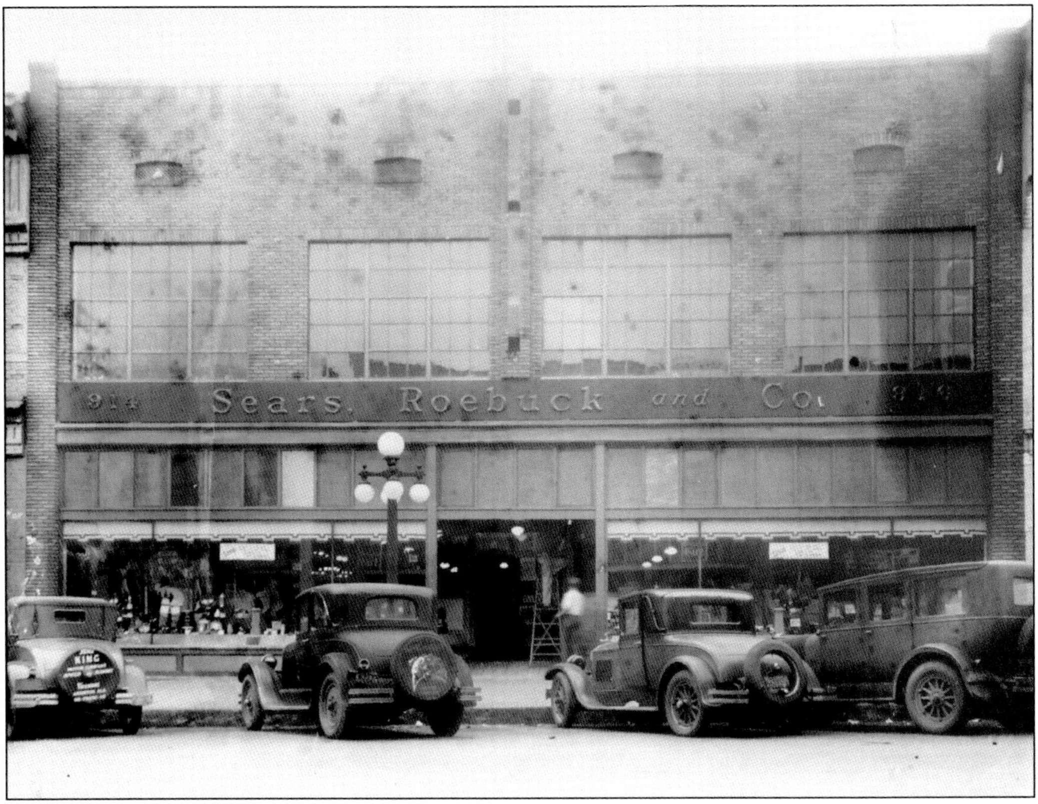

Around 1951, Claude Kitchens, who was associated with Belk Hudson's, opened Kitchens Thrift Store, a discount department store, at 914–916 Noble Street. This location had briefly housed Sears in the 1920s. Kitchens Thrift Store operated at this location until 1974, when it closed. Claude Kitchens moved on to open the Withit Shop and Kitchens Department Store. In the early 21st century, the building was occupied by the US Bankruptcy Court.

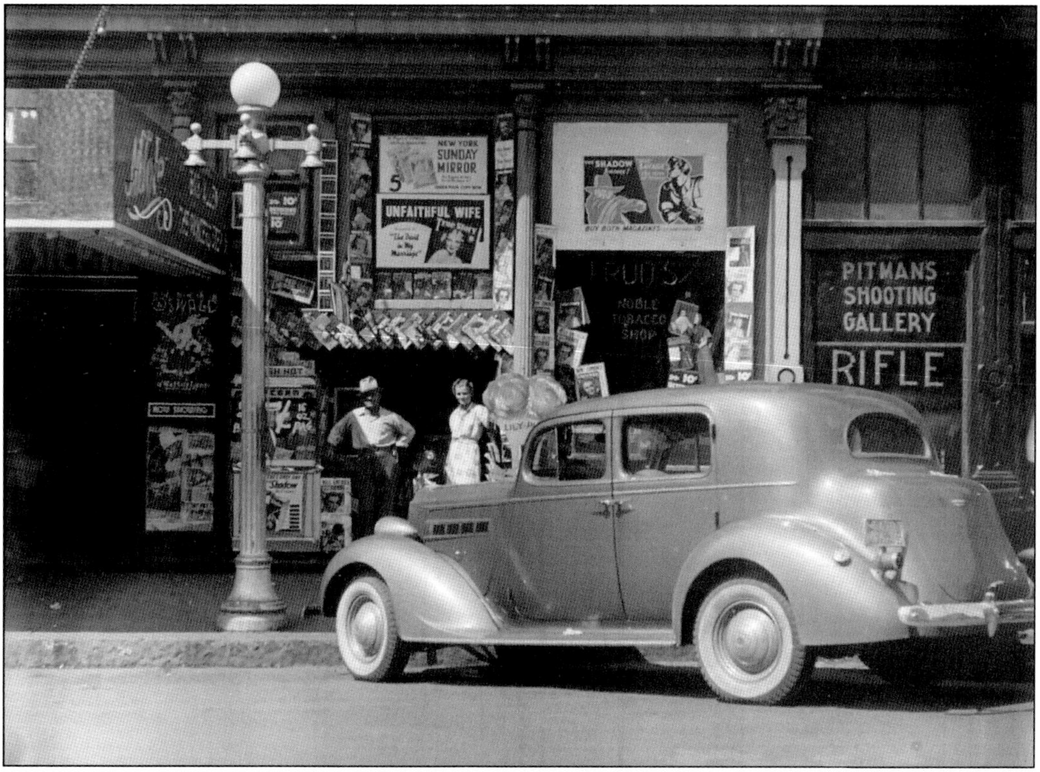

Tobacco shops and pool halls were plentiful on Noble Street. The Noble Tobacco Shop, at 928 Noble Street (seen around 1937), was part of the Noble Theatre. Next to this tobacco shop was Pitman's Shooting Gallery, a billiards hall. These two locations saw various tenants until 1962, when the Noble Theatre building was slated for demolition.

The 900 block of Noble Street had always been the hub of the city. In the 1940s, the block was home to the Liles-Wilson Building, the Noble Theatre, various lunch counters, billiard halls, shoe shops, and a laundry. The two-lane street featured angled parking at the curb, like many small towns of the day.

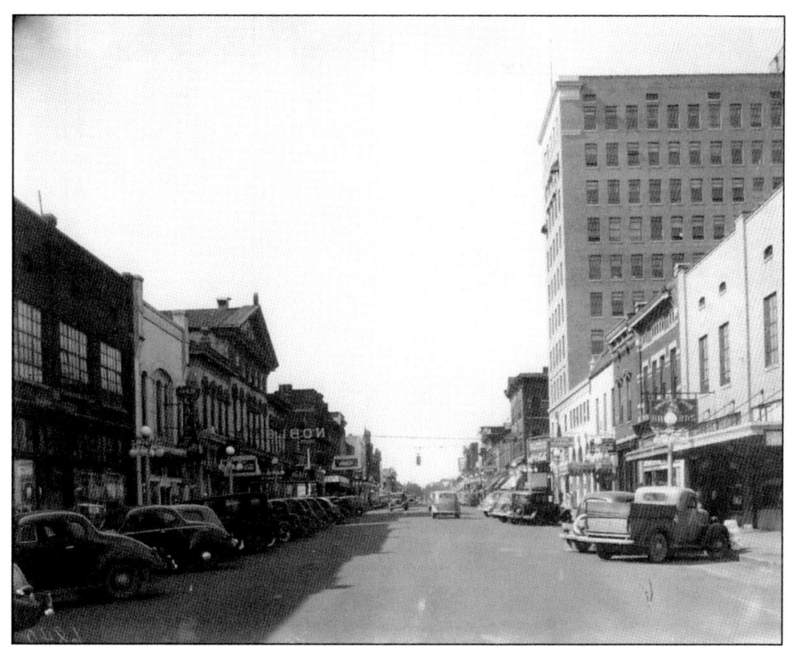

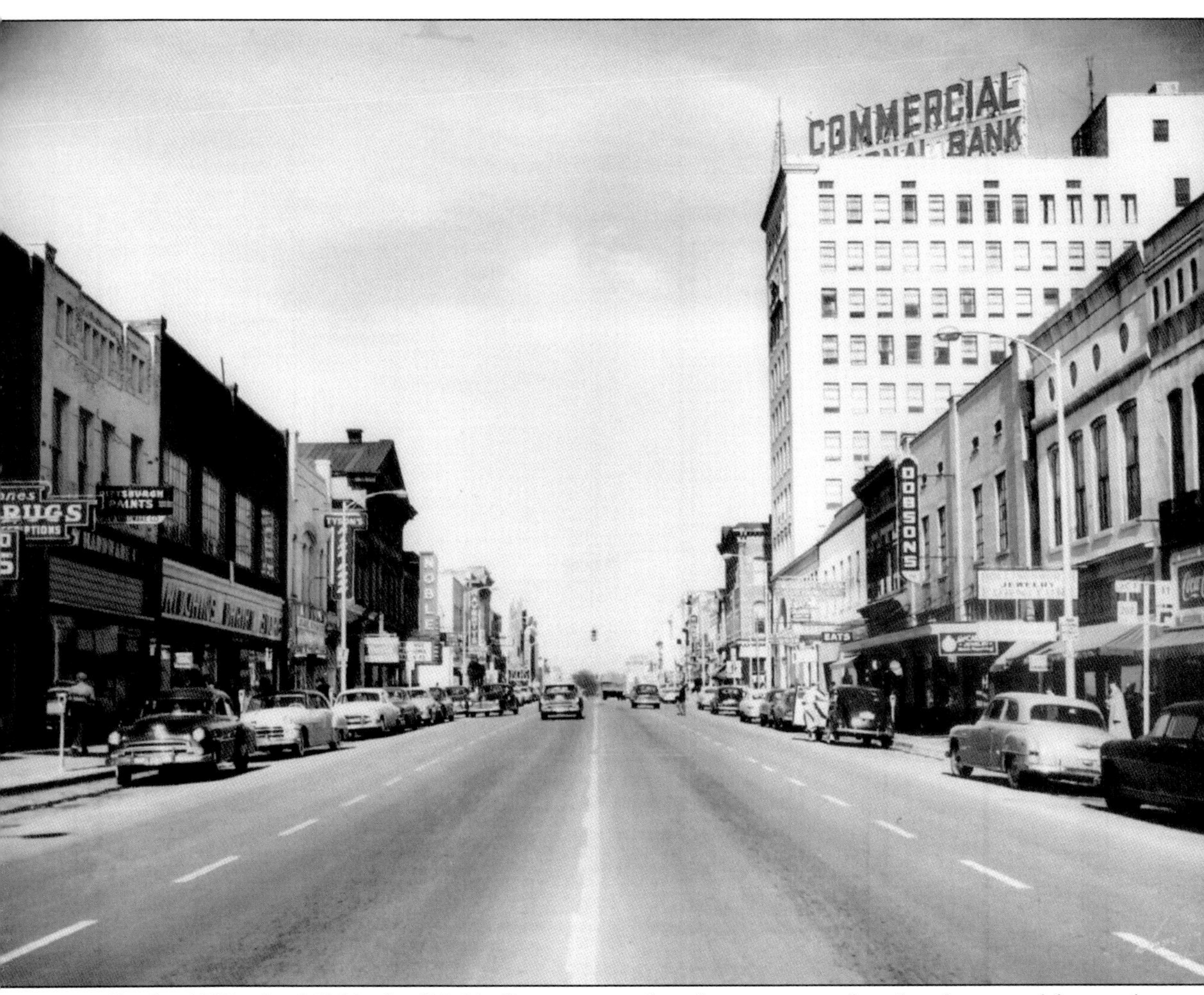

By the 1950s, the 900 block of Noble Street was widened to accommodate four lanes and featured parallel parking. During this time, the block housed several jewelry stores, clothing stores, drugstores, an auto-parts store, and a hardware store. By 2014, several restaurants, government agencies, and antique stores occupied the block.

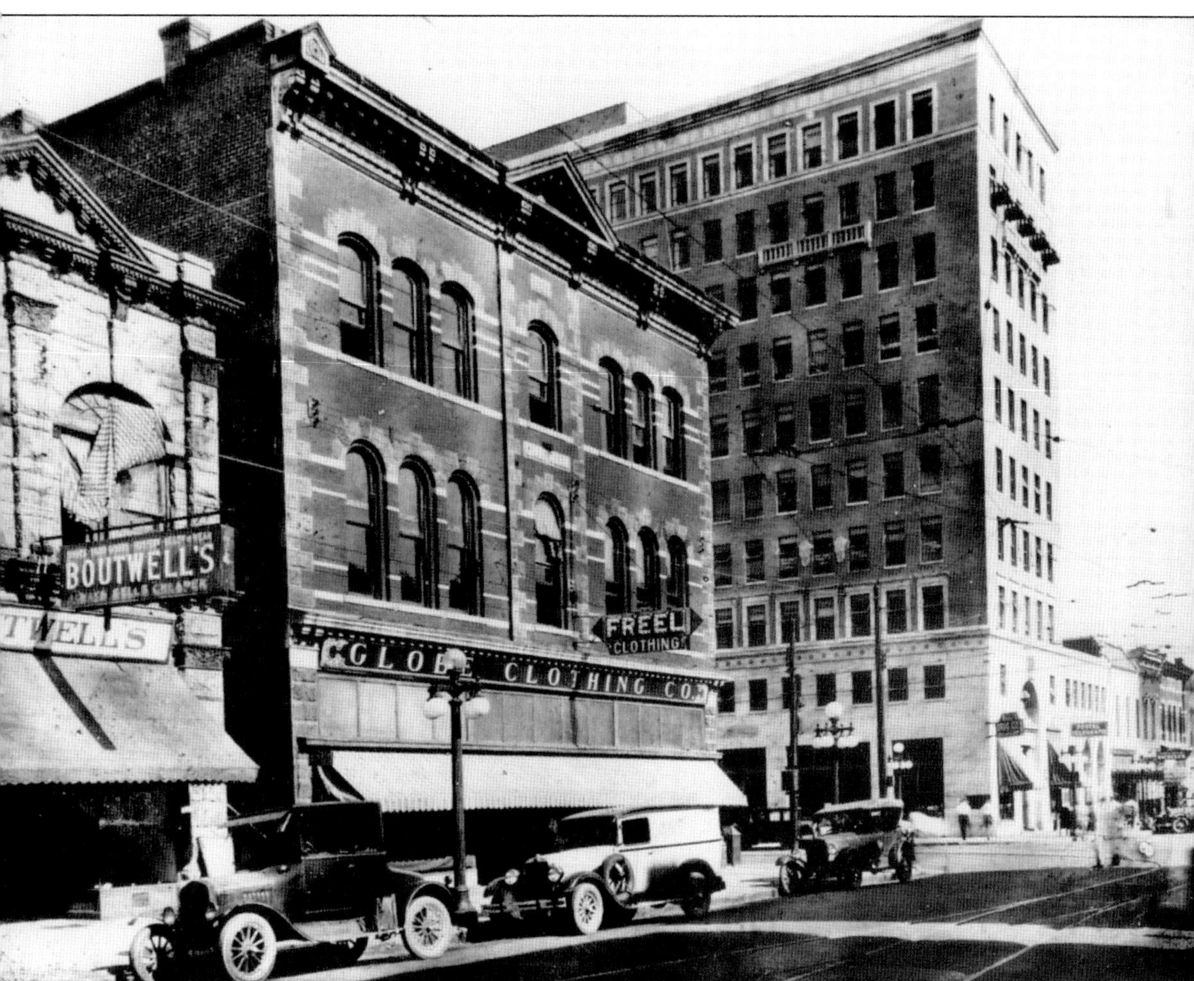

The Caldwell Building, located at 1001 Noble Street, was built on the first lot sold in Anniston. The lot, purchased by W.H. Williams in June 1883, was the original site of the Woodstock Iron Company's Episcopal church building. John M. Caldwell, the attorney for Woodstock Iron Company, built the three-story Italianate structure in 1889. The Globe Clothing Company, a men and boy's clothing store, occupied the building from around 1900 to 1929. It is seen here around 1925. By 1931, Mangel's, a women's apparel store, had moved in, remaining until 1979. Through the years, the upper floors of the building have been used as office space.

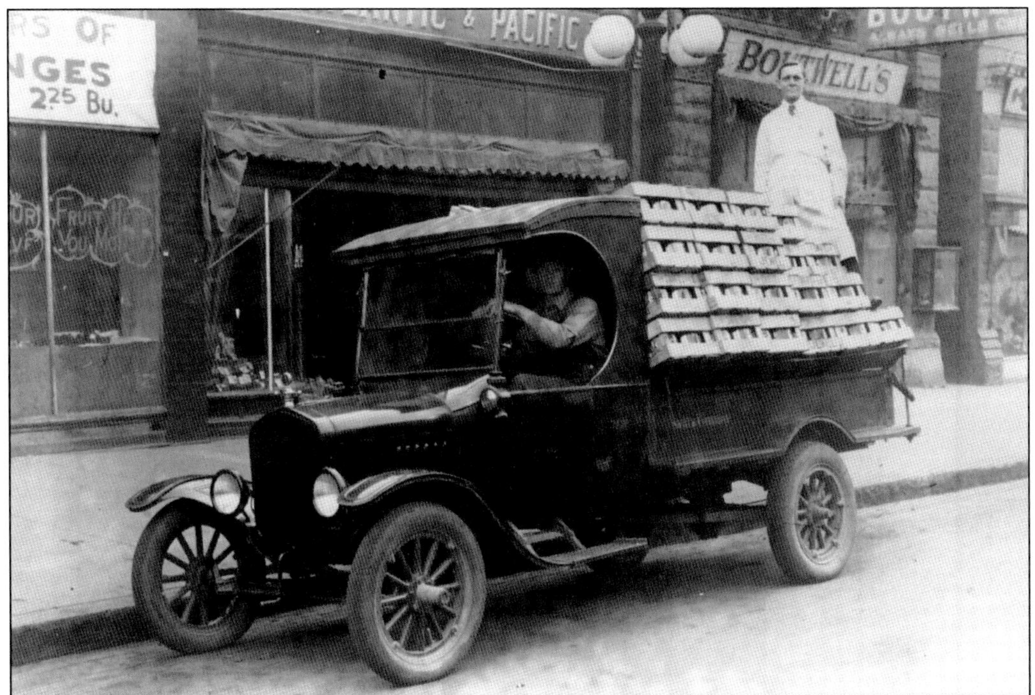

The Great Atlantic & Pacific Tea Company, better known as A&P, entered Anniston not long after the end of World War I. The grocery chain operated multiple stores in Anniston and throughout Calhoun County. The company started out as a delivery grocer, but changed over time to a "cash-and-carry" business. It incorporated its A&P brands, such as Eight O'Clock Coffee. This photograph was taken around 1920.

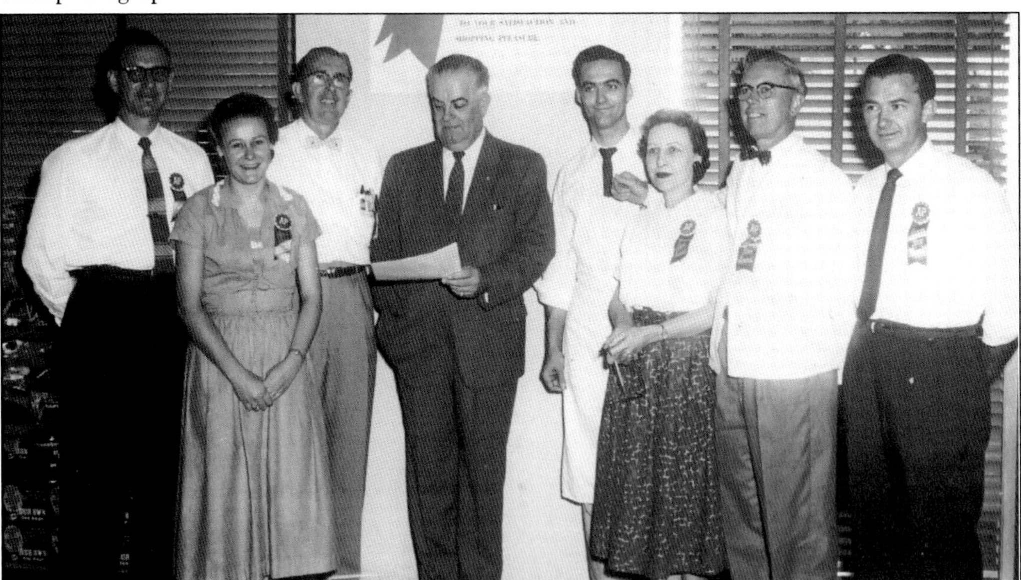

The A&P stores did well in the area, but after the death of the chain's founders in the 1950s, the company lost direction. By the early 1970s, the business faced heavy financial losses due to poor management and began closing stores. All of Anniston's A&P stores had closed by the mid-1970s. Here, employees of the A&P store at 620 Noble Street gather around 1965. (ERY.)

Hudson's Department Store was opened in August 1936 by Michael Hudson and Gray L. Hunter in the 1100 block of Noble Street. The Anniston Belk's store was the chain's first establishment in Alabama. In 1940, the store moved to 1017–1021 Noble Street, then expanded into a modern building in 1972. After Hudson's closed in 1997, the Stewart Building was renovated as office space. In this photograph of a parade, taken around 1950, Hudson's is the second building from the right.

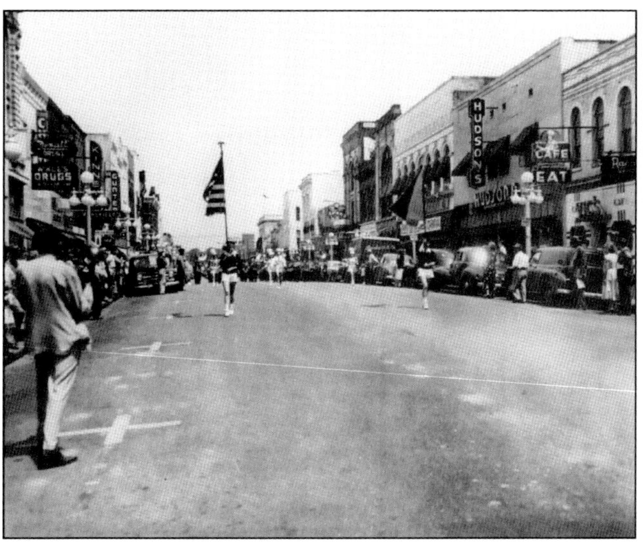

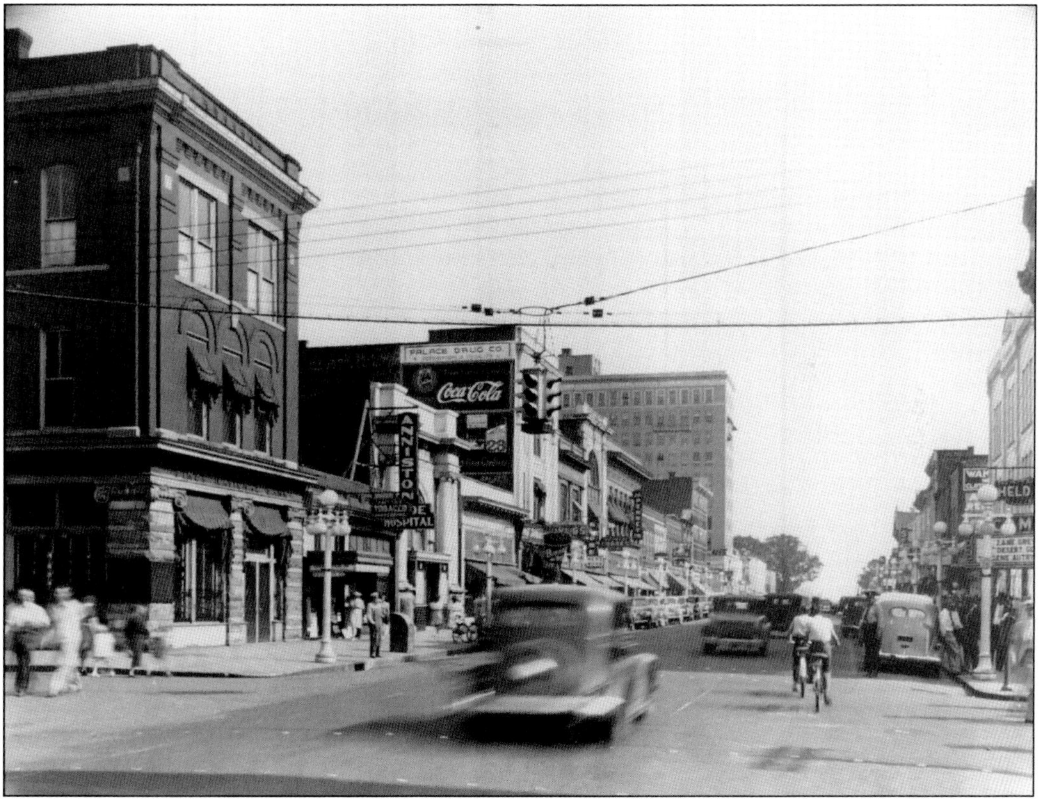

Around 1915, Palace Drugs opened at 1025 Noble Street. It is seen at center in this c. 1936 photograph. The drugstore was affiliated with Jitney Drugs, as well as Curry and Broadnax Drugs. Joe Broadnax was the manager of the drugstore until it closed in 1952. The building housed many different businesses, including the Cheese Deli and a finance company. In 1942, Electrik Maid Bakery moved next door at 1023 Noble Street, where it remained until 1988.

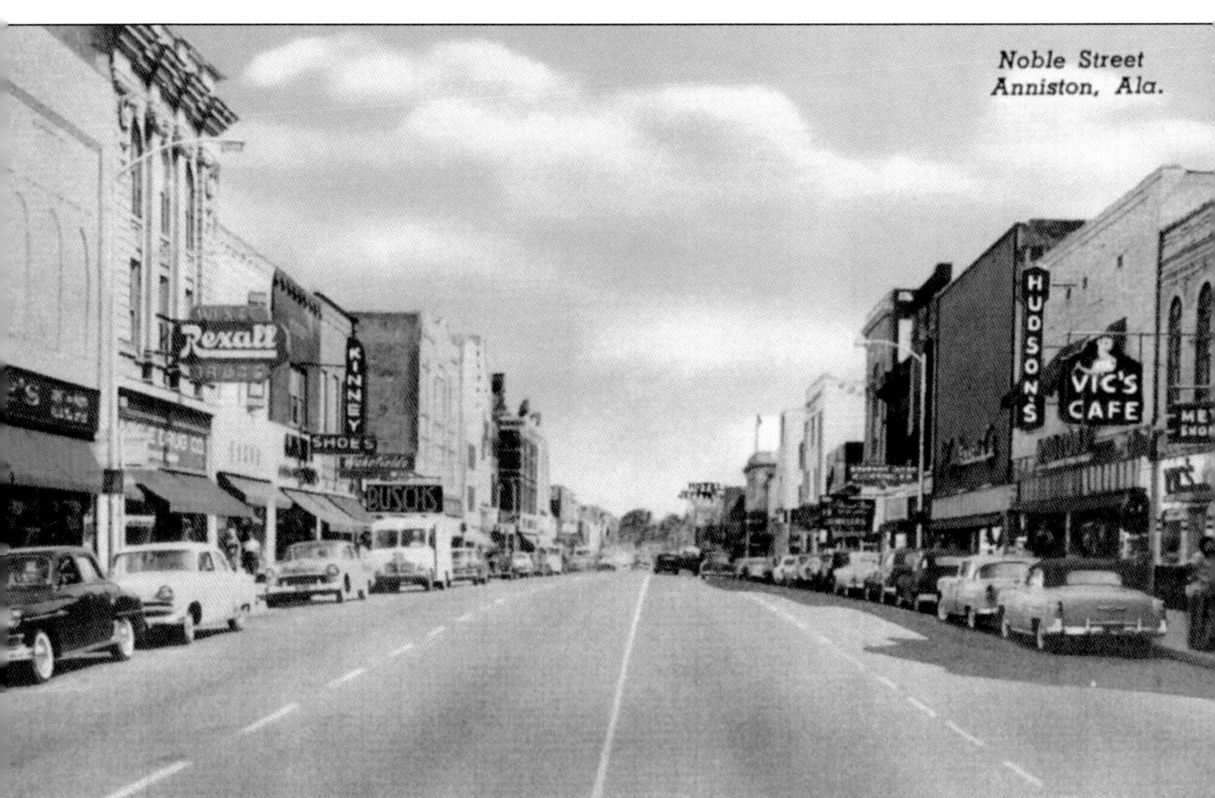

Wikle's Drug, seen here at left around 1950, was one of the first buildings constructed in Anniston. Dr. Jesse L. Wikle came to Anniston in 1880 to run the Woodstock Iron Company Lab. By 1883, he opened Wikle's Drug at 1010 Noble Street, where it remained, under various managers, until 1999. Dr. Wikle retired from the drugstore business in 1917, but continued to be active in civic life by serving on the city council, in the state senate for two terms, and as mayor three different times until his death in 1940. (PLACC.)

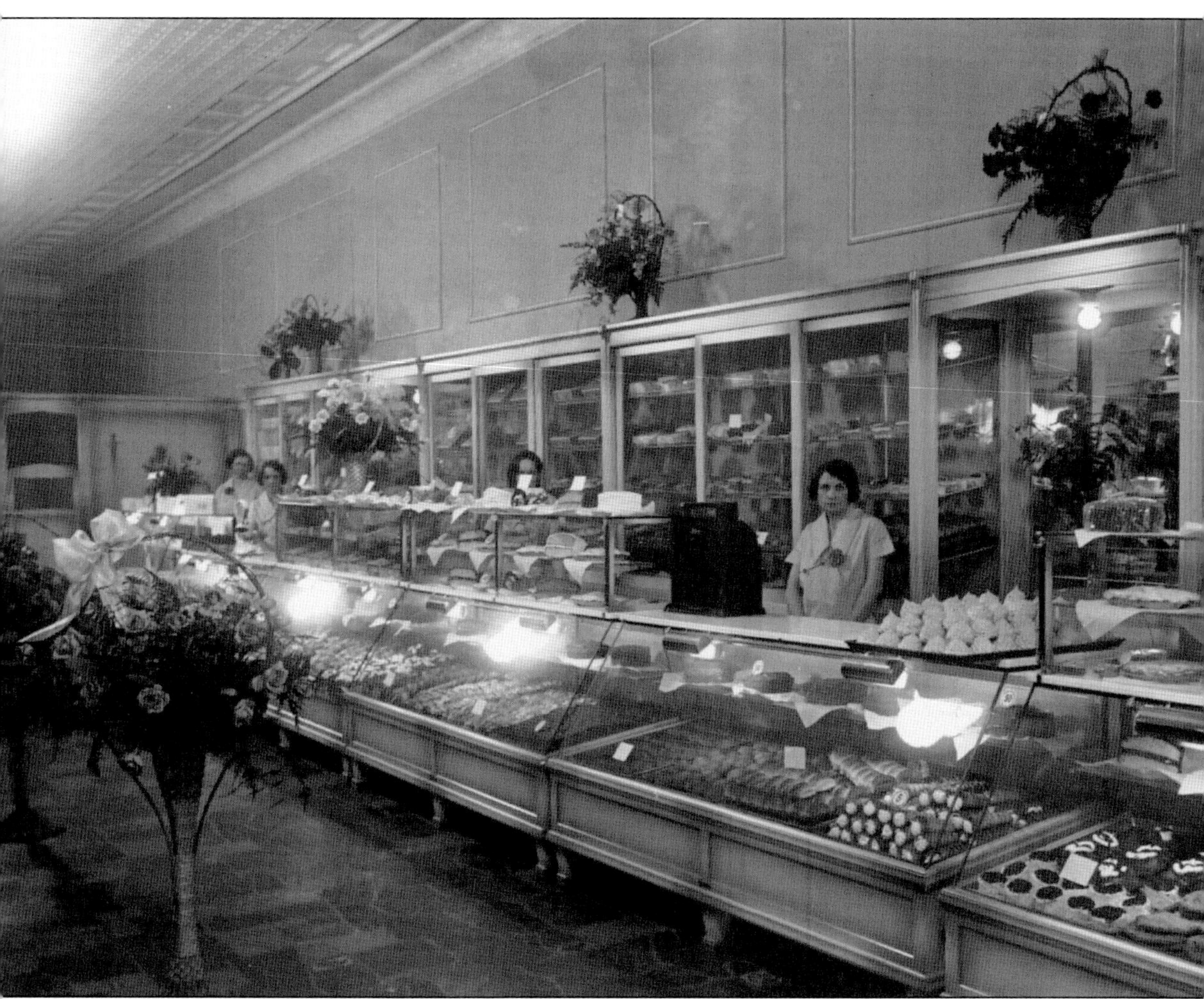

Bakeries were plentiful in Anniston in the 20th century. E.O. Lloyd opened Lloyd's Bakery in 1919, which became Hart's Bakery in 1952. Lloyd's Sweet Shop & Cafe, seen here around 1931, was at 1012 Noble Street on the first floor. In 1932, the second floor was renovated to serve as a ballroom for private dances, banquets, and parties. In addition to sweets and pastries, Lloyd's served homemade ice cream as well as full meals. The Sweet Shop was destroyed in 1939 by a fire. Other bakeries in town included Little Chef in the 1800 block of Noble Street and Electrik Maid, located in the 1000 block of Noble Street.

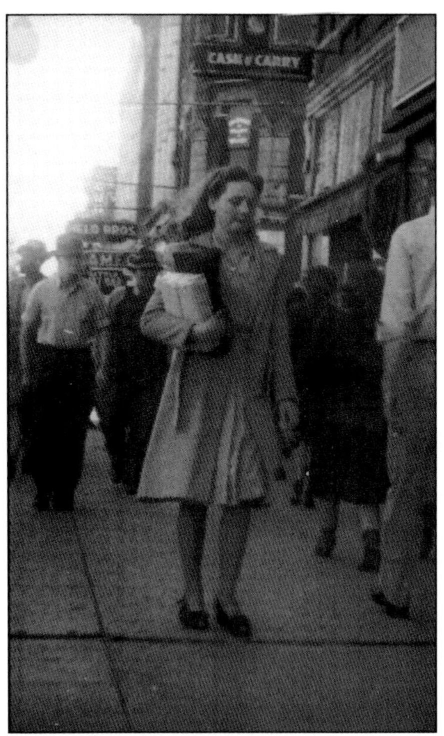

The Held Brothers' Department Store and the Cameo Theater were located in the 1000 block of Noble Street, seen here around 1940. In the 1930s and 1940s, Held Brothers' sold clothing, shoes, and furnishings. The Cameo Theater, managed by the Alabama Theater Corporation, operated from February 1939 until it closed in late September 1950. The site was remodeled a few weeks after closing to accommodate a retail merchandise establishment. (ERY.)

F.W. Woolworth, a successful five-and-dime enterprise in the 20th century, located in Anniston at 1026 Noble Street by 1917. It is seen here at center around 1920. From around 1929 to 1939, Woolworth's operated at 1120 Noble Street. By 1942, the store had moved back to the 1000 block in the Levi Building (far left). The building was remolded to include brick in the upper-floor windows. Woolworth's Anniston store closed in 1972. The Levi Building was restored to house the Classic on Noble.

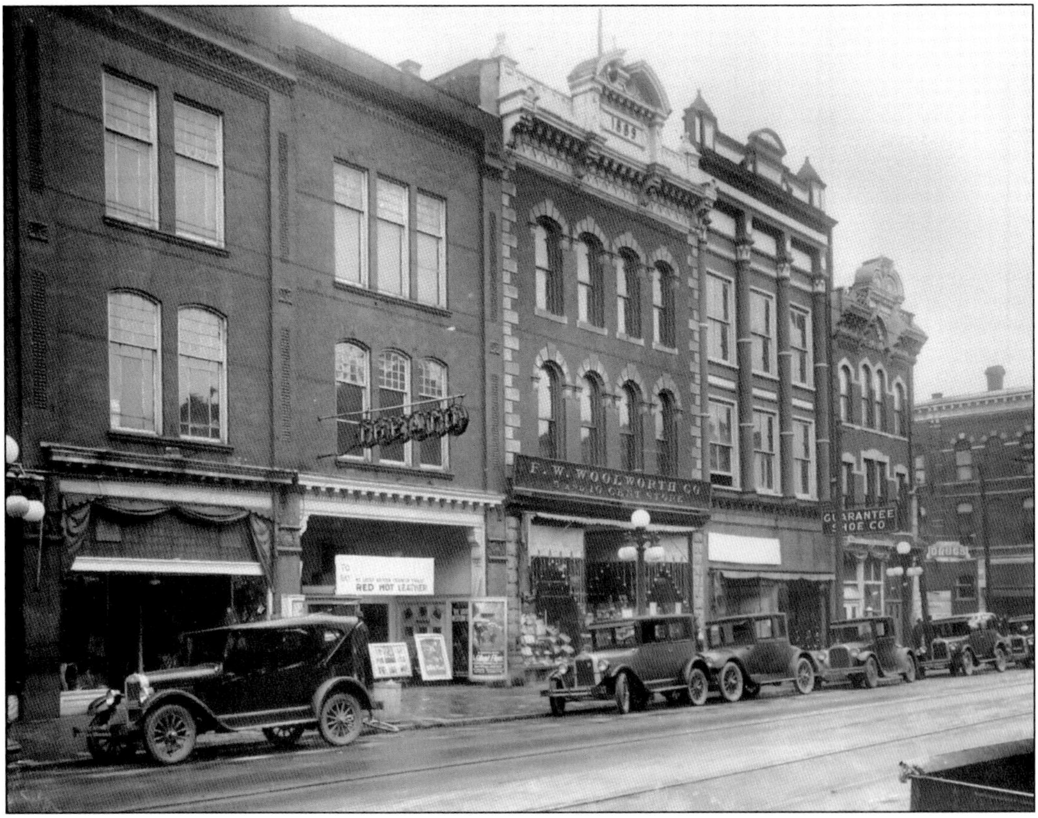

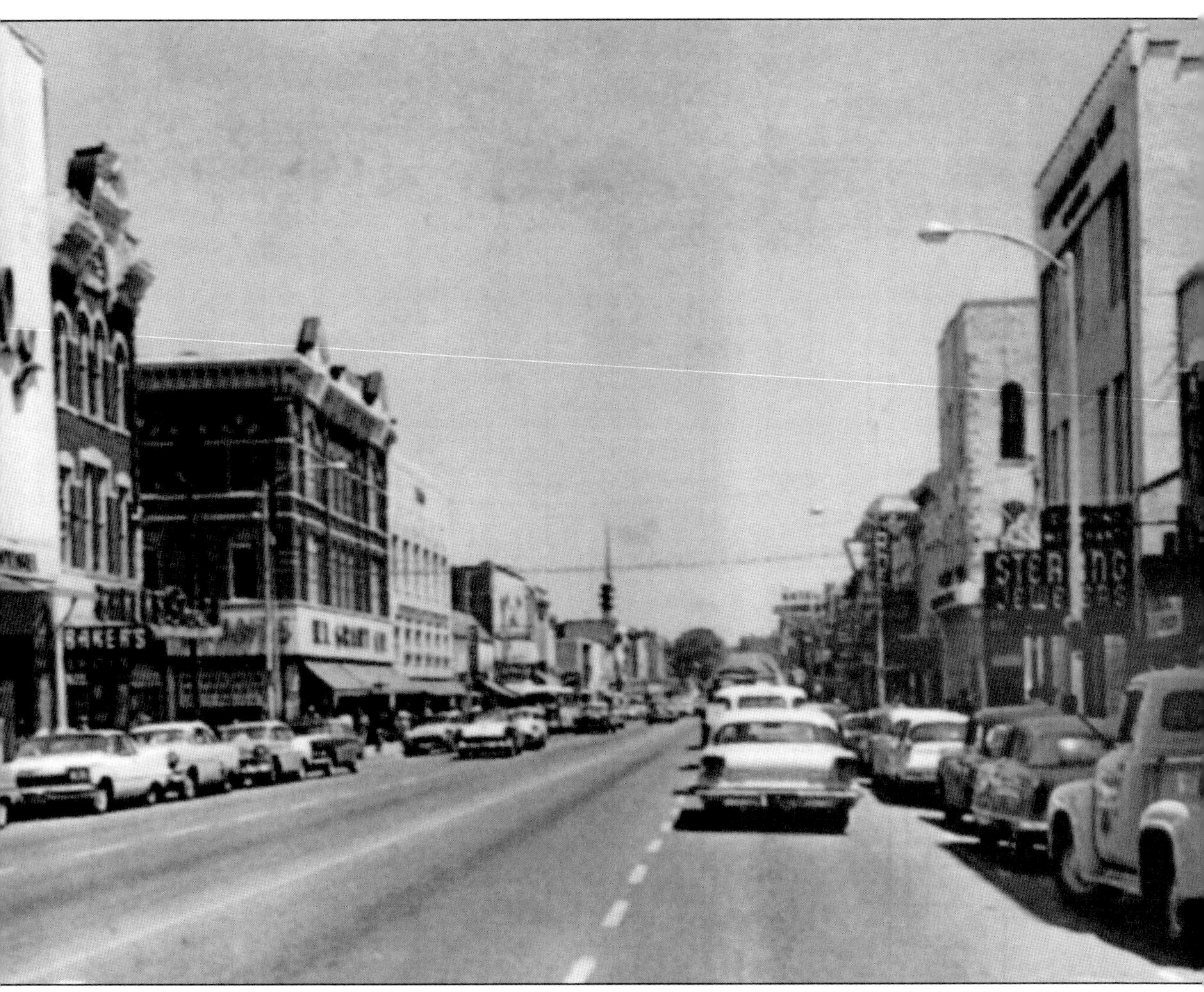

The heart of downtown Anniston was filled with clothing stores. The Smith Building (third on the left), at 1100–1104 Noble Street, was built around 1890. At various times, it housed Wakefield's, Held Brothers', and the W.T. Grant Company. Grant's, a 25¢ store founded around the turn of the 20th century, operated in Anniston from 1932 to 1976, when the company filed for bankruptcy. In the 1940s, a renovation enlarged Grant's retail space to encompass the entire building. Eventually, the retail space was replaced with a city parking lot.

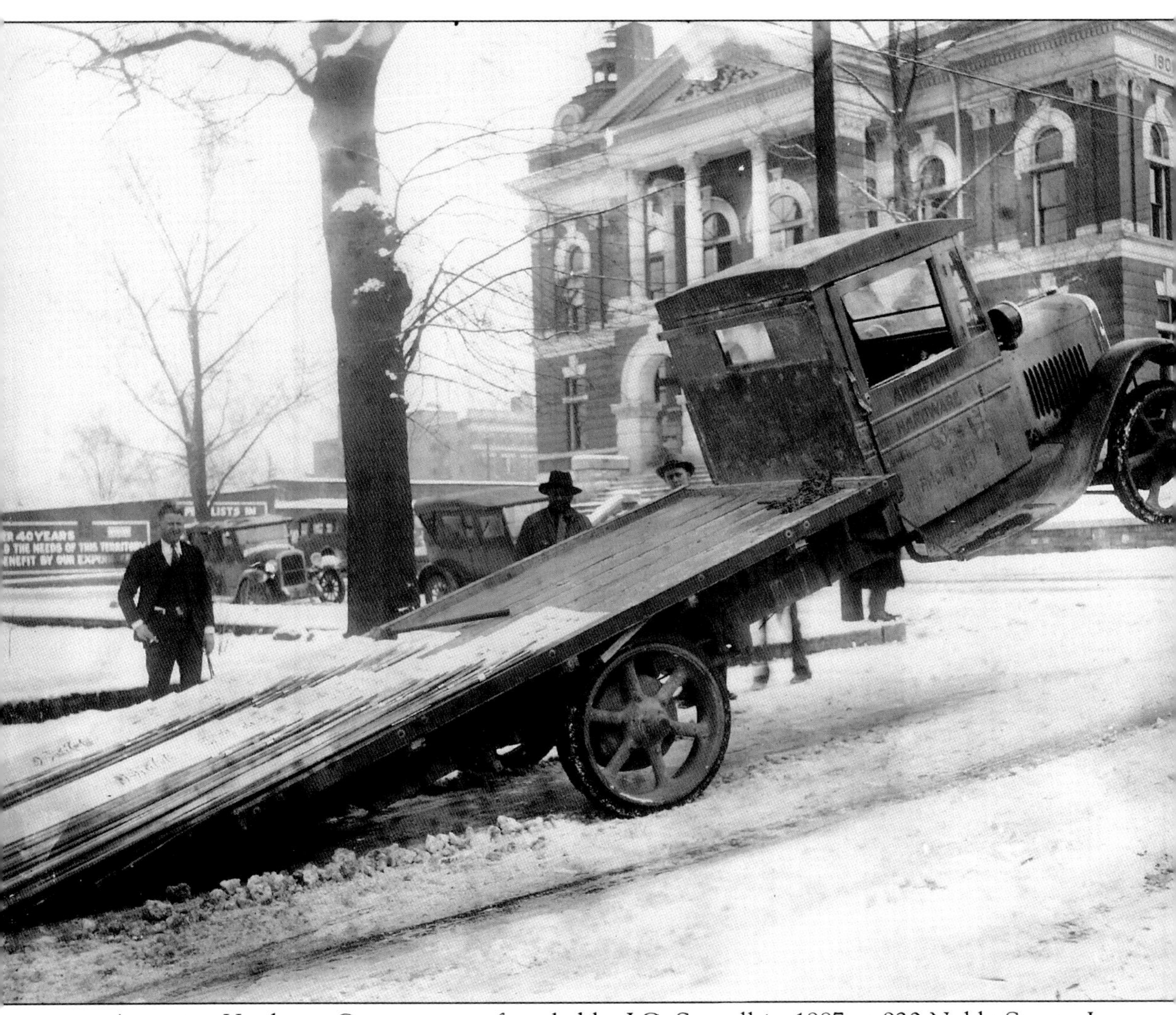

Anniston Hardware Company was founded by J.C. Sproull in 1887 at 920 Noble Street. In 1898, the business moved to 1118–1122 Noble Street. The company added a 40,000-square-foot warehouse on Twelfth Street, directly behind the three-story main store, by 1935. The store not only sold hardware and supplies, but also had a bridal registry with dishes and other household items. By 1958, the company was a wholesale dealer located at 1117 Court Avenue. In the 1960s, the company moved to West Anniston. By 1982, it had returned to 227 Noble Street. After 1984, the company no longer used the Anniston Hardware name. This c. 1920 photograph shows an Anniston Hardware delivery truck next to the Calhoun County Courthouse.

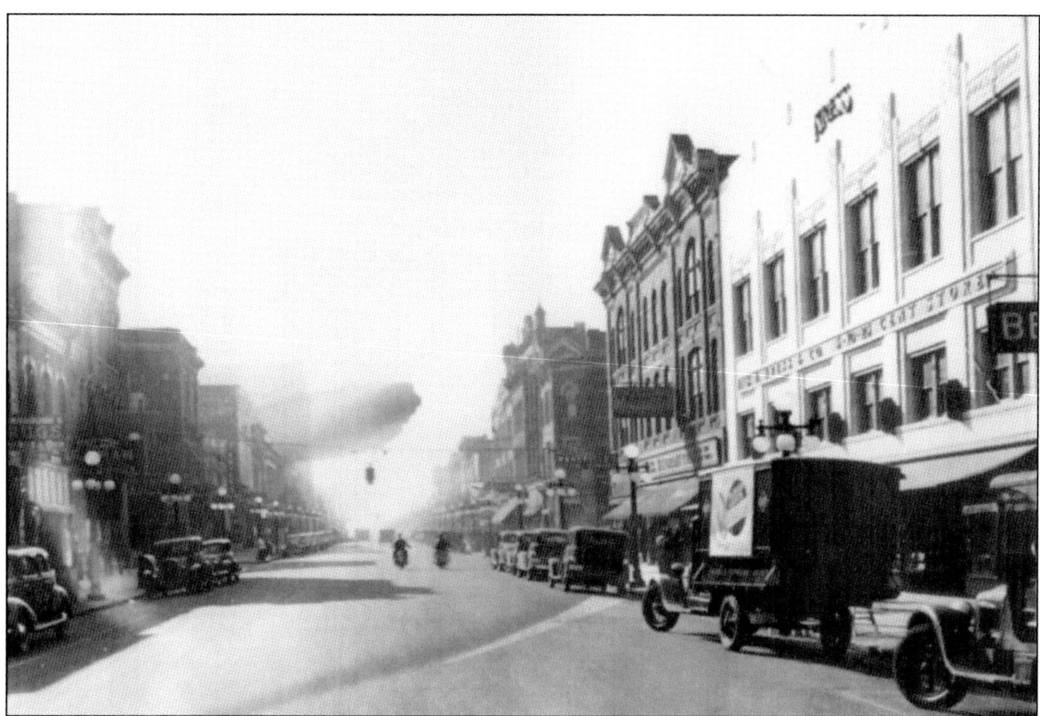

In this photograph, taken around 1920, the Kress Building is at far right. S.H. Kress & Company's 5&10 Store was built around 1917 at 1106 Noble Street on the site of the old Commercial Hotel. The establishment sold housewares and notions. S.H. Kress employed its own architects and designers in an architectural division. In 1930, they renovated the Anniston store to include a new Art-Deco facade and incorporated the Wakefield's building to the right.

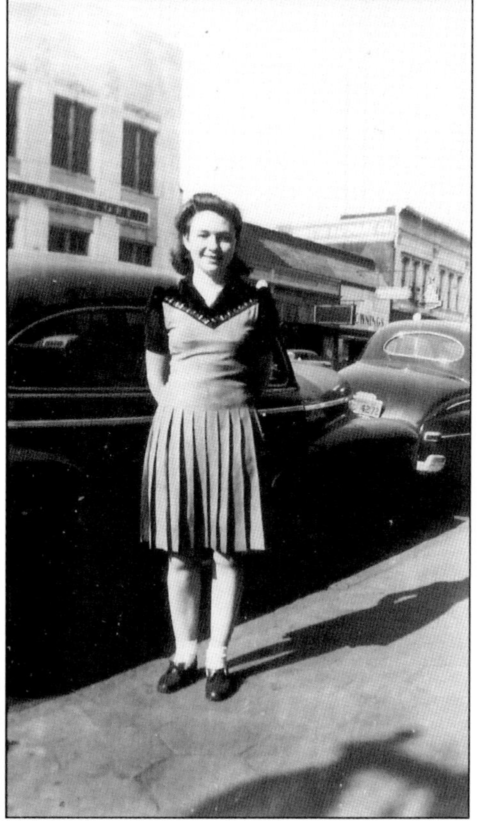

The two-story Kress Building contained a mezzanine. By the late 1950s, a stairway to the basement was constructed to open the lower floor for commercial use. In 1980, Kress's Anniston location closed, and the building was occupied by a furniture store, then a department store. In the 21st century, the Super 10 Store occupied the site. Anniston Hardware Company can be seen in the background at far right. (ERY.)

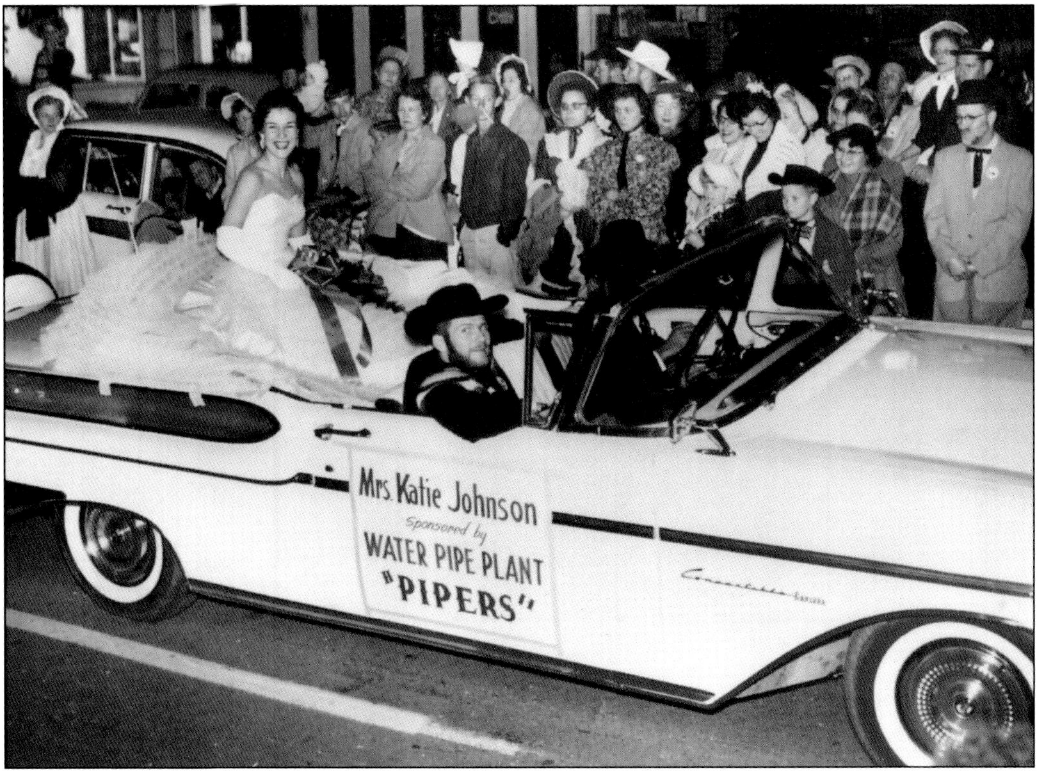

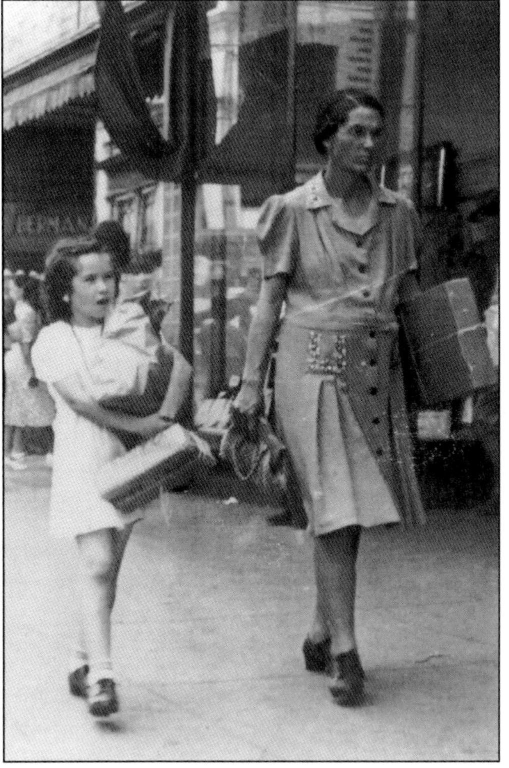

Russell Brothers Photography Studio was founded in 1883 by brothers Samuel and Robert Russell at 1213 Noble Street. By 1889, brother W.P. joined the family business. When W.P. died in 1943, the Russell Brothers gift business was sold to Fred Couch Sr. The photography store, shown at far left in this 1958 photograph, was sold the previous year to Lance Johnson. Both Couch's Jewelers and Lance Johnson Studio were operated by the sons of the founders. (PLACC.)

Berman's, seen here in the background around 1943, was founded in 1900 by Jacob Berman. The shop, originally located in the 1200 block of Noble Street, was relocated to 1112 Noble Street by 1938. After the building burned down in November 1961, the women's clothing store New Berman's opened in a modern building with a new proprietor, Sam Routman, owner of Gayle's Department Store. In 1974, Routman combined his department stores and operated Berman-Gayle's until the business closed in the 1990s. (ERY.)

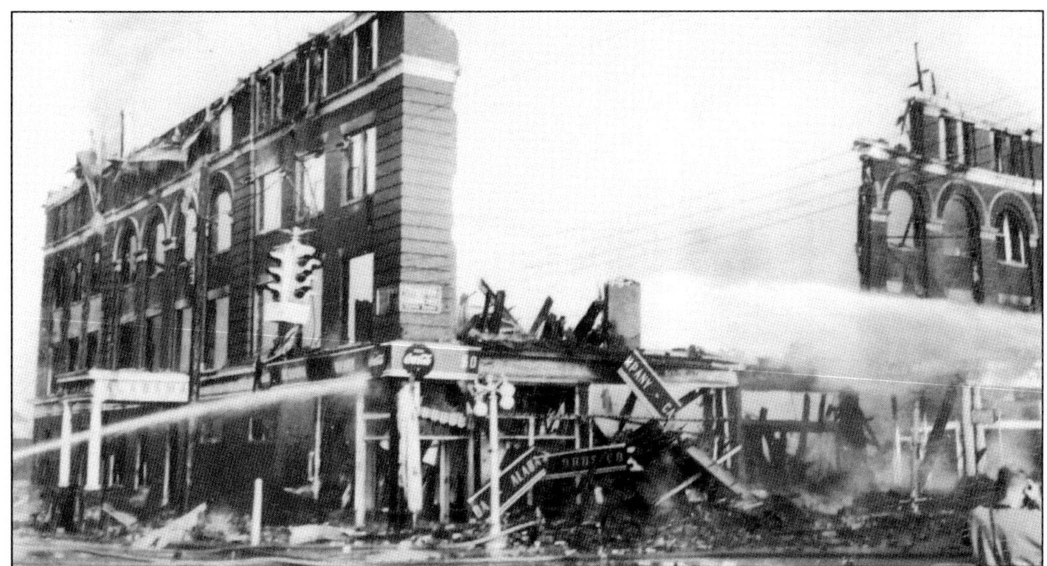

The Alabama Hotel was built around 1905, largely with the help of William Zinn, who kept a room at the hotel for many years. The 94-room hotel, located at Twelfth and Noble Streets, was popular with travelers for its dining room, coffee shop, and spacious lobby. In September 1944, the hotel was destroyed in one of the worst fires in Anniston's history. The blaze claimed two persons, including a young Army wife. (ERY.)

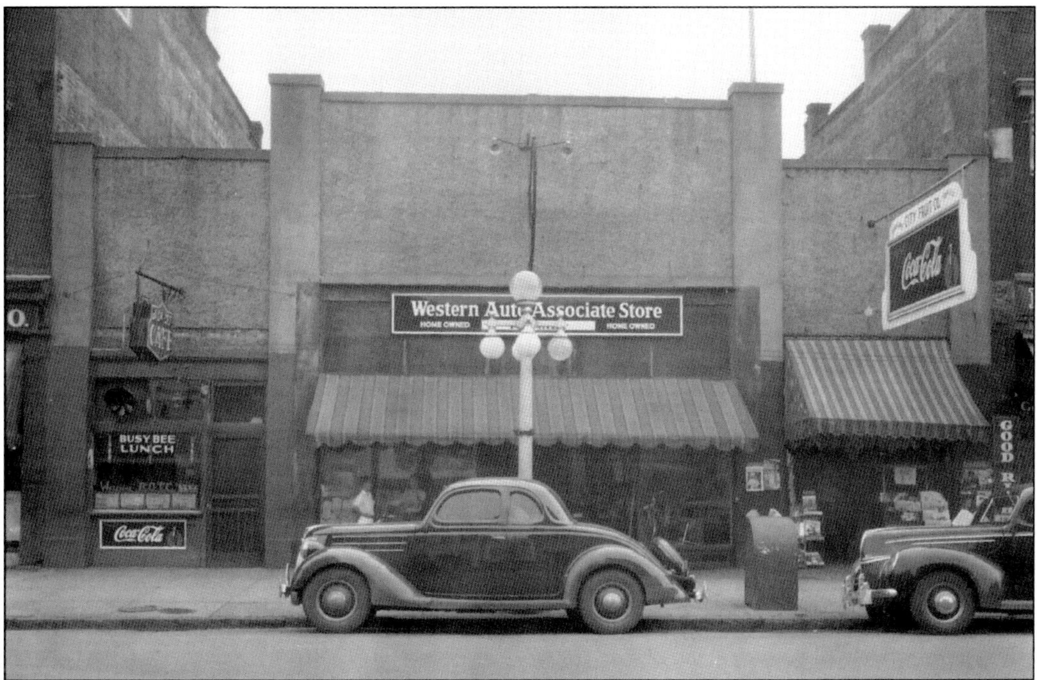

In the 1930s, the 1200 block of Noble Street, seen here around 1938, was home to the Busy Bee, Western Auto, and City Fruit. With an influx of GIs training at Fort McClellan, L.H. Carre decided that the site would be better utilized as an entertainment venue. In 1942, the Calhoun Theater, with 1,081 seats, opened at 1220 Noble Street on the site of the World War I–era Garden Theatre. The Calhoun, part of ABC Southeastern Theaters Inc., closed around 1983.

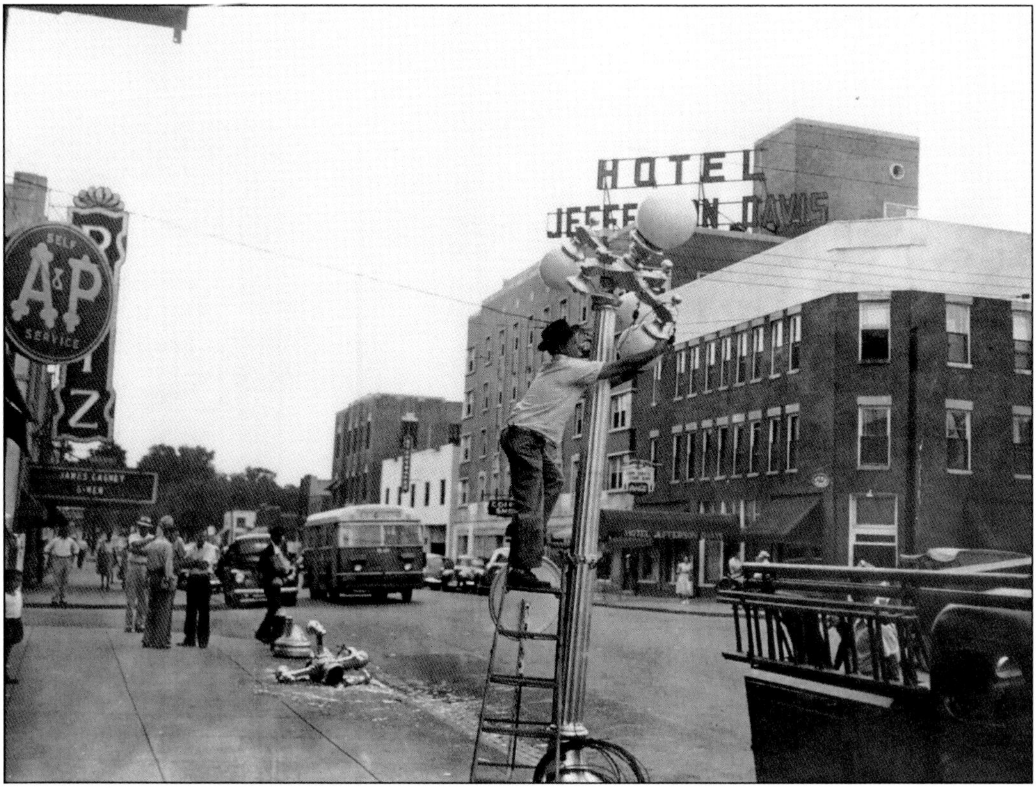

The Hotel Jefferson Davis is seen in the background around 1950. Formerly called the Manhattan Hotel, it was constructed in 1917 at 1301 Noble Street. The Manhattan Hotel had a European plan, which meant that meals and rooms were priced together. The hotel was originally a three-story structure located on the corner. An addition to the main building was erected in 1942. In the 21st century, the Homestead, an independent living community for seniors, occupied the space, along with a barbershop and cafe.

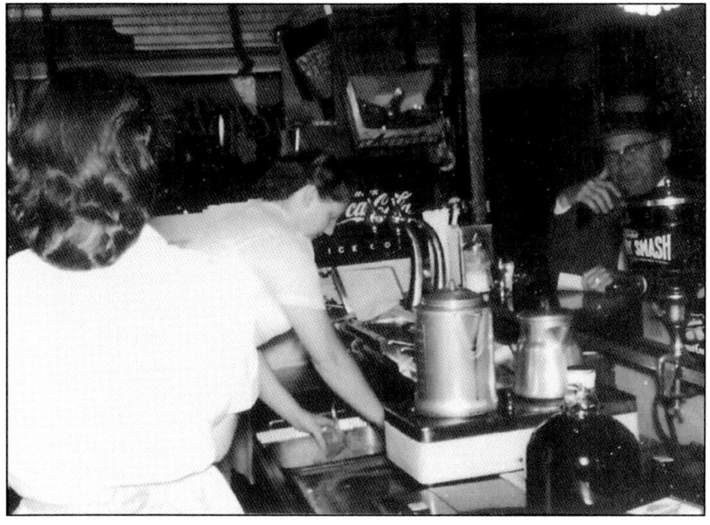

The Hotel Jefferson Davis included a barbershop, beauty shop, dining room, and snack bar. The Jeff Davis Snack Bar and Sundries, seen here around 1955, was housed on the first floor. John W. Burgess managed the snack bar from 1951 until 1965, when the hotel changed its name to American Host. The snack bar provided sodas, fountain service, sundries, and sandwiches as well as candies and tobacco. (ERY.)

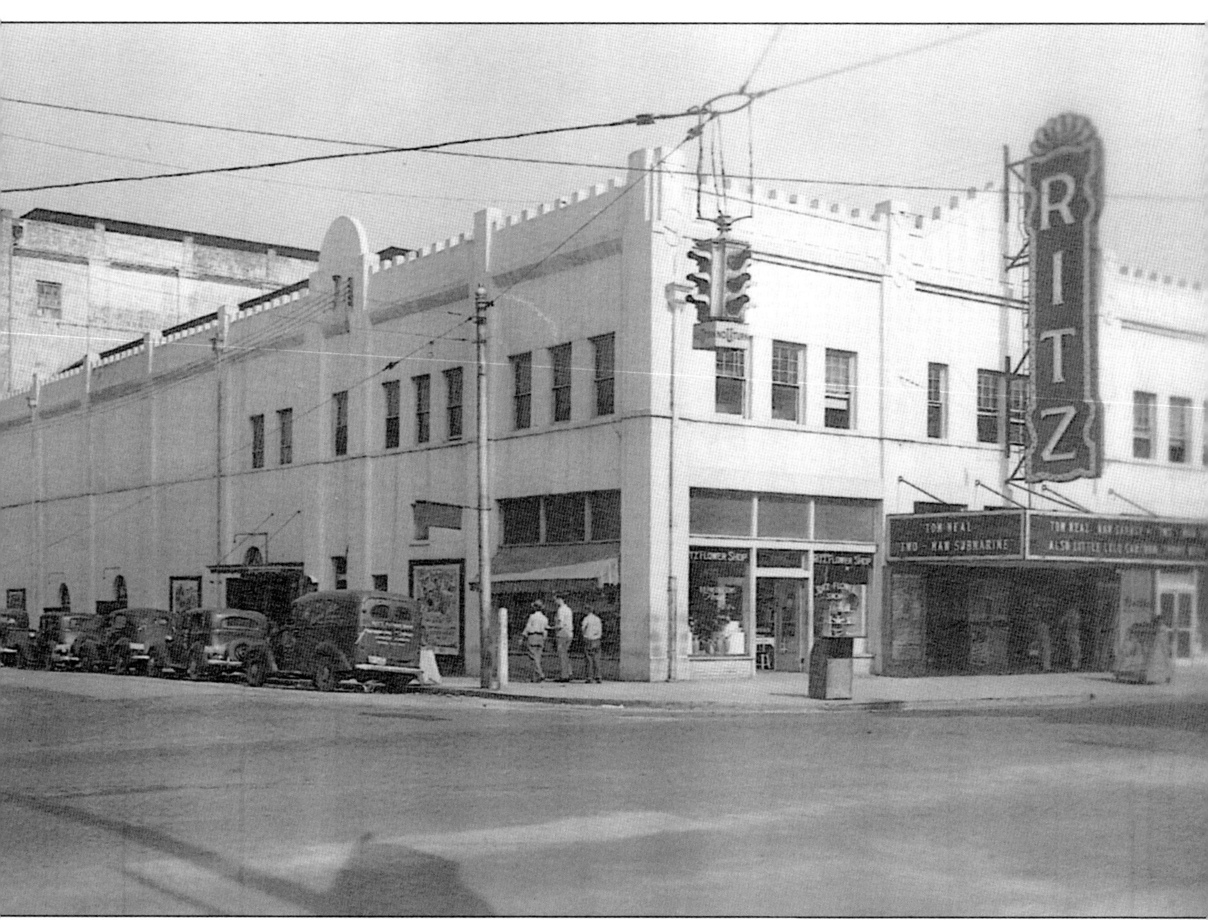

The Ritz Theater was launched as the Lyric Theater when the Anniston Theatre Company constructed the building at 1302 Noble Street in 1918. A year later, the building was sold to the Anniston Amusement Company. For 10 years, the theater was used as a stage for the Keith Vaudeville circuit. In 1928, motion pictures overtook vaudeville in popularity, and the building was remodeled by the motion-picture company Publix, which renamed it The Ritz. In the 1930s, a subsidiary of Paramount Pictures leased the building. The Anniston Little Theater purchased the building in 1973, but abandoned it by 1980. The Ritz sat vacant until the 1990s, when the theater was gutted and adapted as multiuse office space. (PLACC.)

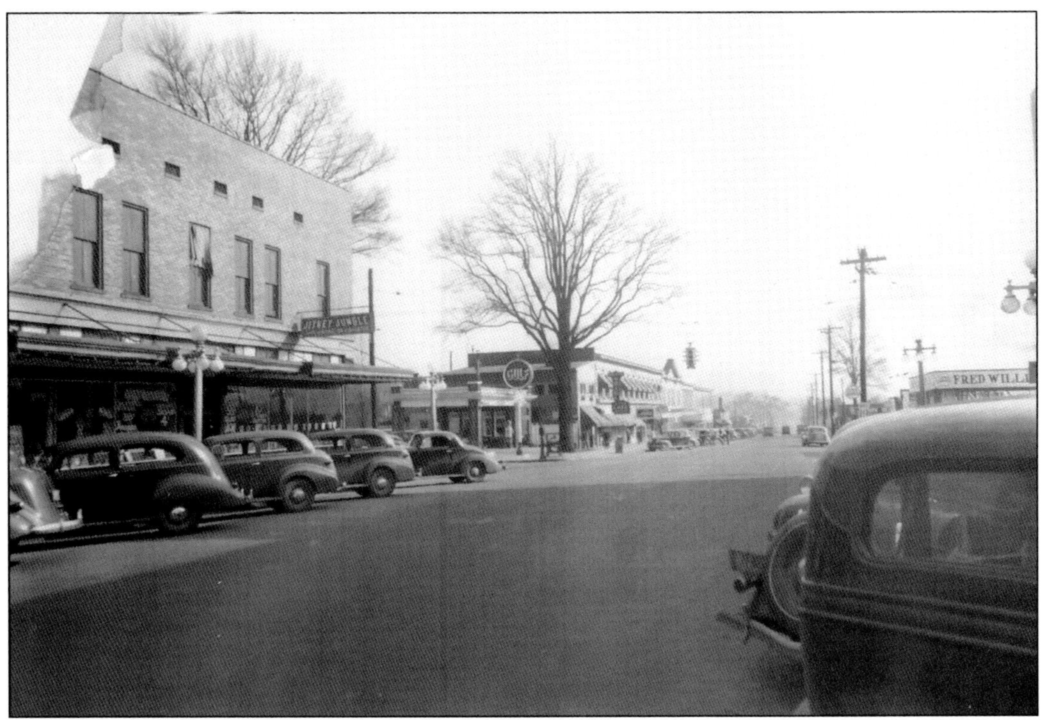

Prior to the 1930s, most people purchased goods from a local grocer, who kept an account for the customer. When Jitney Jungle was founded in the early 20th century, it was designed on a "cash-and-carry" principle instead of a "charge-and-carry" format. The chain grocery store began in Jackson, Mississippi, then expanded throughout the Southeast. Jitney Jungle was popular in Anniston, where it had three locations: 1623 Noble Street (shown below around 1940), which became the site of the Anniston City Meeting Center in 1995; 13 East Twelfth Street; and 901 Noble Street (shown above around 1940). The Jitney Jungle stores in Anniston began to fade away in the 1950s. The company was acquired by Winn-Dixie in 2000, and the remaining Jitney Jungle stores throughout America were rebranded.

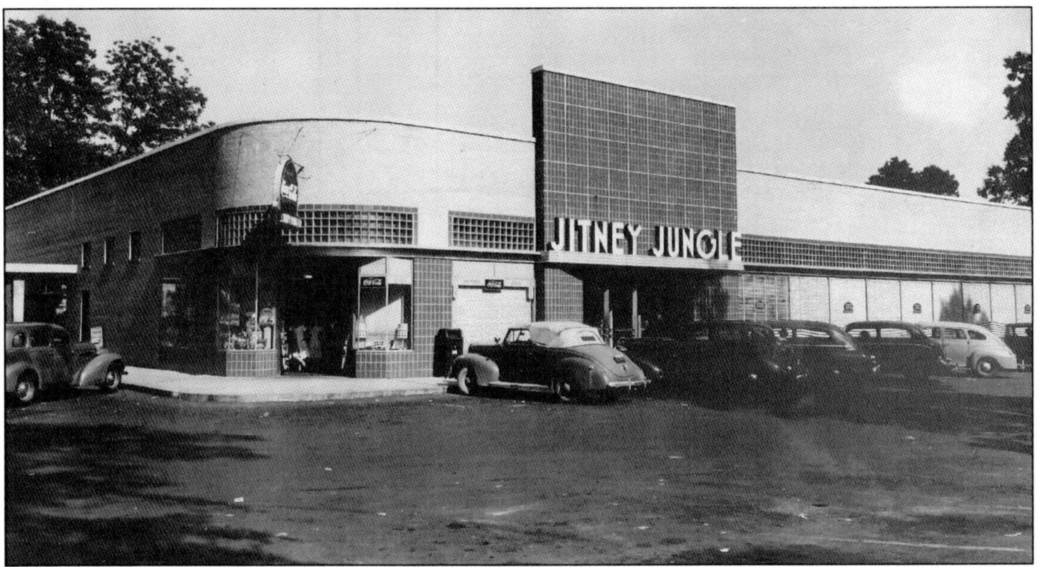

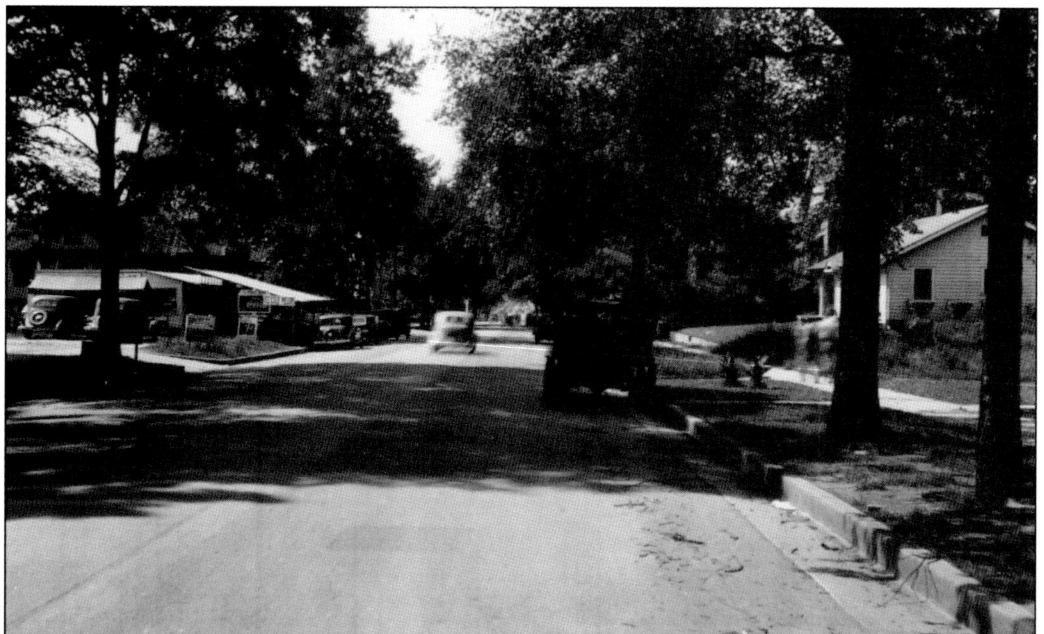

In the late 1930s, Paul F. Fite opened a fresh-fruit market, The Fruit Bowl, at 1605 Noble Street. It is seen here on the left around 1940. Fite added a donut shop, The Sugar Bowl, to his fruit market in the early 1950s. From 1958 to 1970, the site was occupied by a dry cleaner. Various enterprises occupied the site through the rest of the 20th century. By 2015, the lot was occupied by DaVita Dialysis Center.

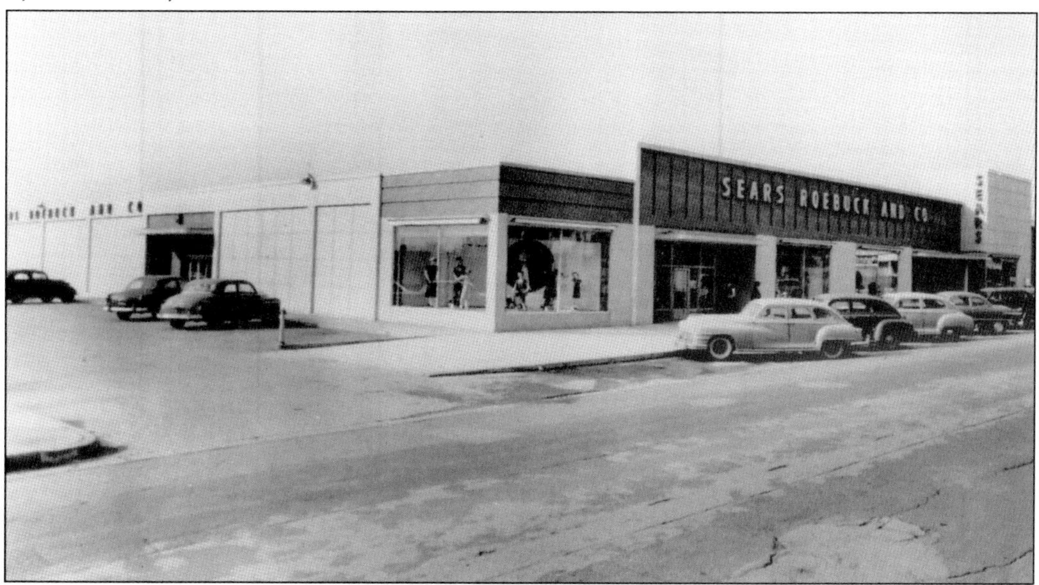

In May 1940, Sears, Roebuck, and Company decided to return to Anniston in the newly rebuilt Constantine Building. The company relocated to a single-floor plan layout in a modern building at 1702 Noble Street (pictured) in February 1950. Sears operated a retail store in this location until 1986, when the company moved into the former Mason's space in the Quintard Mall. The Noble Street building was renovated and opened in 1988 as the Calhoun County Administration Building.

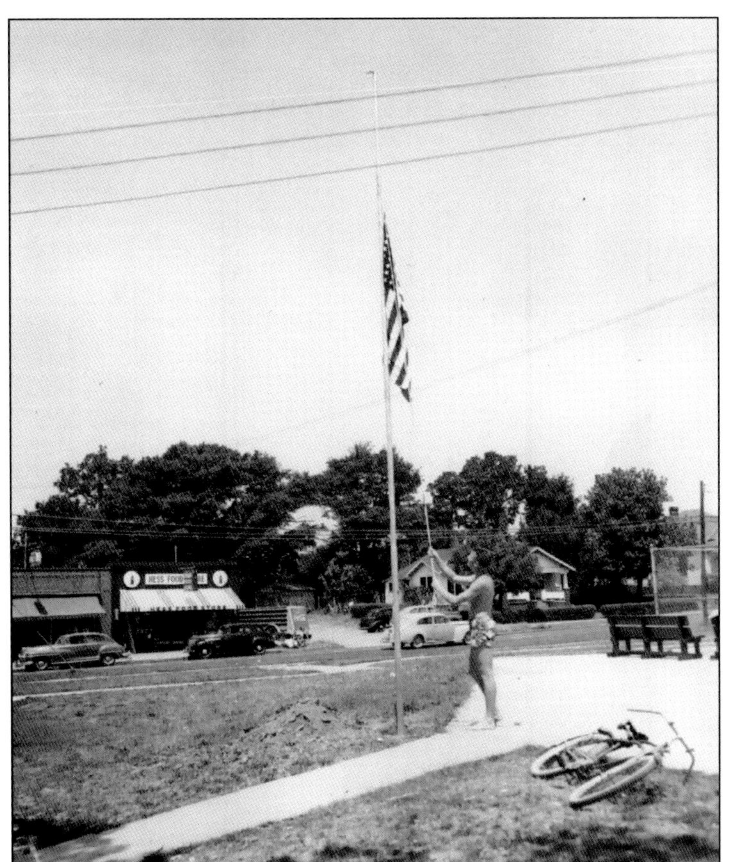

The North Noble Community developed in the 1930s, and by 1938, it had a grocery store, later Ward Hess' Food Store No. 3, at 2208 Noble Street. The store is seen here in the background around 1947. Economy Drug, located at 2204 Noble Street, arrived in the 1940s and remained in operation until 1970. Eventually, the retail area at Twenty-second Street grew to include A&P Grocery and a Masonic hall. (PLACC-BC.)

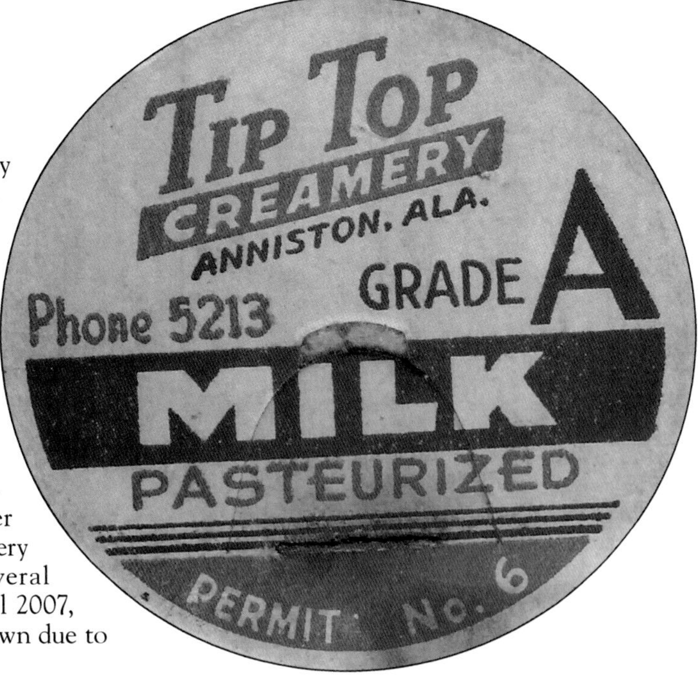

Tip Top Creamery, founded by dairy farmer Joe McClellan in 1949, was located at 2716 Noble Street. McClellan produced his own milk for the creamery until 1964, when he began purchasing milk from local farmers. The creamery was known for McClellan's homemade ice-cream recipes, such as Cherry Garden. When McClellan was killed in a 1972 automobile accident, his sister Moree Trammell ran the creamery until it closed in 1989. Several tenants occupied the site until 2007, when the building was torn down due to environmental issues. (ERY.)

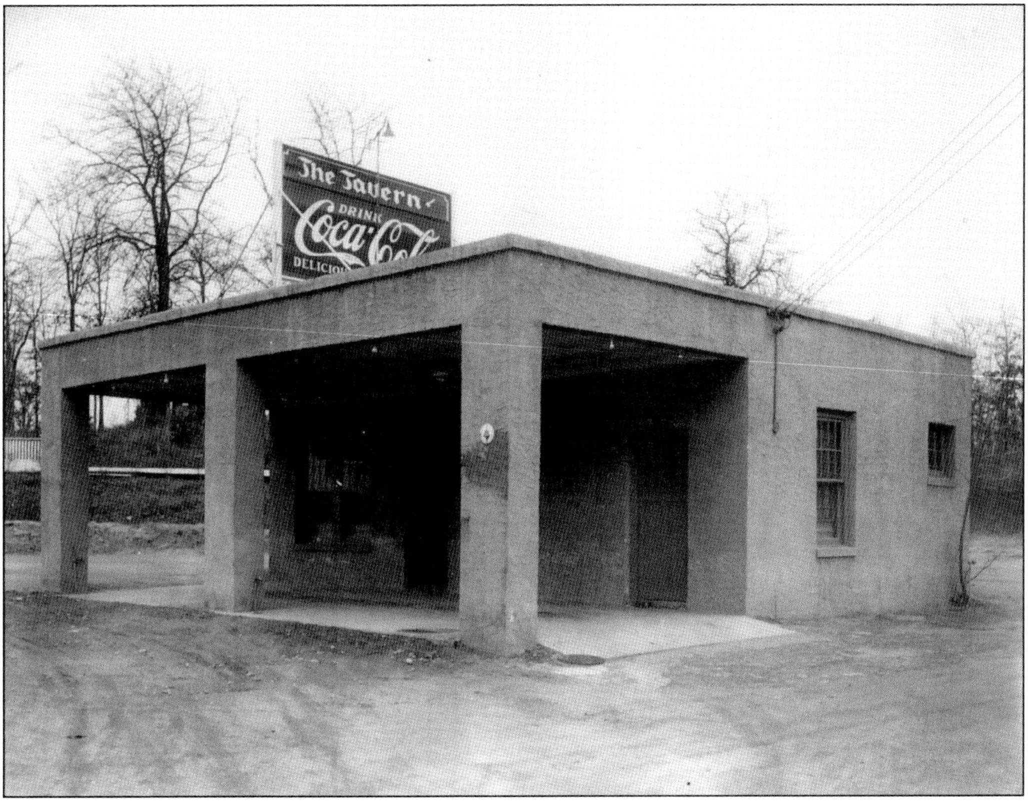

Built in the late 1930s, The Tavern Drive-In at 3101 Noble Street was known for its barbeque and curb service. By 1961, the establishment advertised that it was "Open 24 hours and serving Breakfast, Dinners, and Sandwiches of All Kinds." The Tavern had a fast-service window and three fully air-conditioned dining rooms for patrons. Located behind The Tavern was Edgemont Cemetery, a 50-acre city cemetery that dates to the 1800s, with an estimated 30,000 graves, including some that were unmarked.

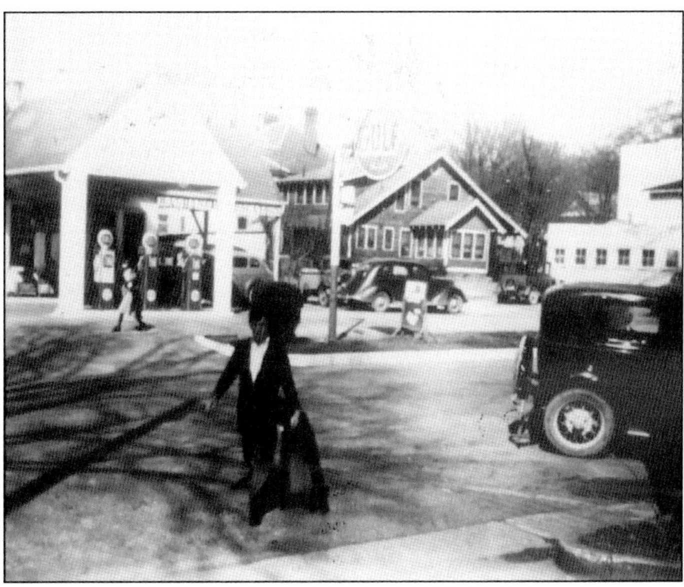

In the 1930s, when automobile travel was becoming prevalent, service stations sprang up throughout Anniston. These stations were staffed by attendants who filled up the gas tank, washed the windows, and checked the oil. A full-service garage was also available for repairs. The stations were affiliated with brands such as Pure, Sinclair, Shell, and Texaco. This photograph, taken around 1930, shows a Gulf station on Wilmer Avenue. (PLACC.)

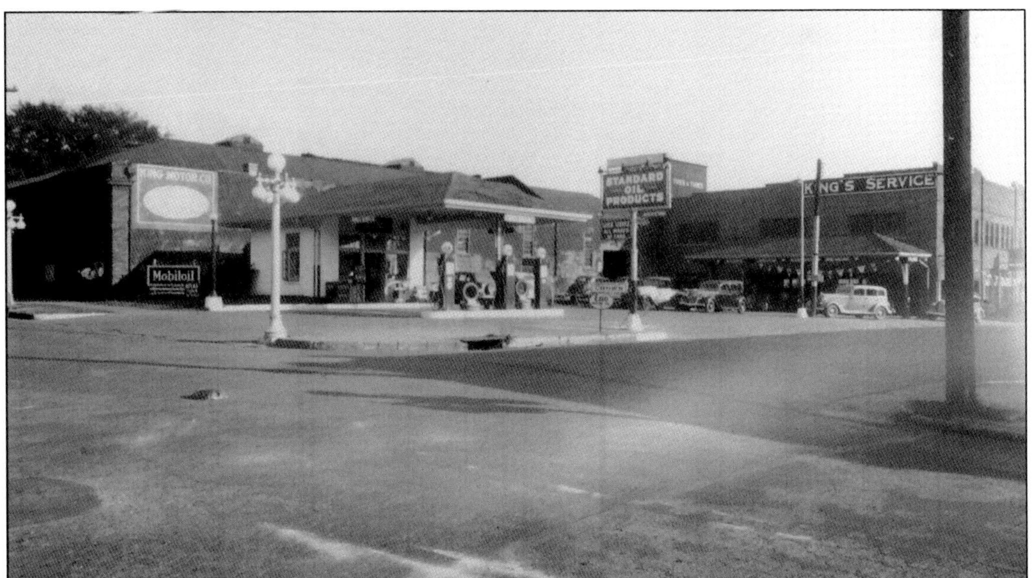

King Motor Company (above) holds the distinction of being the oldest continually operating dealership in Anniston. The company was organized in April 1922, with J.F. "Gerald" King as president and E.D. King as vice president. By 1946, Gerald had become the president of the local Lincoln-Mercury dealership. Then, 10 years later, E.D. left the company to his son E.D. "Sunny" King Jr. The showroom, first located on the southeast corner of Eleventh Street and Wilmer Avenue (shown below around 1940), moved to 1507 South Quintard in January 1971. The King Motor Company was active in fleet sales to the City of Anniston and Calhoun County, and supplied trucks and school-bus chassis to the State of Alabama starting in 1946. After Sunny King's death in 1990, the King family continued to operate the dealership and expanded to include Honda (1976), Toyota (1989), and Scion (2006).

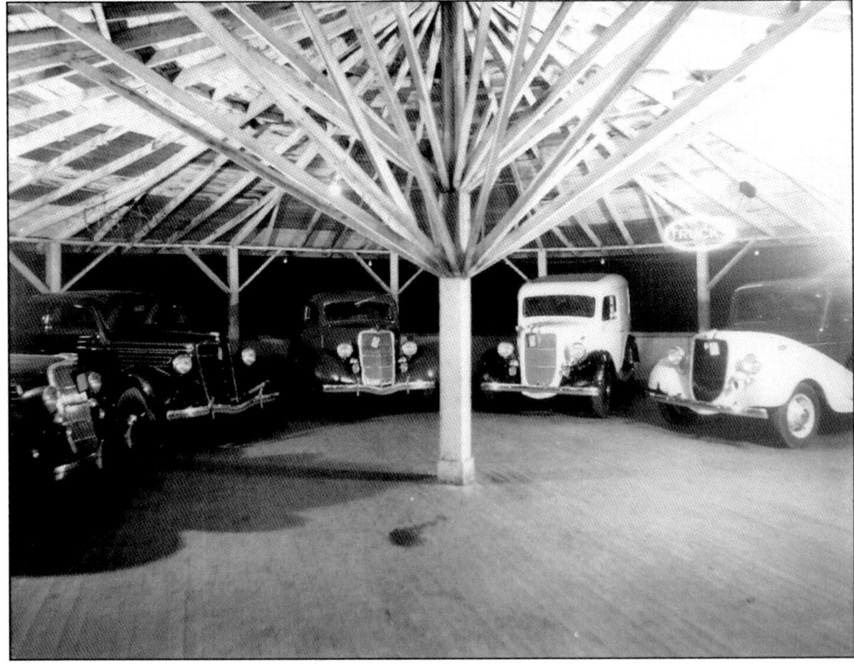

The Dr. Pepper Bottling Company was established in Anniston in 1937. The Anniston franchise of Dr. Pepper operated at 1020 Wilmer Avenue from 1937 until the early 1950s. It is seen here around 1930. The franchise was sold to Royal Crown Bottling Company in 1966. To the left of the bottling company was the Anniston Fire Station No. 3. Eventually, this site became a parking lot.

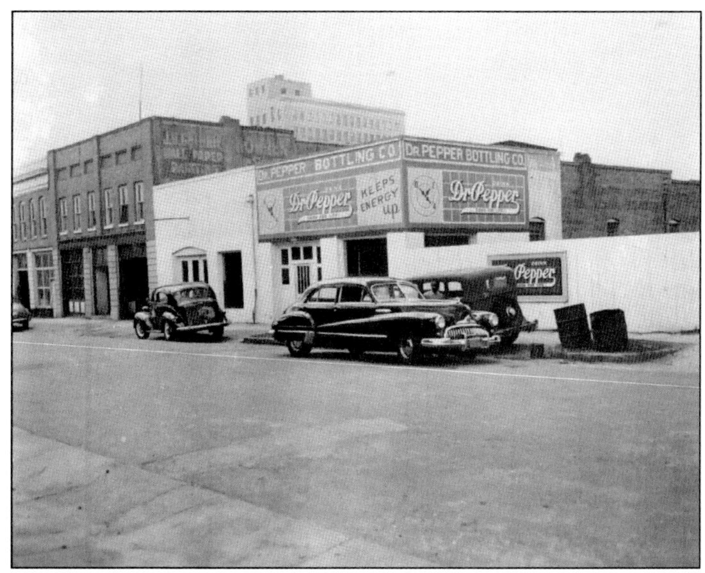

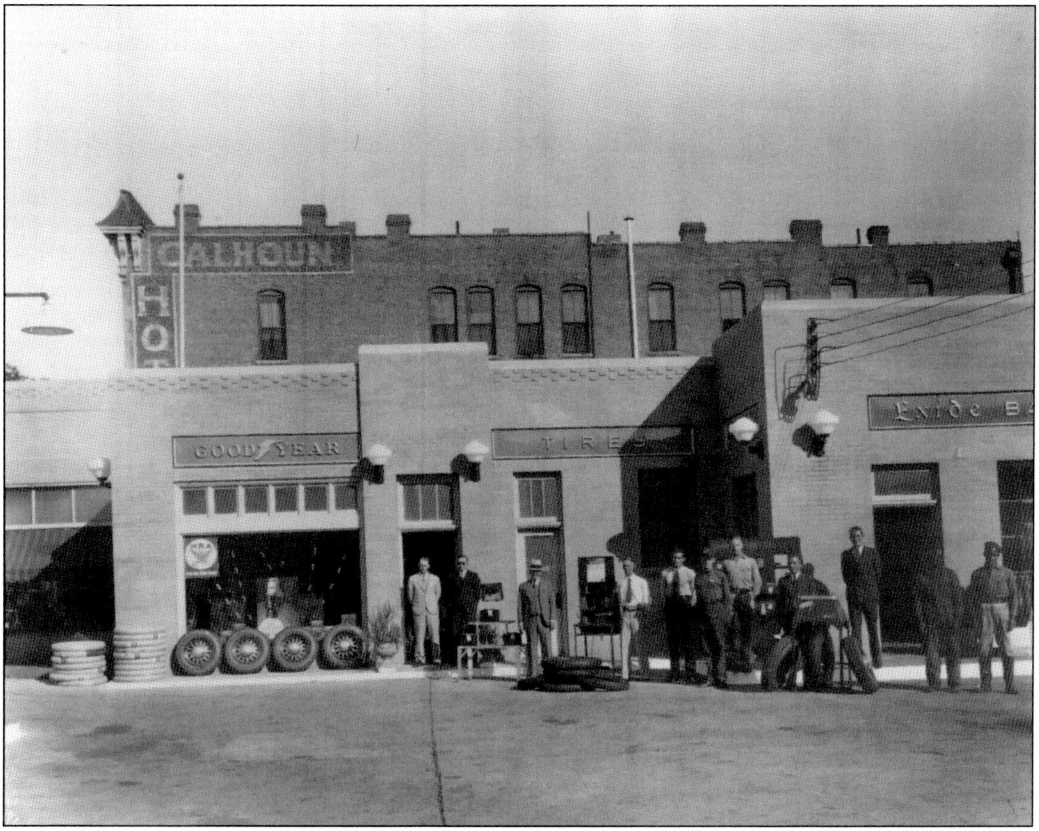

The Calhoun Hotel is seen in the background of this photograph, taken around 1935. It was built on the southwest corner of Tenth Street and Wilmer Avenue around 1888, originally as the Wilmer Hotel. The hotel underwent several name changes through the years, including the Victoria Hotel (1905), the New Anniston Hotel (1913), and the Calhoun Hotel (1924). The building was known as the Keener Hotel from around 1938 until 1961.

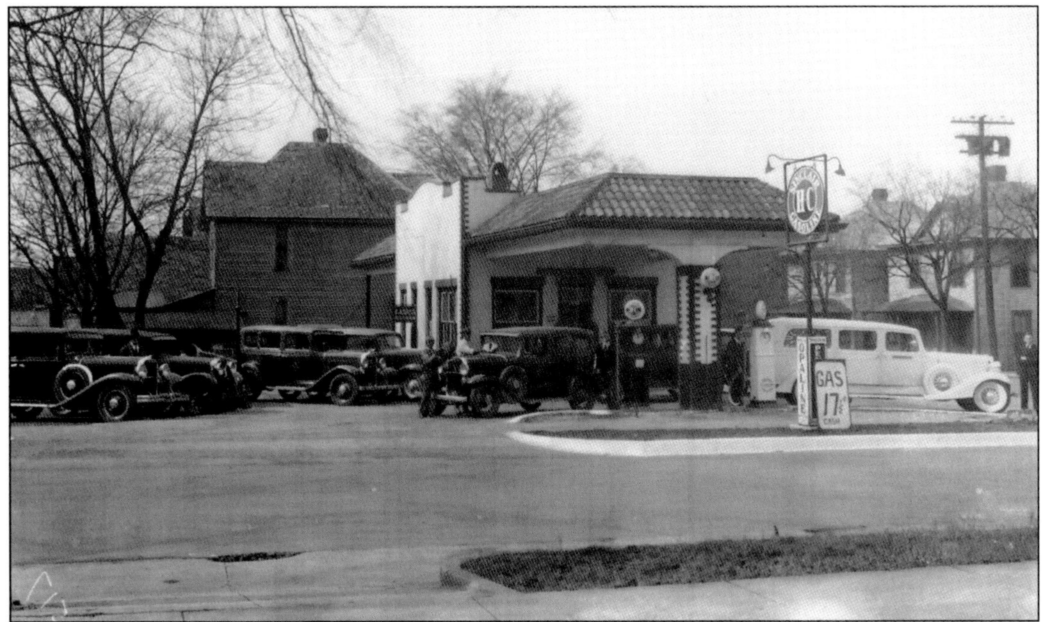

Seen here around 1935, the building at 1230 Wilmer Avenue was erected as a Sinclair-affiliated service station around 1930. Several different proprietors operated the service station until the 1970s. In the 1940s, Robert Clark operated a filling station and dairy at the site. One of the longest occupants was Anniston Safe & Lock Company, a locksmith business, which relocated to the site in 1989.

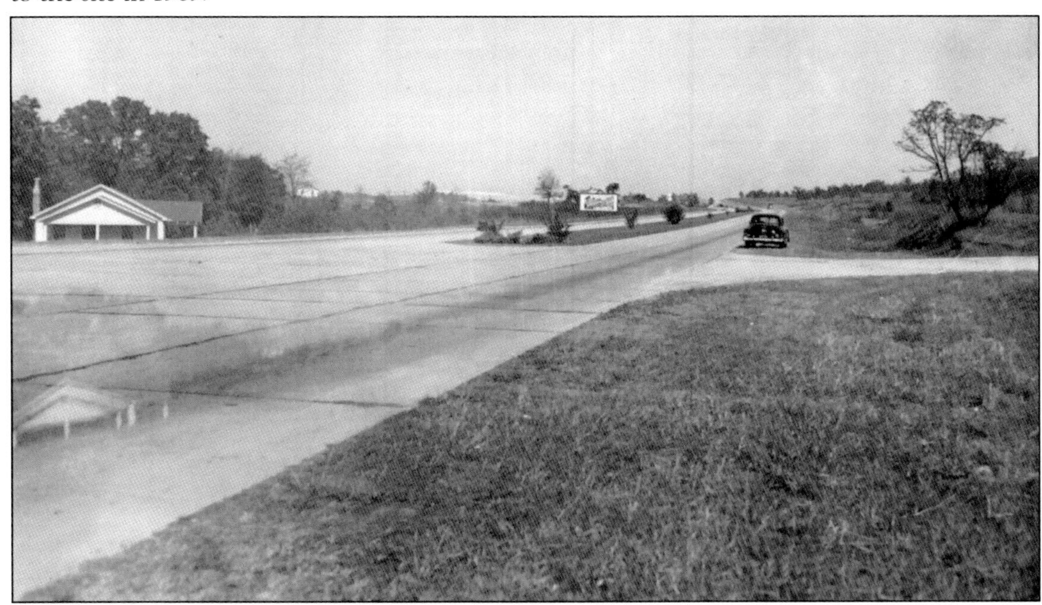

As early as 1941, discussions were under way to open Quintard Avenue north of Twenty-second Street. An access road from Summerall Gate to Twenty-second Street was cut by late 1942. Despite the residents being upset with the new access road intruding into a residential area, a World War II beautification project was established by the City of Anniston. Businesses began locating to the area in the early 1950s, when the bypass for US 431 was constructed. This photograph looks north on Quintard Avenue toward Twenty-eighth Street. (PLACC-BC.)

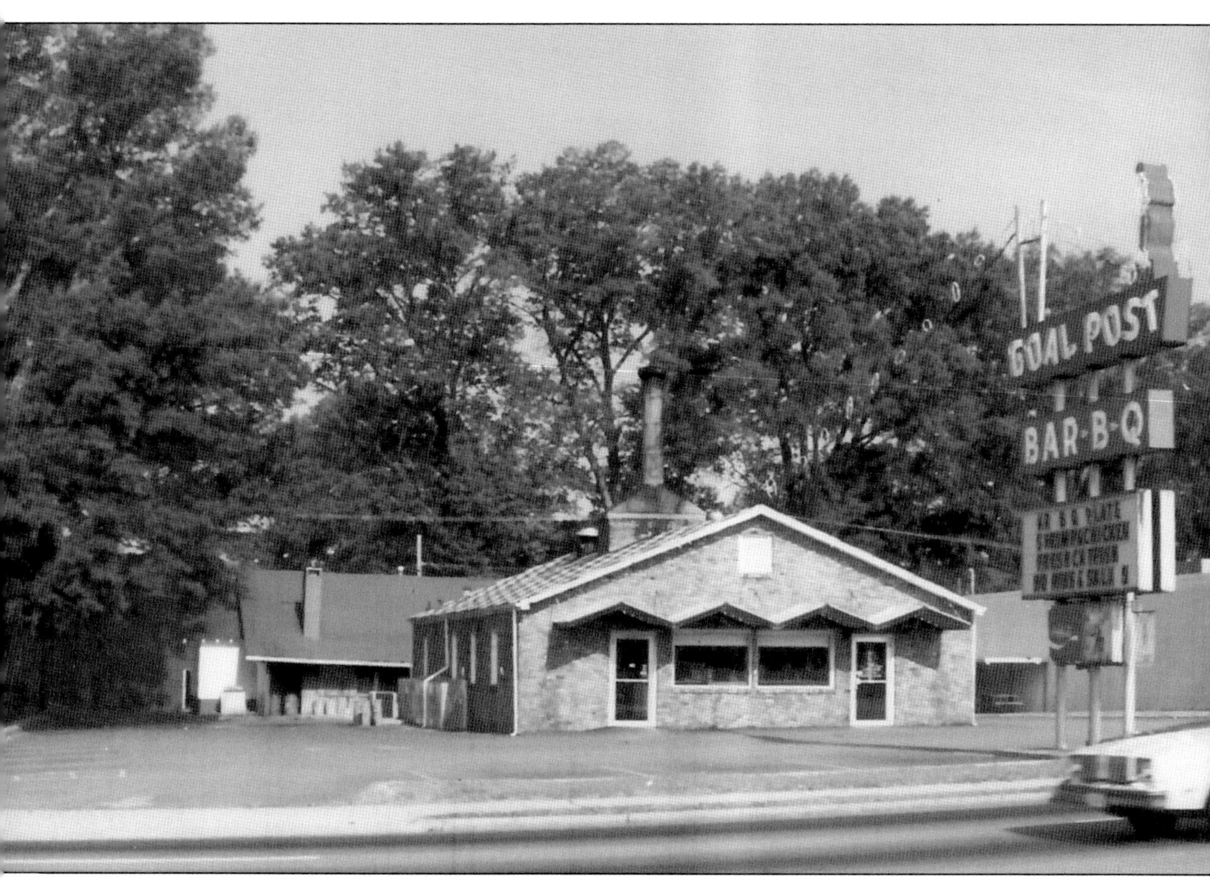

The Goal Post Drive-In was founded by S.A. Pruett in 1959 on the northwest corner of Fourteenth Street and Wilmer Avenue. The barbeque restaurant served hams and shoulders, along with catfish, fried chicken, salads, and "a meat and three." In 1964, Pruett relocated the Goal Post to 1910 Quintard Avenue (seen here around 1980), where he used the house on the property as a cooking pit, storage, and living space. B.B. Ballard purchased the restaurant in 1968 and remained as the operator until the business was sold in 1975 to Roy Young. Young owned the restaurant until 1998, when he sold the business and property. The business operated until 2014, when it was closed and the property sold to Verizon Wireless, which demolished the building. The iconic neon sign was relocated to South Quintard Avenue. (ERY.)

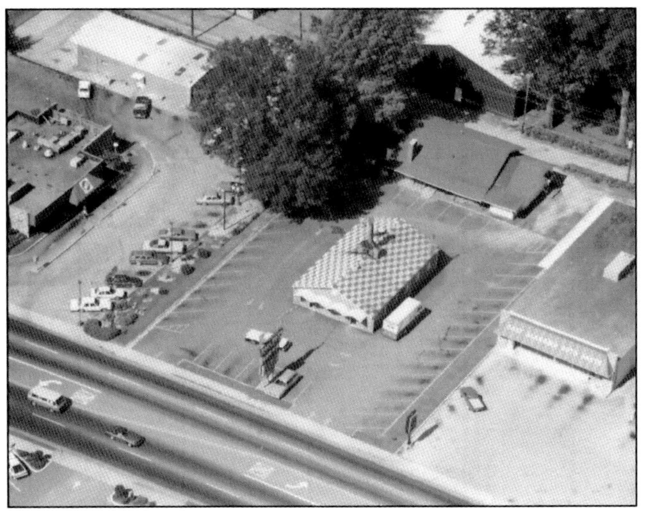

By the 1960s, businesses were locating to North Quintard Avenue to take advantage of the newly opened four-lane road. At far left in this c. 1980 photograph is Jack's, part of a chain started by Jack Cardwell in the Birmingham area. By 1963, Jack's had opened in Anniston, serving 15¢ hamburgers and other staples such as shakes and fries. The first building, located in the 1900 block of Quintard Avenue, was a slant-roof walk-up stand. In the late 1960s, the building was expanded to include a dining area. (ERY.)

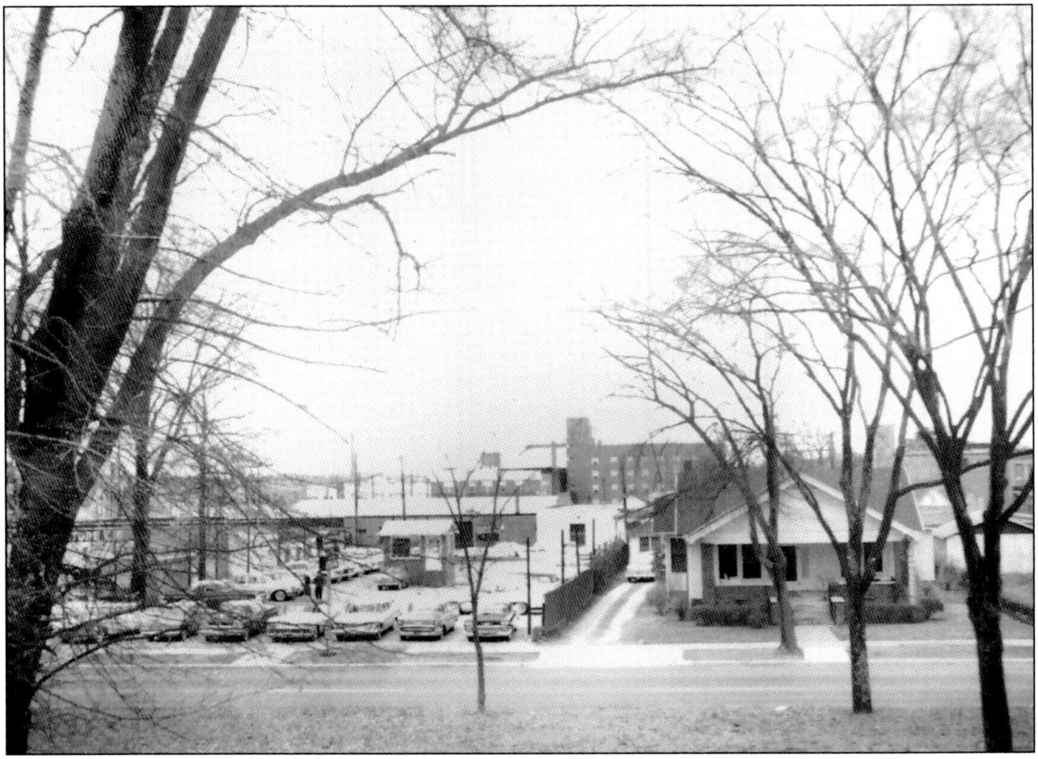

Many of the homes on Quintard Avenue were transformed into apartments by the 1950s. Businesses began locating to Quintard Avenue, including Fant and Turner Car Lot, seen here in the 1300 block around 1960. The proximity to Noble Street made Quintard Avenue a logical place for expansion of business. The Young, Wollestein & Jackson Law Firm built a new structure on the lot in the 1990s. (ERY.)

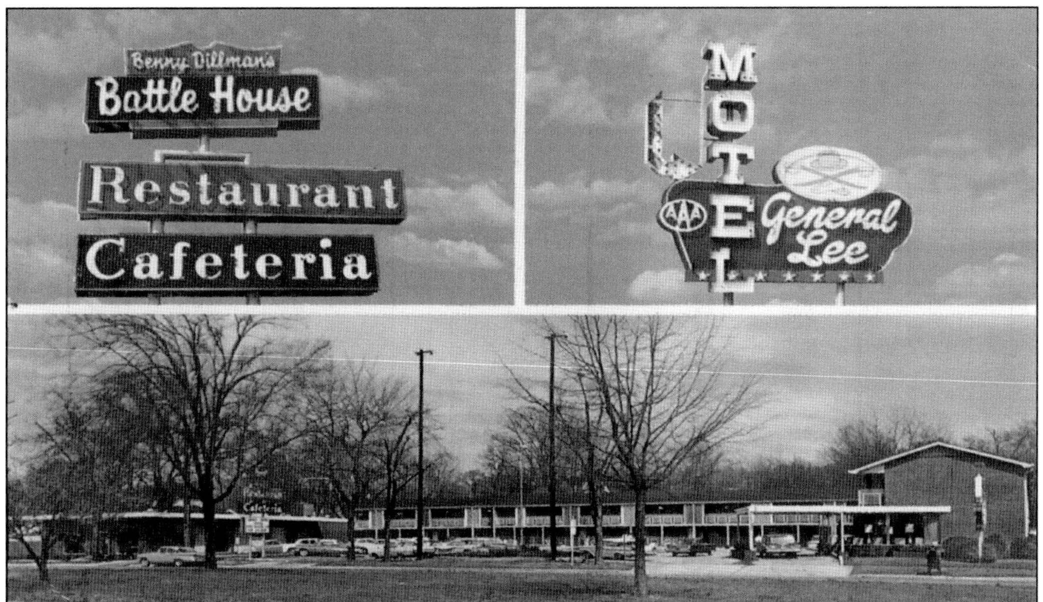

Benny Dillman's Battle House Restaurant Cafeteria opened in January 1964 on Fourteenth Street and Quintard Avenue. The restaurant seated 175 people and had private dining facilities for 150 people. Next to it was the General Lee Motel, operated by E.F. Lee. In 1967, Lee sold the motel to D.E. Locklear, who remodeled the structure and changed the name to Heritage House. The motel operated under various names until it closed in 2002. By 2006, CVS Pharmacy had built a store on the site. (ERY.)

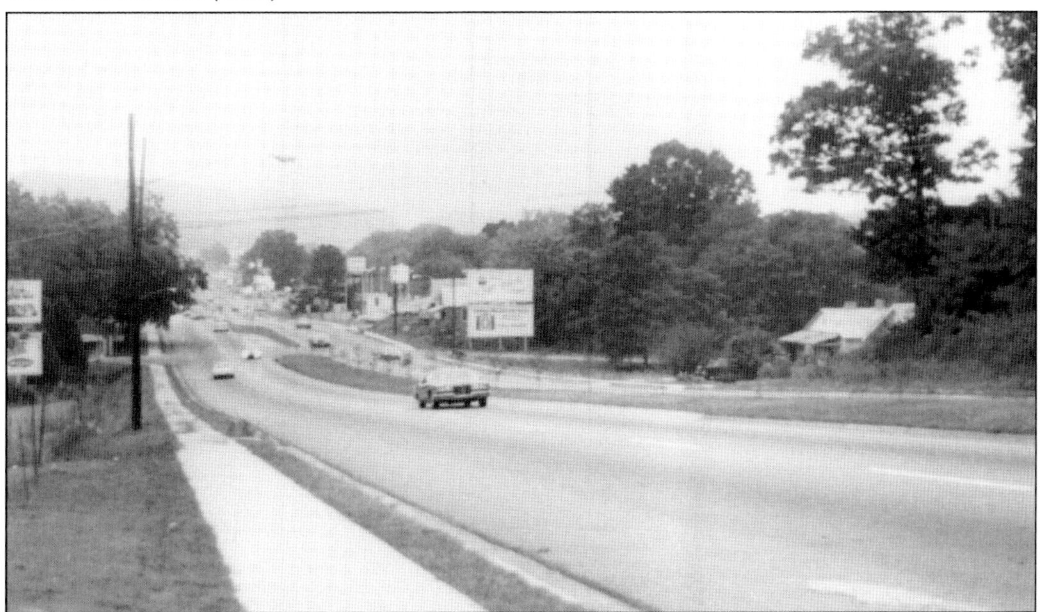

To access South Quintard Avenue prior to the late 1950s, travel was routed onto Leighton and Wilmer Avenues as well as onto Noble Street. Once a bypass route for US 431 was decided in the mid-1950s, the houses between Fifth and Third Streets on Quintard Avenue were destroyed, and a road was cut through to allow access. The road, seen here around 1970 looking south toward B Street, became a busy six-lane highway connecting I-20 to US 431. (PLACC.)

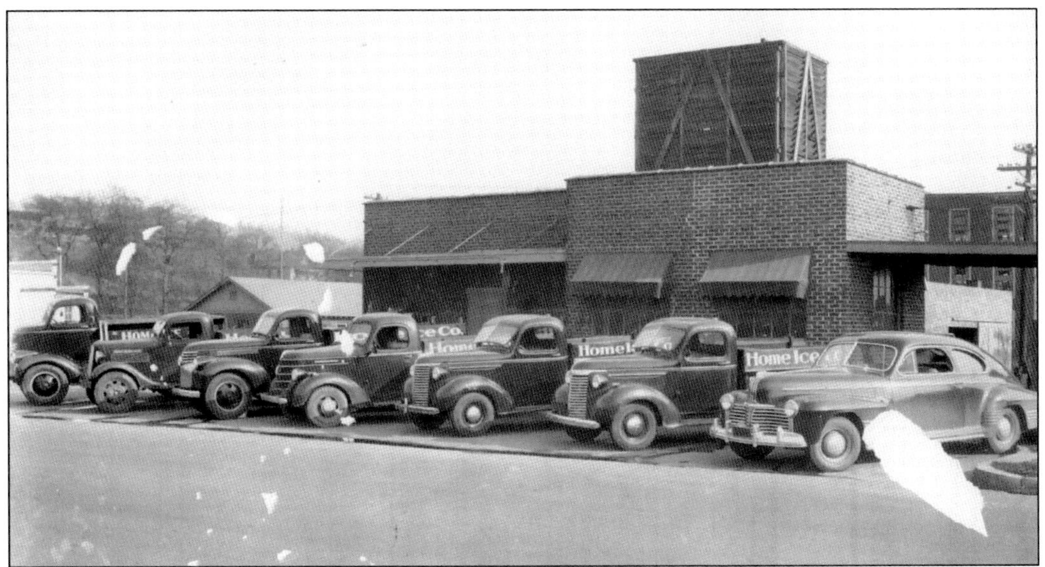

The Home Ice Company, located at 16 West Fourth Street, was founded in 1932 by A.H. Little and W.K. Pollack. The business is seen here around 1940. Ice companies also sold coal to heat the homes of consumers. By 1938, Home Ice Co. had added a second location on South Leighton, as well as a coal station at 1006 West Fifteenth Street. In 1962, the business name was changed to Alabama Ice Industries Inc., which sold ice for commercial purposes until 1973. The property sat vacant for a year before the Salvation Army obtained the property.

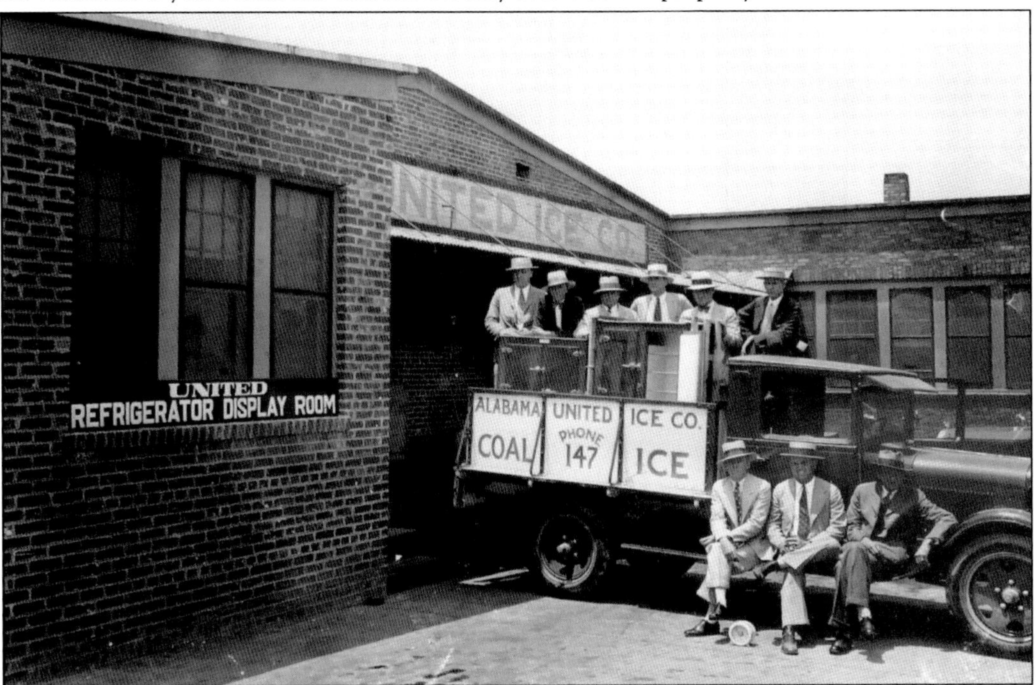

Founded in 1929, Alabama United Ice Company was located at 100 West Ninth Street under the management of T.H. Riley. The business was a manufacturer, wholesaler, and dealer in both ice and coal. By 1954, the establishment was vacant, most likely due to icemakers being built into home refrigerator units.

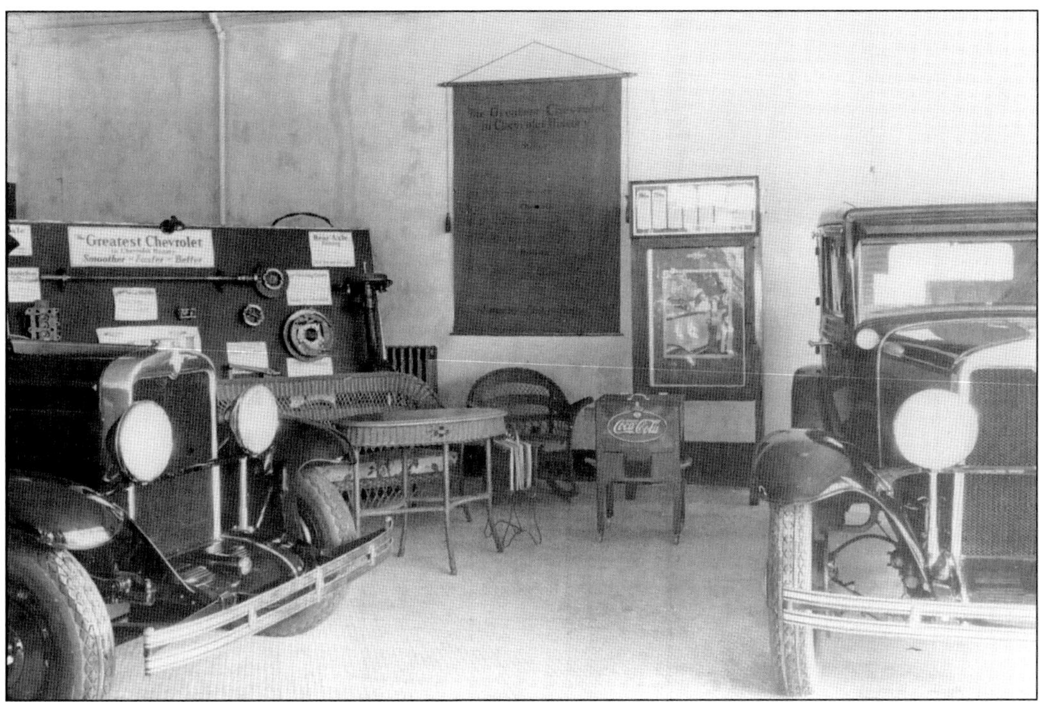

Adams-McCargo was chartered in 1927 by Virgil C. Adams and Dewitt McCargo Jr. as a Chevrolet dealership. In the 1930s, the showroom was located on Twelfth Street and Gurnee Avenue. It is seen in the above photograph around 1927. By 1939, a new showroom was built at 111 East Tenth Street, on the site of an old livery stable that had burned down. The dealership sold over 31,000 cars and trucks in 38 years of business. The business survived through the Great Depression, two world wars, several strikes, and a February 1945 fire that destroyed the garage. A fire wall saved part of the business, and the company was rebuilt. It is seen below around 1960. In April 1965, the Chevrolet dealership was sold to Ron Shafer.

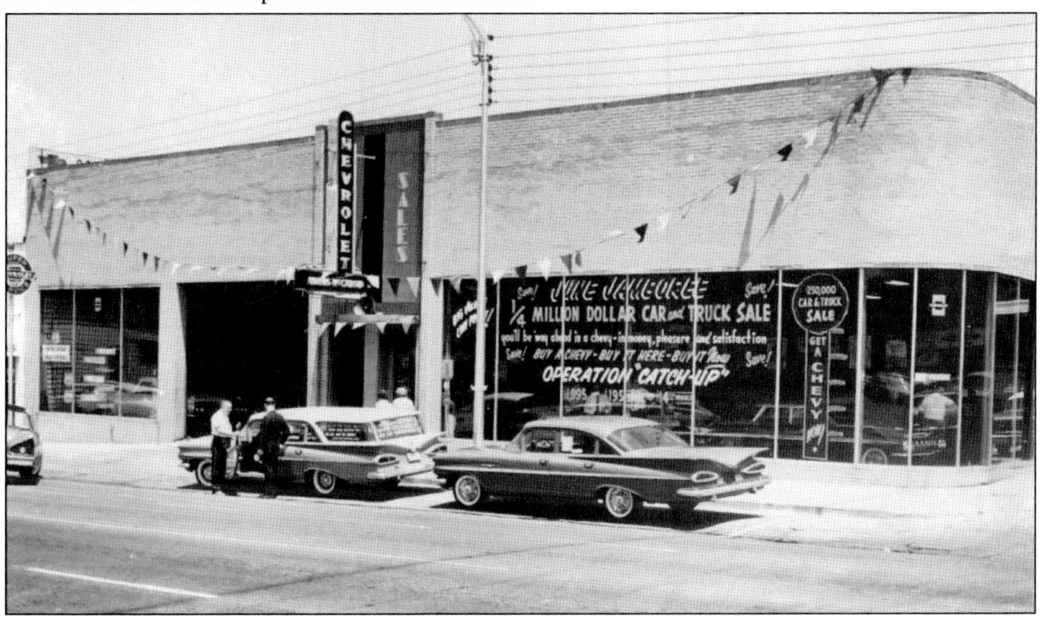

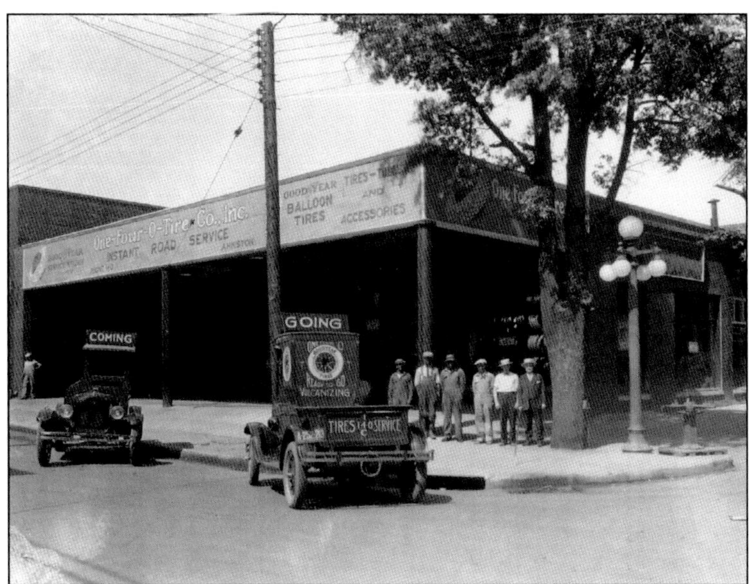

One-Four-O-Tire, located at 101 East Tenth Street, was one of the earliest companies to provide services for automobiles, including washing, greasing, and tire and tube sales, as well as expert tire repair and a cavity mould system. The company lasted throughout the 1920s and was replaced by Sinclair Oil and Anniston Auto Motors by 1931.

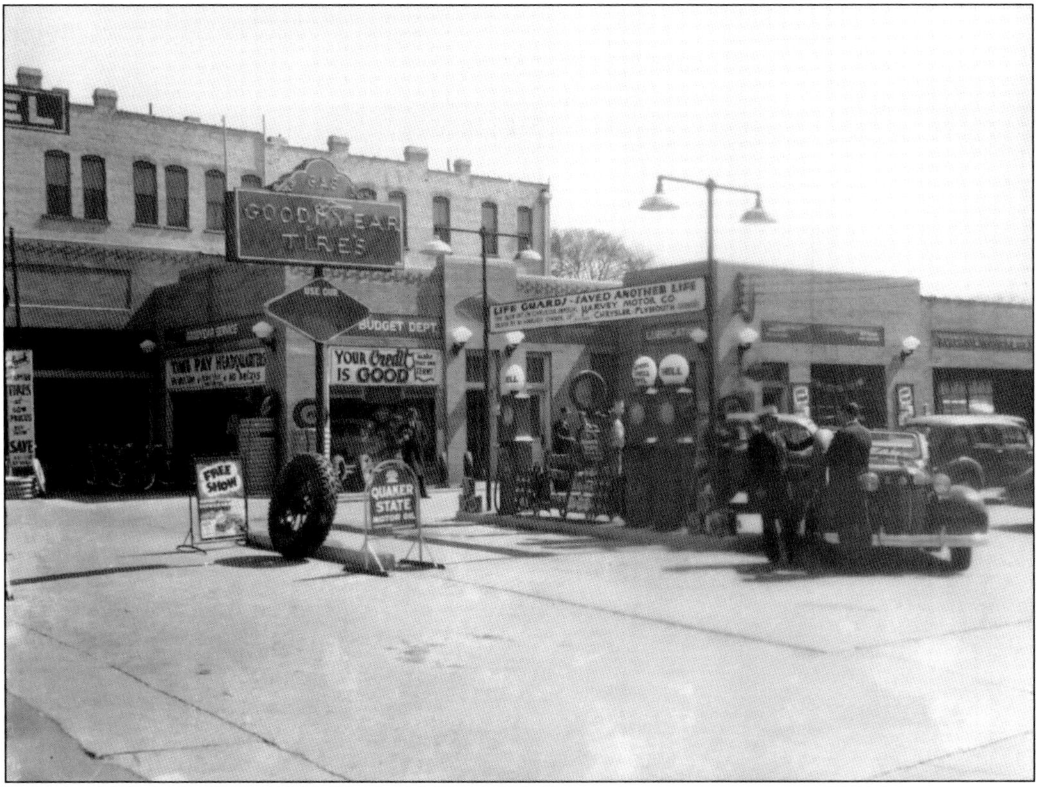

The Goodyear Tire Service Store was built next to the Calhoun Hotel in March 1931 by the Duke-Stickney Construction Company for $12,000. The tire store property at 10–16 East Tenth Street was leased out by the Calhoun Hotel Company, headed by L.B. Liles. The shop had a 50-foot open paved court and a 30-foot-by-120-foot building. The structure was built with brick, similar to the Liles Building, located to the west and adjacent to the property. By 2006, Regions built a bank branch on the site.

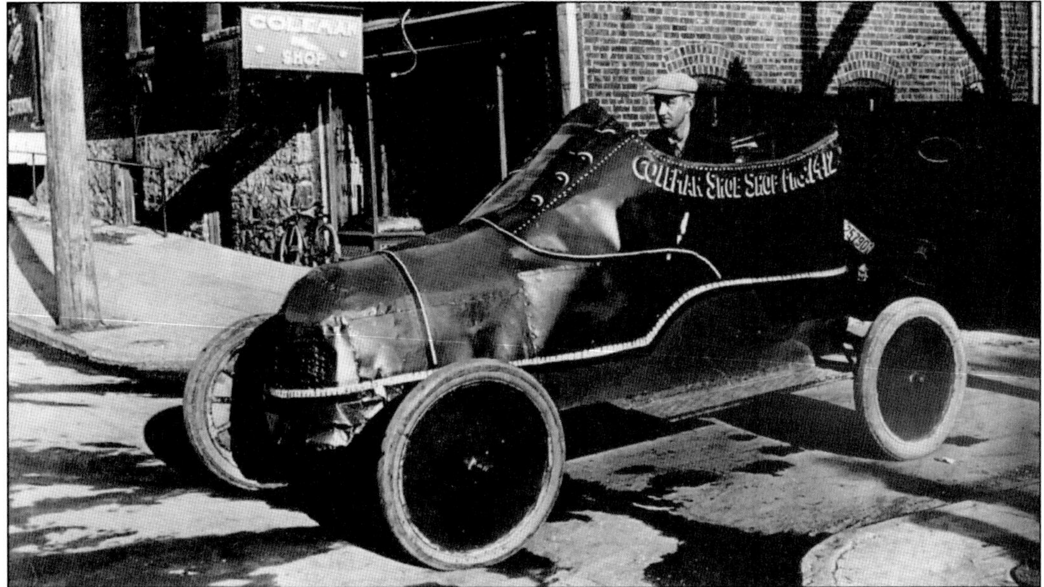

Until recent times, shoe soles of leather and rubber were made to be repaired. Throughout the 1920s, Jesse B. Coleman operated Coleman's Shoe Repair at 10 West Tenth Street, behind the Noble Theatre. Seen here around 1925 is the company's delivery truck. In April 1933, E.L. Crossley purchased the business and renamed it the Blue Ribbon Shoe Shop. A 1933 advertisement listed a man's shoe sole and heel for $1.75, while a woman's sole was 50¢ to 60¢ and heel taps were 10¢.

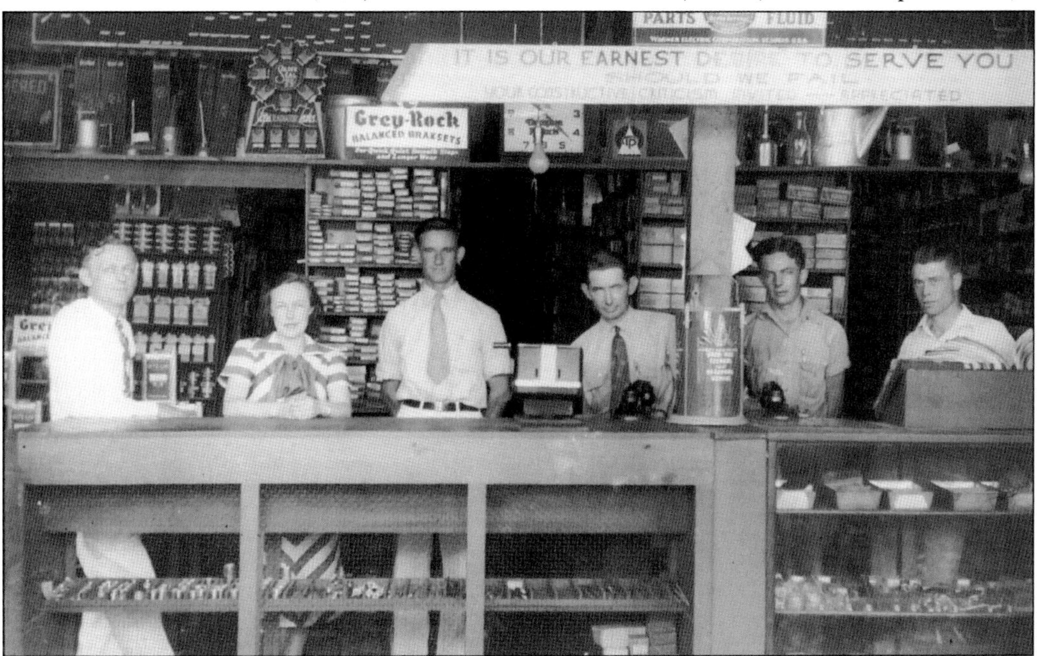

Auto-parts stores were prevalent starting in the 1930s. Claude Hearn opened East Alabama Auto Parts around 1935 on West Tenth Street. Employees of the store pose here around 1940. By 1953, Hearn's widow had sold the business to the Sawyer family. Originally located at 102 West Tenth Street, the auto-parts dealer moved to 909 West Tenth Street in 1960. The business remained there until 1977, when it moved to 1920 Quintard Avenue. East Alabama Auto Parts closed in 2000.

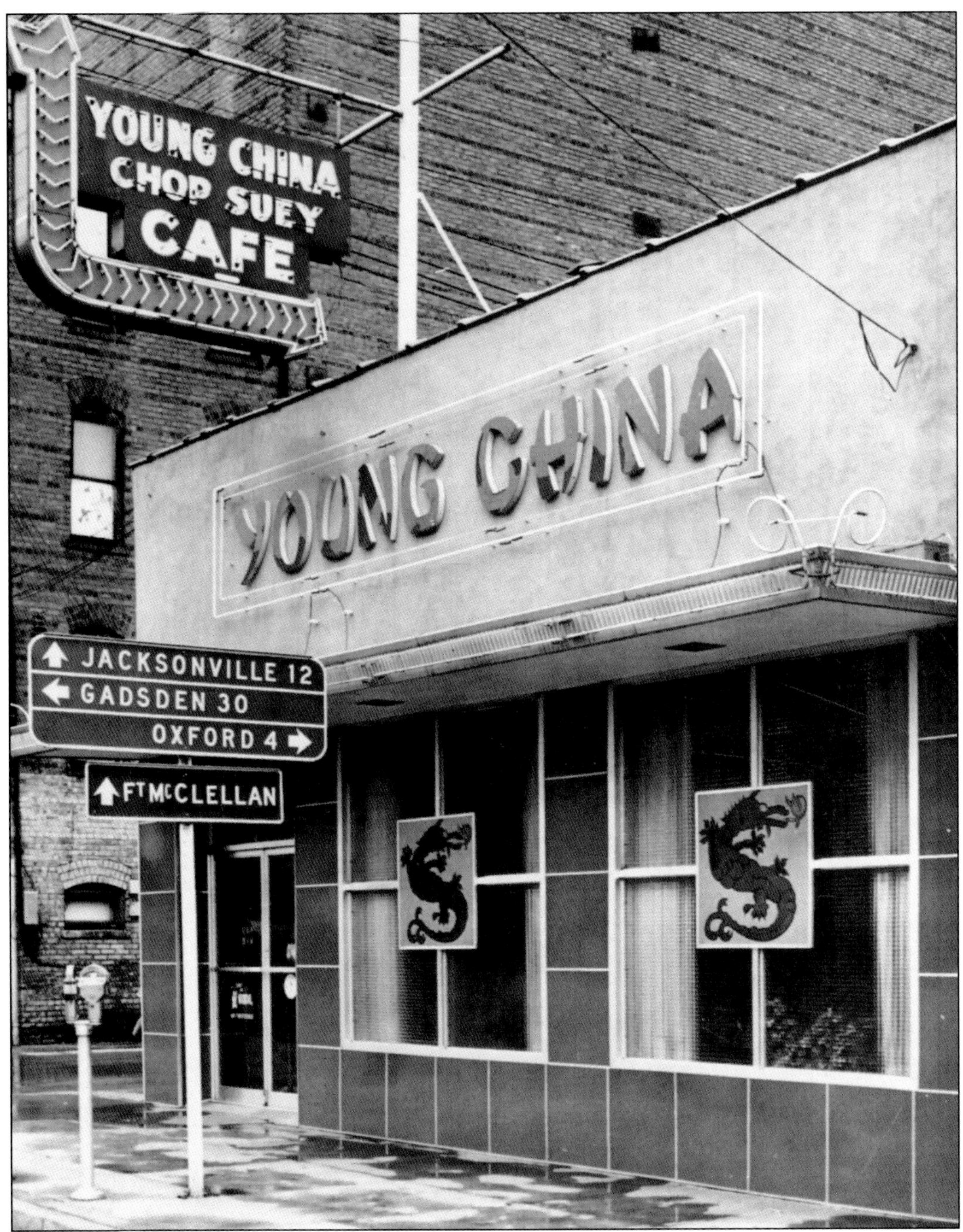

After moving around the United States, Charlie Lee settled in Anniston in 1915 to open Charlie Lee Chinese Laundry on Ninth and Noble Streets. In the early 1940s, Lee helped open Young China Cafe on West Tenth Street. During World War II, he enlisted in the Army and was stationed at Fort McClellan as a mess sergeant. When he died in 1963, he left the restaurant to Lynn Mok, a widow he had helped move to a house at 709 Quintard Avenue. In 1970, the Young China Cafe moved to Mok's home, where it operated until 1979. Lee, who never wanted to leave Tenth Street, was buried in Hillside Cemetery.

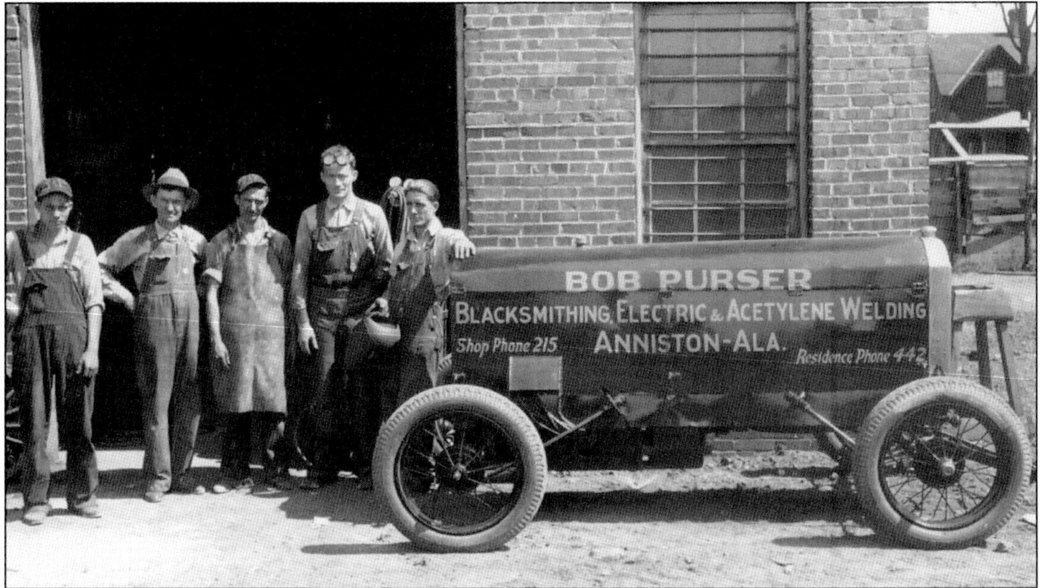

Anniston's early blacksmiths shoed horses and repaired metal objects. Some blacksmiths became early automobile makers and mechanics, while others, like Bob Purser, moved from blacksmithing into welding. Purser, seen here around 1930, opened his shop at 120 West Eleventh Street before 1929, and 10 years later, had added welding. By 1956, Purser had moved into the metal-fabrication business with his son Elbert. Bob Purser's Steel Fabrication shop operated until Elbert retired in 1974.

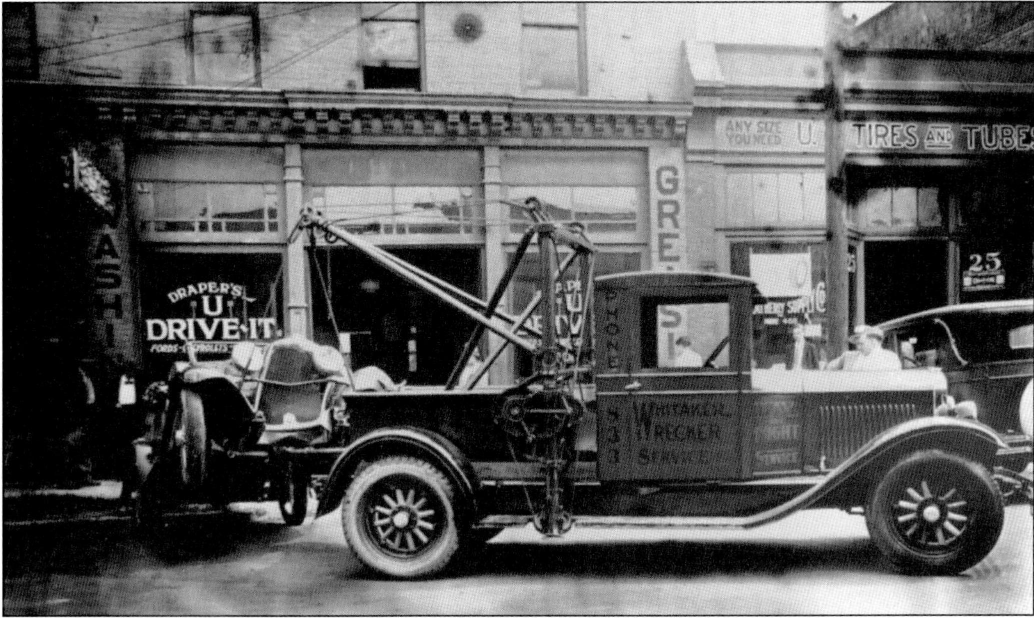

From the mid-1920s to the mid-1930s, Lucius A. Draper operated his automobile rental business, Draper's U-Drive-It, at 18 East Eleventh Street. The business, seen here around 1931, also served as a modern auto-repair shop. A new Draper's U-Drive-It, at Thirteenth and Noble Streets, was operated by L.A. Draper Jr. from 1959 to 1961. The business rented Chevrolet, Ford, and Edsel trucks.

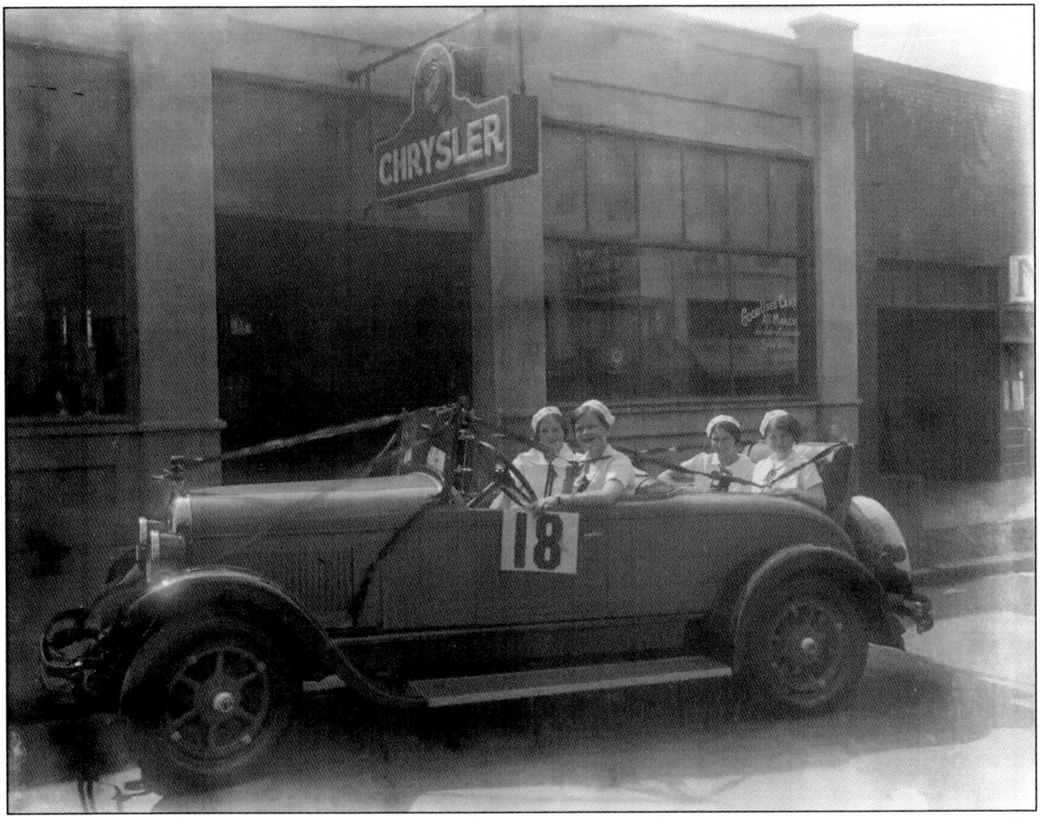

Cooper & Sons Motor Company Inc. was founded in the mid-1920s by Davis C. Cooper, the mayor of Oxford. The Chrysler dealership was located at 22 East Eleventh Street. Constantine & Cooper Home Furniture was next door. In the 1920s and 1930s, East Eleventh Street was at the center of the automobile culture in Anniston. These women are posing in front of Cooper & Sons Motor around 1926.

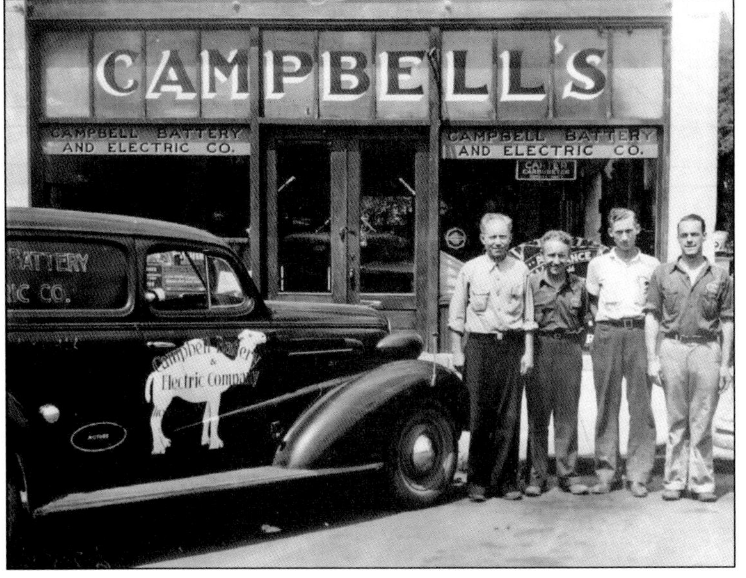

W.L. Campbell started his battery shop in 1921 in a small section of a Woco-Pep Station on Wilmer Avenue. The business specialized in batteries, and as it grew in the 1930s, Campbell Battery relocated to a larger store at 1020 Wilmer Avenue, then to 27 East Eleventh Street. The larger shop offered drive-in battery service, radio repair, and electrical service on cars.

The Motor Parts Company operated a store at 113 East Eleventh Street. It is seen here around 1935. When King Motor Company expanded in the early 1940s, this site became the motor lot. The King Motor Lot remained at the location until 1965. The site has since been occupied by a savings-and-loan bank and Wells Fargo.

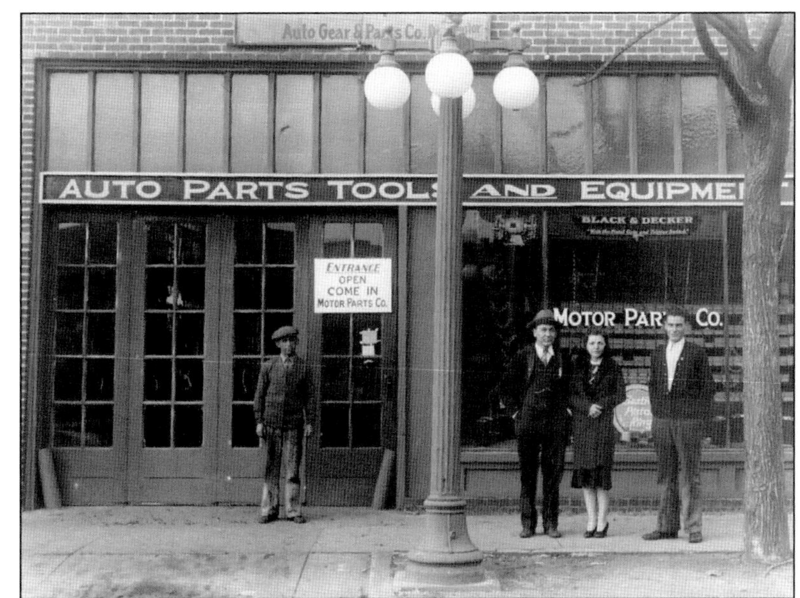

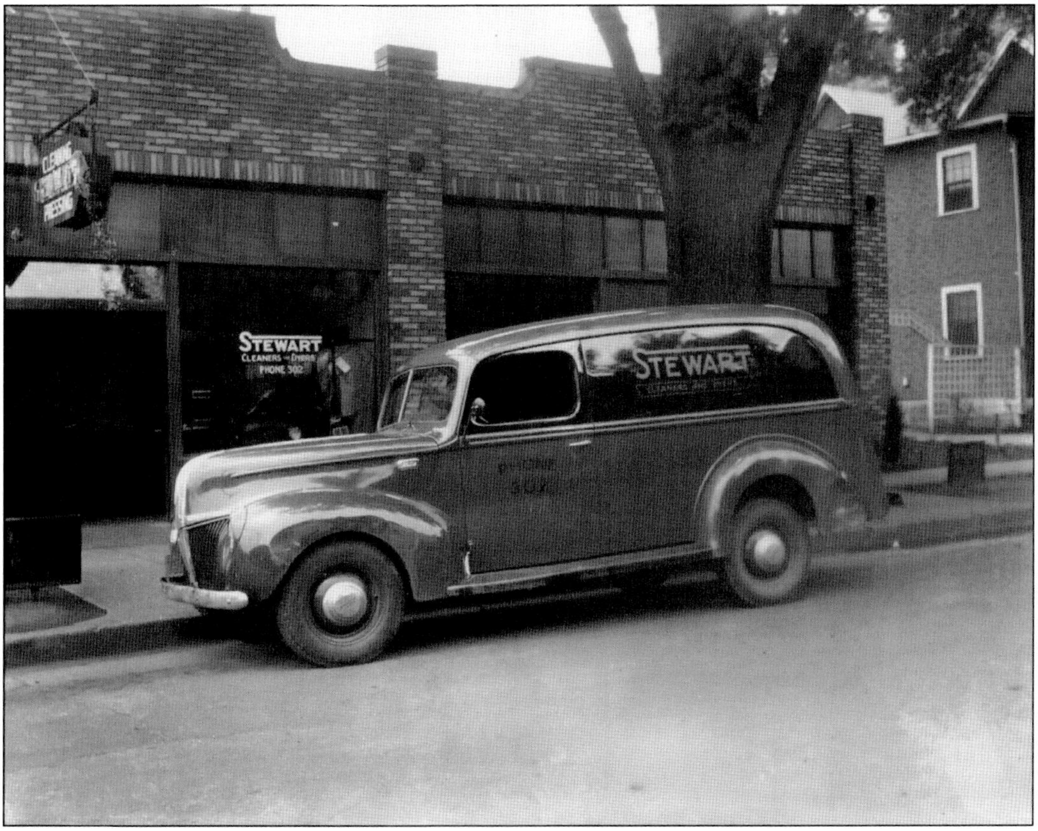

In the late 1920s, Rose-Stickney Shoe Repair & Dry Cleaning opened at 121–123 East 11th Street. By the mid-1930s, Sam Stewart purchased the building and opened Stewart's Dry Cleaners. The company, seen here around 1940, was sold in 2003. Lander's Boarding House (far right) was next door to the cleaners. In the 21st century, it was the site of Cheaha Bank.

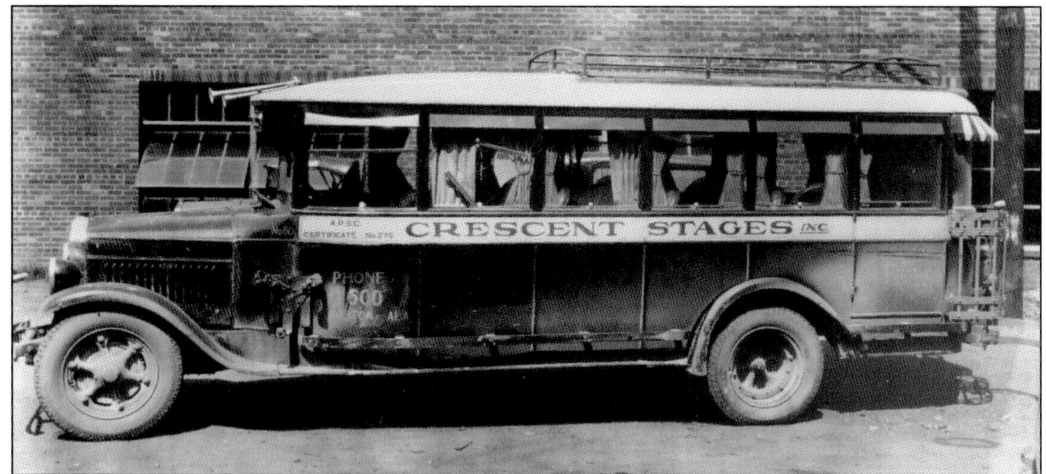

The Anniston trolley-car system was transferred to Alabama Power in 1912, but, due to the rise of competition from the Crescent Stage Line, the trolley system lost money. By 1932, trolley cars no longer operated, and the streetcar rails were eventually taken up and used for scrap metal during World War II. The trolleys were replaced by buses, which in turn were replaced by the family car.

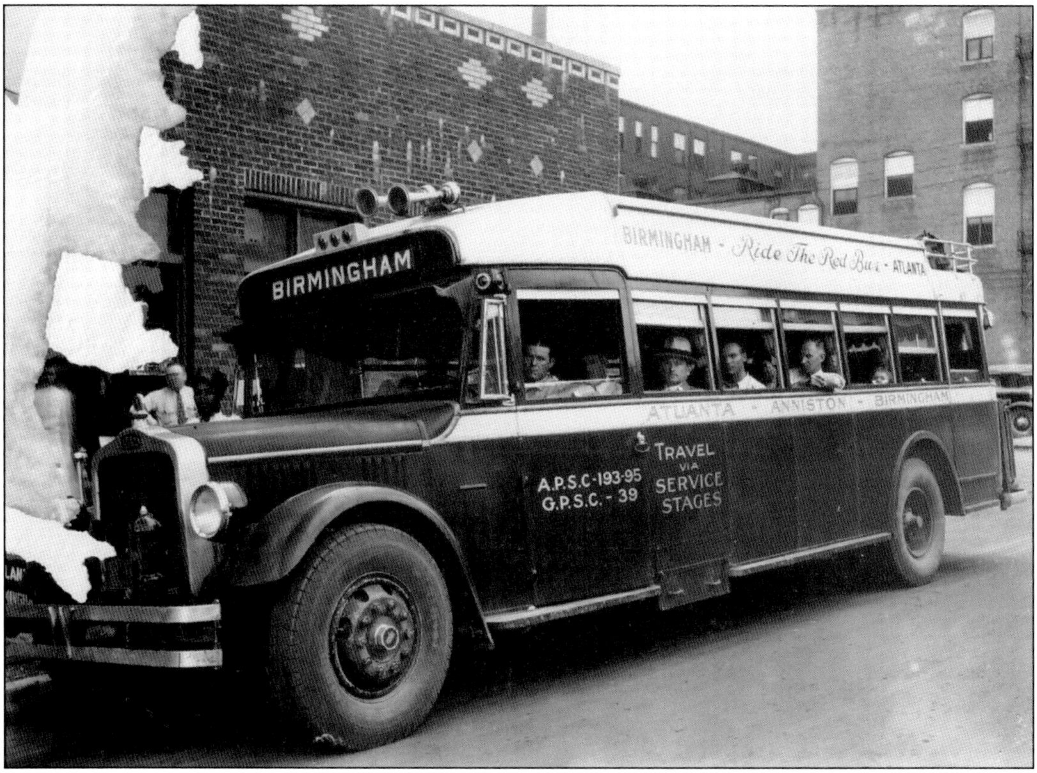

Crescent Stage Line operated Clipper buses from Anniston to points including Montgomery, Birmingham, and Huntsville, and as far as Rome, Georgia. Incorporated in 1928 as Dixie Stage Lines, the bus line reorganized in 1931 as Crescent Stages. In 1938, Crescent Stages joined Trailways and, by 1953, was sold to Transcontinental Bus System. The bus terminal, seen here around 1930, was located behind the Alabama Hotel, near the train station.

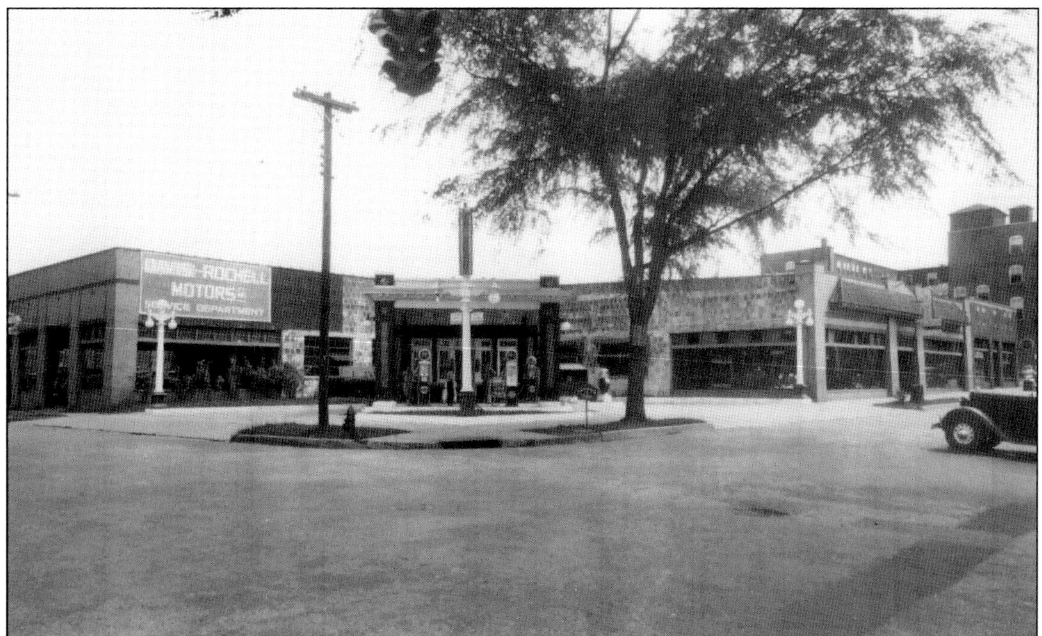

Davis-Rochell Motors was chartered in June 1936 as a Dodge-Plymouth dealer. The dealership was located at 25 West Twelfth Street, behind the Alabama Hotel, at the former Adams-McCargo Dealership. It is seen here around 1936. By 1938, the dealership became Cruse-Rochell Motors. The location housed Fred's Discount Store from 1975 until 2012.

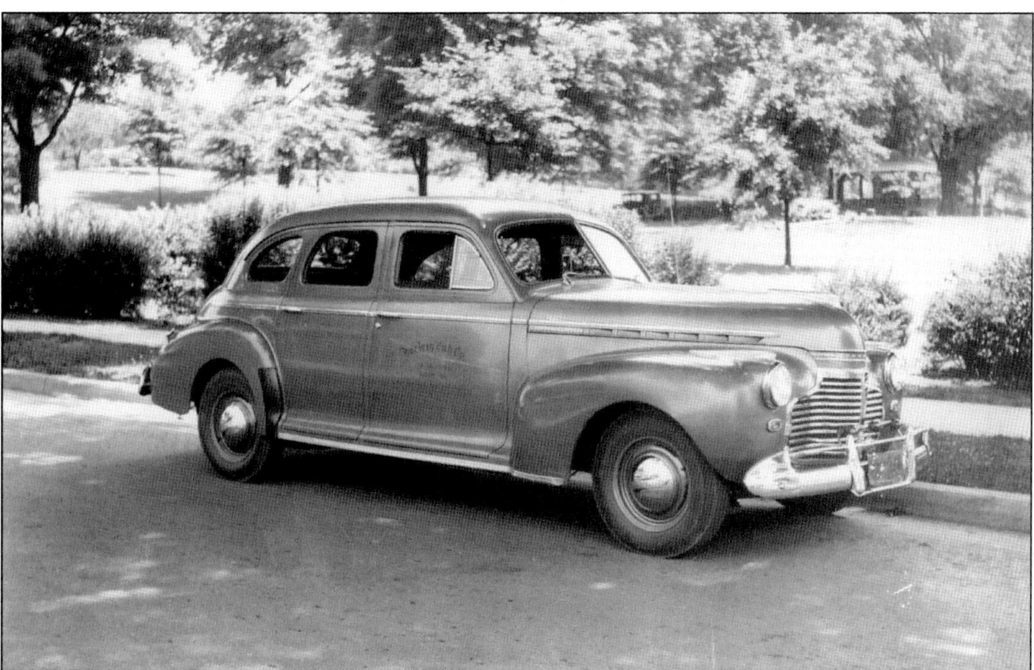

During World War II, Harlem Cab was operated by C.L. "Doc" Henderson at 14 West Thirteenth Street. The company provided safe, fast transportation at the reasonable rate of 2¢ per block. In 1945, Fort McClellan regulated authorized taxi services on post, with the rate from Fort McClellan to Anniston set at $1.

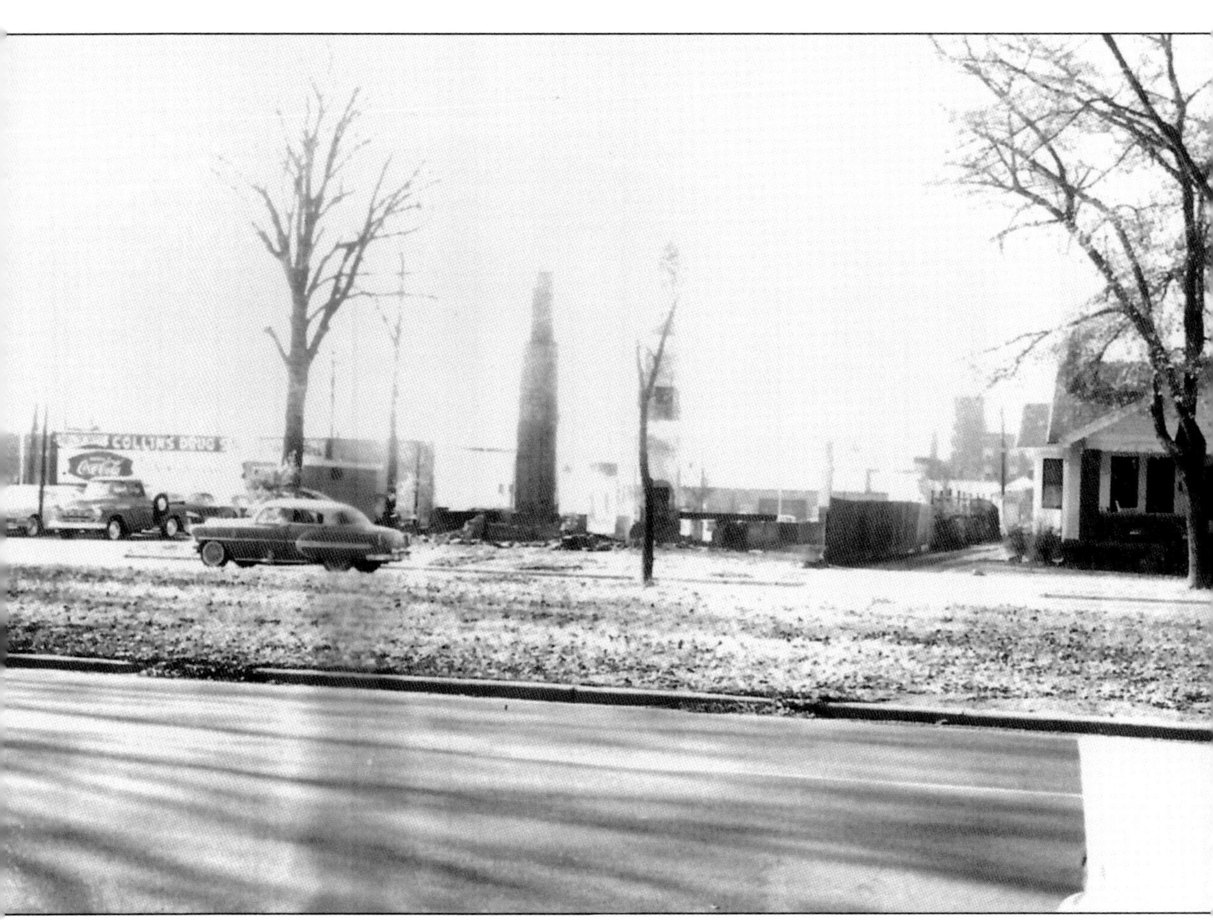

Collins Drug Store, started by W.C. "Doc" Collins in 1917 at 1220 Noble Street, was both a drugstore and soda fountain. In the 1940s, Henry Saxon had a small counter inside the drugstore to sell his wife's homemade chocolates. In 1953, the drugstore moved to 123 East Thirteenth Street (shown at left rear around 1960). The drugstore was sold to Awbrey Burns and became Model City Drugs in January 1963. (ERY.)

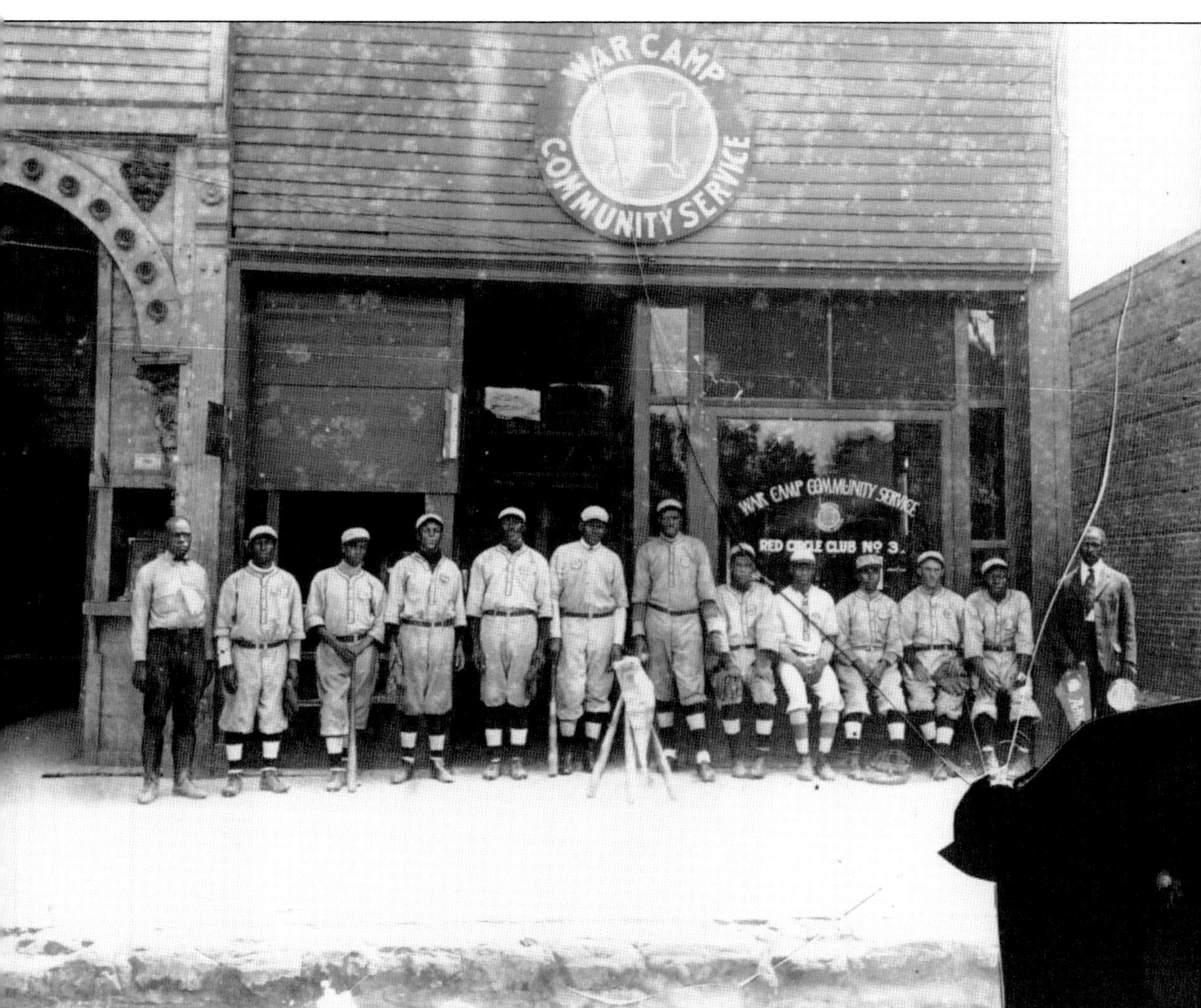

The West Fifteenth Street Business District developed as a secondary commercial district in Anniston specifically for the black community from 1898 to 1935. Not only was the area a business district, it also served as a social center. The Queen Theatre, located at 504–508 West Fifteenth Street, was the only African American vaudeville and motion-picture theater in Anniston. It is seen at far left in this c. 1917 photograph. By 1922, the theater was closed. The building was replaced in 1927 with a single-story commercial building that housed various specialty shops. The War Camp Community Service Center was a recreation center during World War I for black soldiers at nearby Camp McClellan.

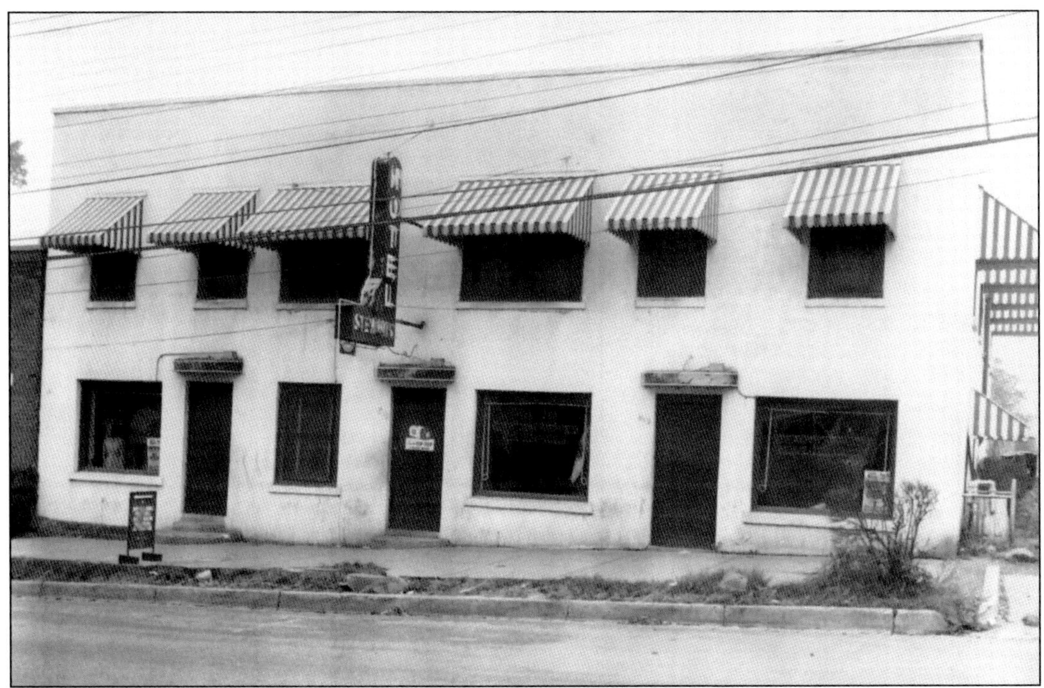

In the 1920s and 1930s, 608–614 West Fifteenth Street was occupied by various businesses, including a dry cleaner, beauty parlor, music teacher's studio, and insurance agency. The Pilgrim Hotel was constructed for the African American community in the early 1940s. By 1945, James Stewart was operating his Stewart's Restaurant and Hotel (pictured). Jonas and Martha Blair operated their Holiday Cafe and Hotel from 1962 until 1975 on the property. The building remained vacant and eventually was demolished.

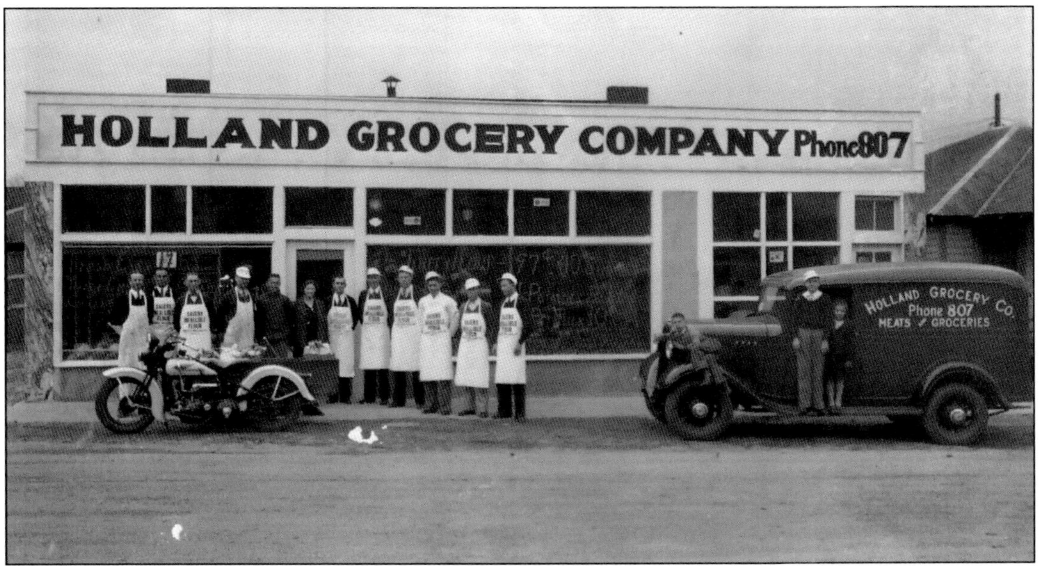

In the 1930s, Holland Grocery Company operated at 102 West Eighteenth Street, across the street from Central Presbyterian Church. Employees pose here around 1930. In 1935, Holland Grocery moved to Oxford, but a series of grocery stores operated in the same location until 1960. For the next 20 years, a school for training "beauty operators in 1,000 hours" occupied the building.

Three

LIFE AND ARTS

From the beginning, Anniston's population built a life around schools, churches, theaters, concerts, museums, parades, libraries, and social organizations. In the 1940s, the park system expanded the number of parks, community centers, and library branches to make culture more accessible to the outlying communities without need for transportation into the city.

In 1883, public schools were under the control of the mayor and the city council; however, there were several fee-based private schools. Samuel Noble funded a Noble Institute for Boys and a separate facility for girls. In 1885, funding for the first black school was appropriated. Overcrowding was an issue from the beginning of the public school system. The system for the city was officially organized under the board of education in 1891. Throughout Anniston's history, several local churches have operated parochial schools. At the turn of the 20th century, education for young women became a priority, with the establishment of Barber Memorial Seminary for young black women and the Southern Female University for young white women. Public school enrollment fluctuated throughout the years, based on military dependents attending local schools. When Fort McClellan closed, there was a steady decline in enrollment.

Samuel Noble established an Episcopal church in the 1870s, with other denominations following soon after. Many early churches met in town buildings or homes until church buildings were constructed in the 1880s. As the town population grew, so did the number of churches of all faiths: Protestant, Catholic, Jewish, and nondenominational. The majority of churches were of the Baptist faith.

Before the town opened to the public, black and white citizens lived side by side. Segregation was based on occupation, but, after 1890, racial segregation appeared. The black business community, including grocery stores, drugstores, furnishing stores, and repair shops, did not emerge until the 20th century. The African American social community was built extensively around the church and a few fraternal organizations, such as the Rising Star Lodge, Colored Knights of Pythias Lodge, and the Calhoun Club. After World War II, segregated parks, pools, and a community center with a library developed in the western part of Anniston.

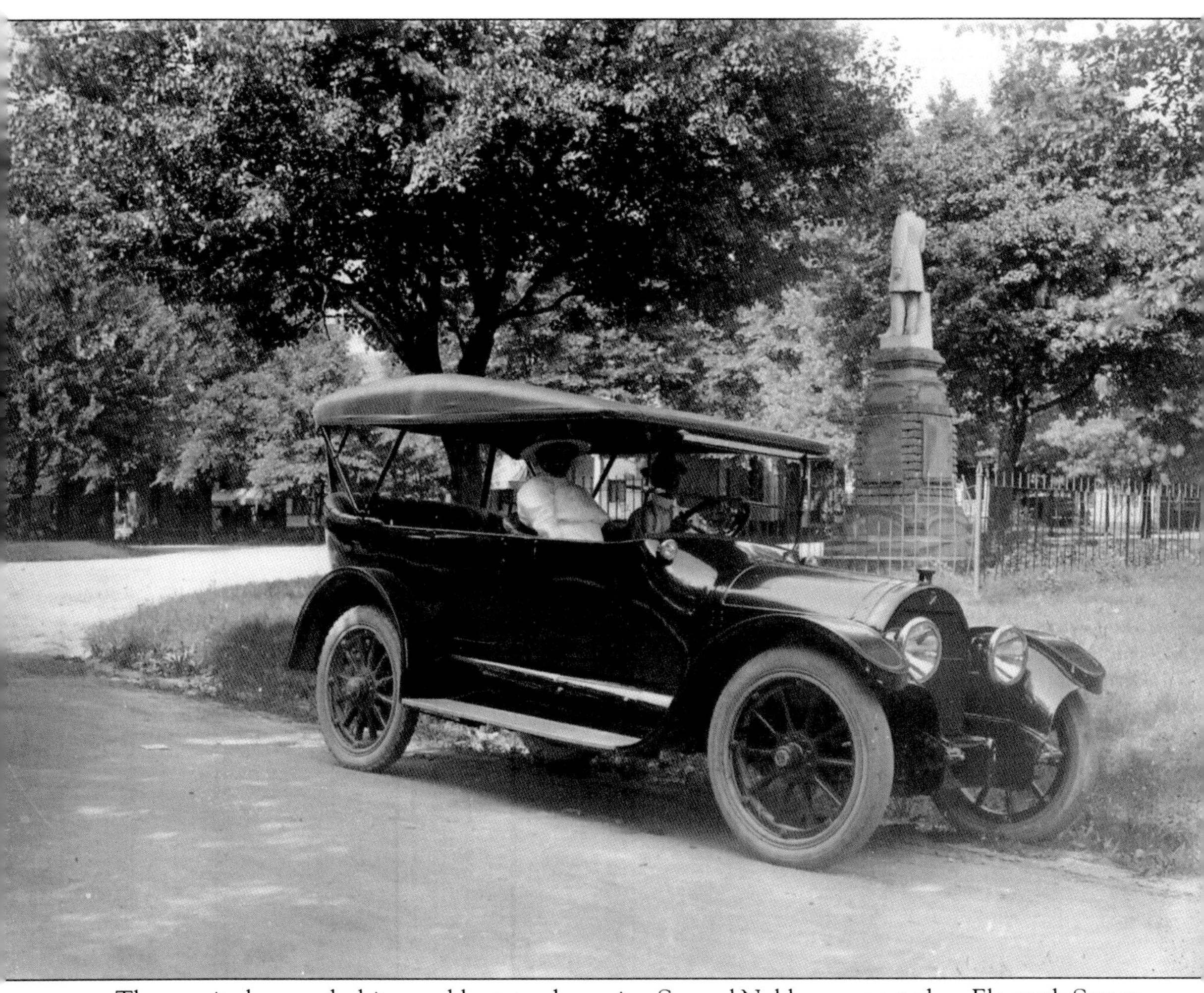

The granite-base and white-marble statue honoring Samuel Noble was erected on Eleventh Street and Quintard Avenue by the citizens of Anniston in 1895, seven years after his death. Founder's Day was celebrated in Anniston on November 22, Noble's birthday, for many years. The tradition was revived briefly in the late 1950s. In 1967, all statues in the park along Quintard Avenue were equipped with lights and refurbished. The Noble statue is seen here around 1915.

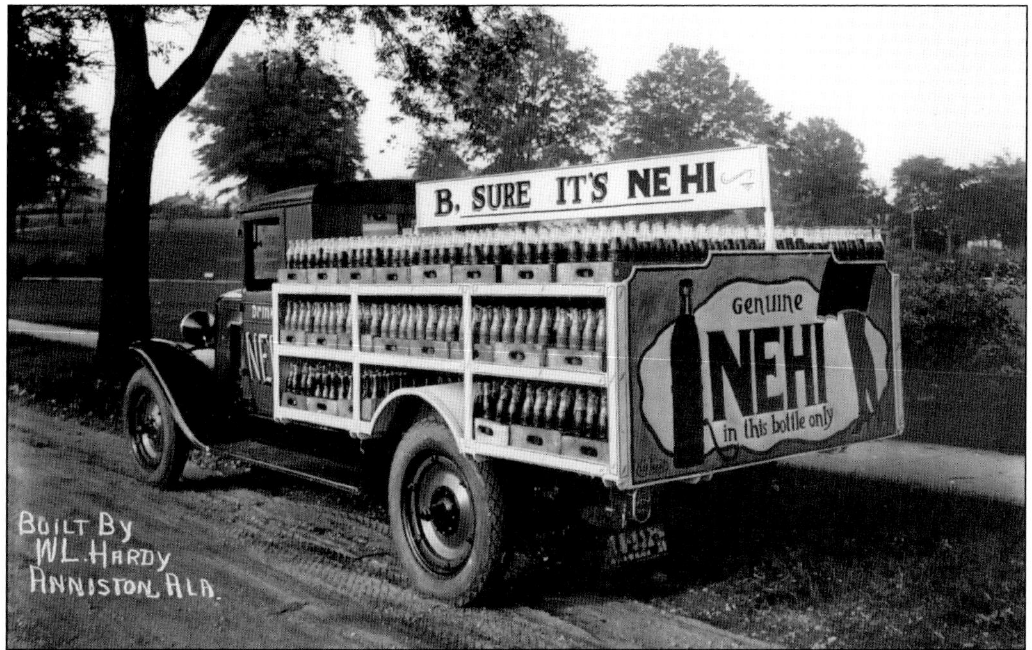

Zinn Park was created after a 1924 bequest from Col. William Henry Zinn. In the above photograph, taken around 1929, the park serves as a backdrop for W.L. Hardy's Nehi truck. Zinn's will provided $10,000 for the establishment of a park if the city purchased land from the Anniston City Land Company encompassing two square blocks between Thirteenth and Fifteenth Streets and Gurnee and Moore Avenues. A provision of the will also included funds for the creation of two additional parks: one for the African American community, and one in South Anniston. The Anniston Park Board was organized in October 1924, with Quintard Avenue and Glenwood Terrace as the only parks. By 1931, there were three white parks (Zinn, Sixth Ward [Ezell], and Glen Addie) and two African American parks (Lincoln and Booker T. Washington), as well as a municipal golf course. The parks system expanded in 1953 to include 10 parks, with baseball fields, playgrounds, and barbeque pits, as well as five pools. The below photograph, taken around 1949, shows an Anniston Parks System truck.

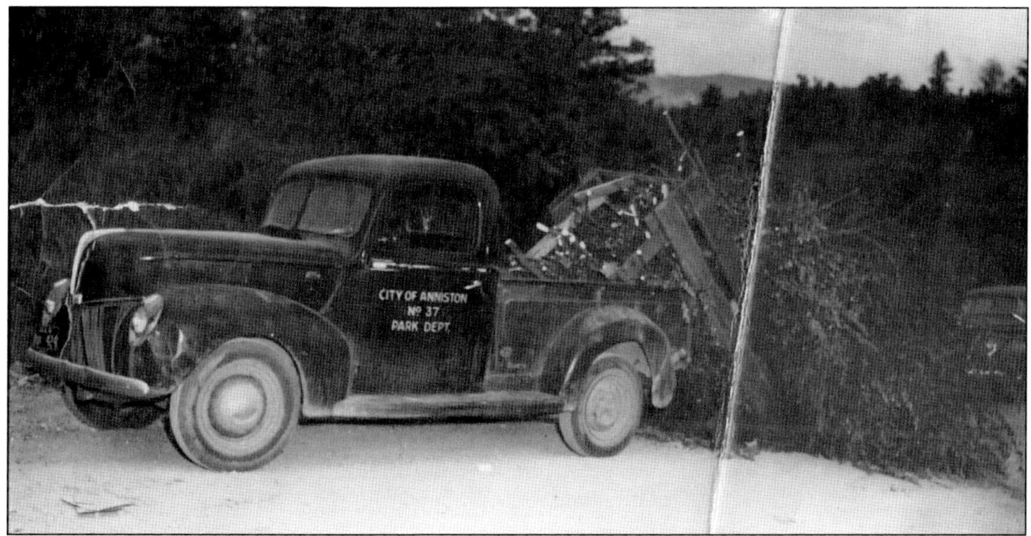

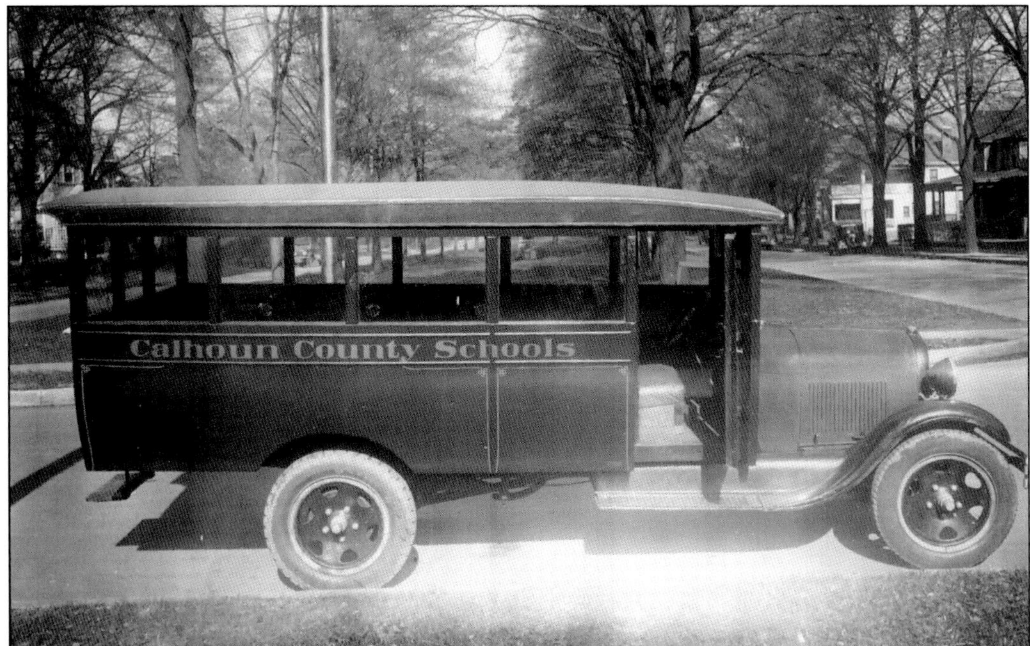

Quintard Avenue was a residential neighborhood starting in the 1870s. The avenue extended from Fifth to Twenty-second Streets. Most of the homes on the northern side of the road sat on steep banks. The northbound and southbound lanes, separated by a large green space, each had one lane. Lanes dedicated to parking were on each side. Quintard Avenue is seen here around 1928.

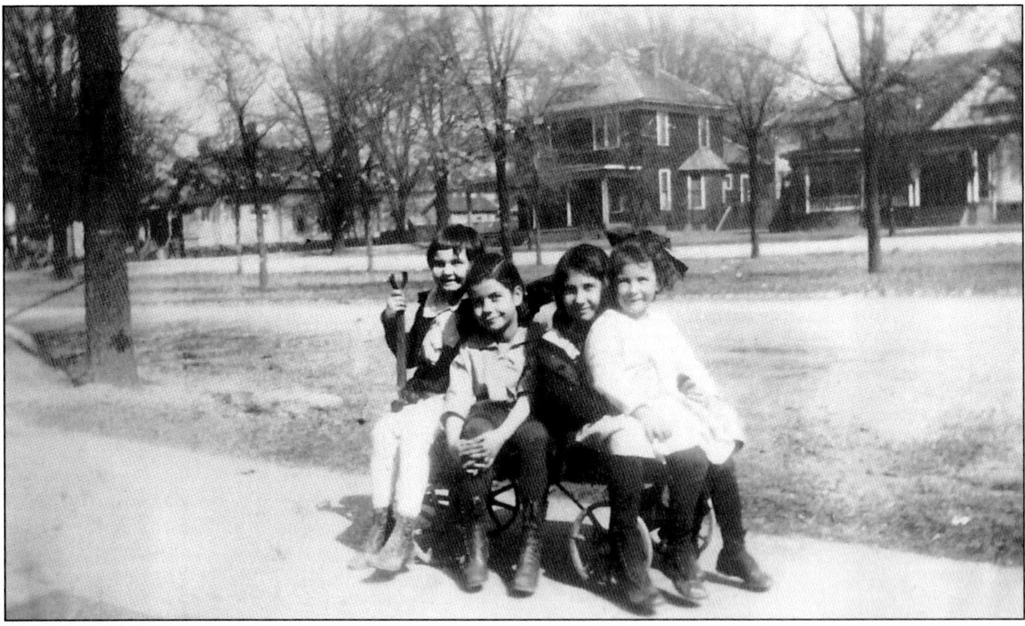

The green space on Quintard Avenue was intended to be a botanical garden. Samuel Noble brought Fredrick Ulbricht, former supervisor of Paris's Tuileries Gardens, to create Quintard Park. Before the park could be completed, Noble died. In the 1920s, the road was paved, but remained a residential area. The green space was maintained as a park administered by the City of Anniston. (ERY.)

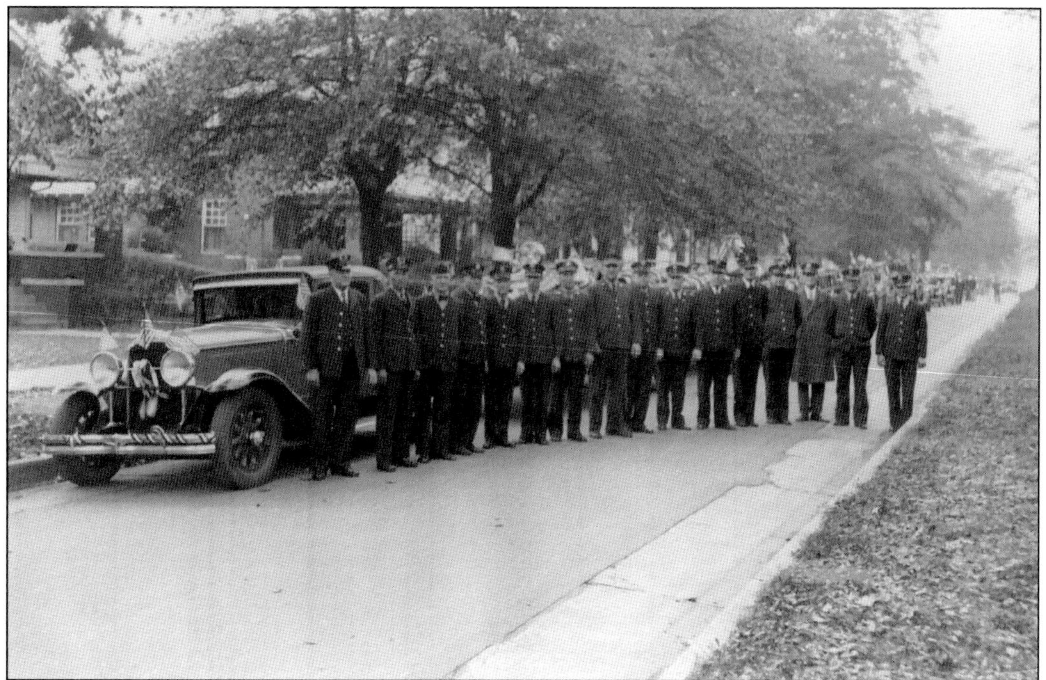

Quintard Avenue, seen here in the late 1930s, was lined with majestic Victorian homes. In the 1940s, the street became an access road for the soldiers at Fort McClellan, much to the dismay of many residents. As traffic increased, the street became a four-lane road.

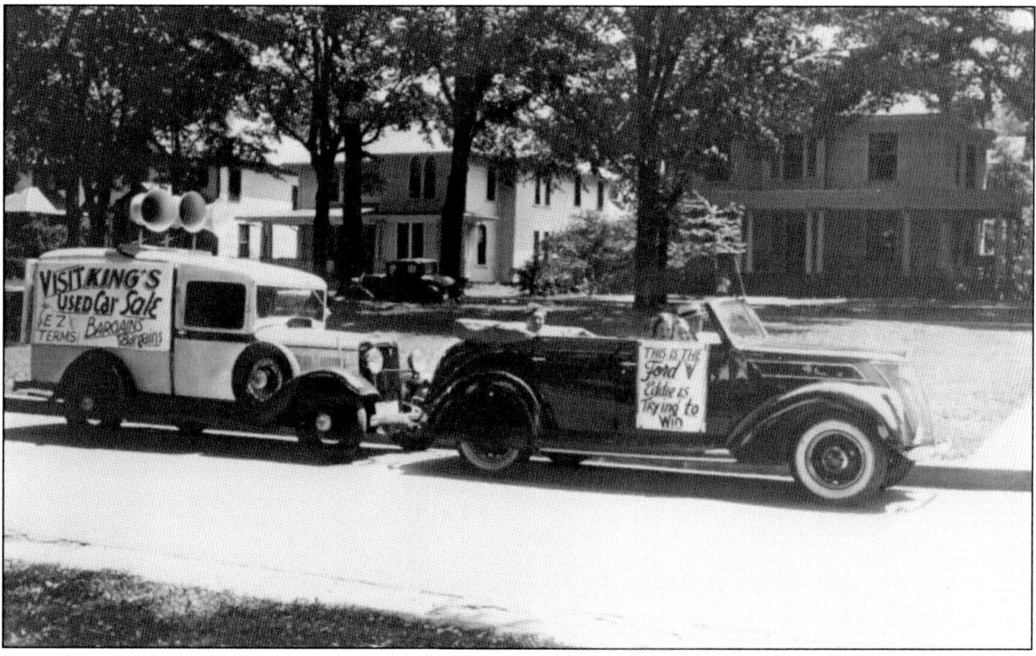

By 1957, Quintard Avenue was opened to the south. The houses near 1101 Quintard Avenue, including the Gilbert House (seen here around 1935), were torn down to build the US Post Office in the 1960s. With progress came an addition of another lane. Along with turn lanes, this created a six-lane road that ultimately became the route for both Highways 21 and 431.

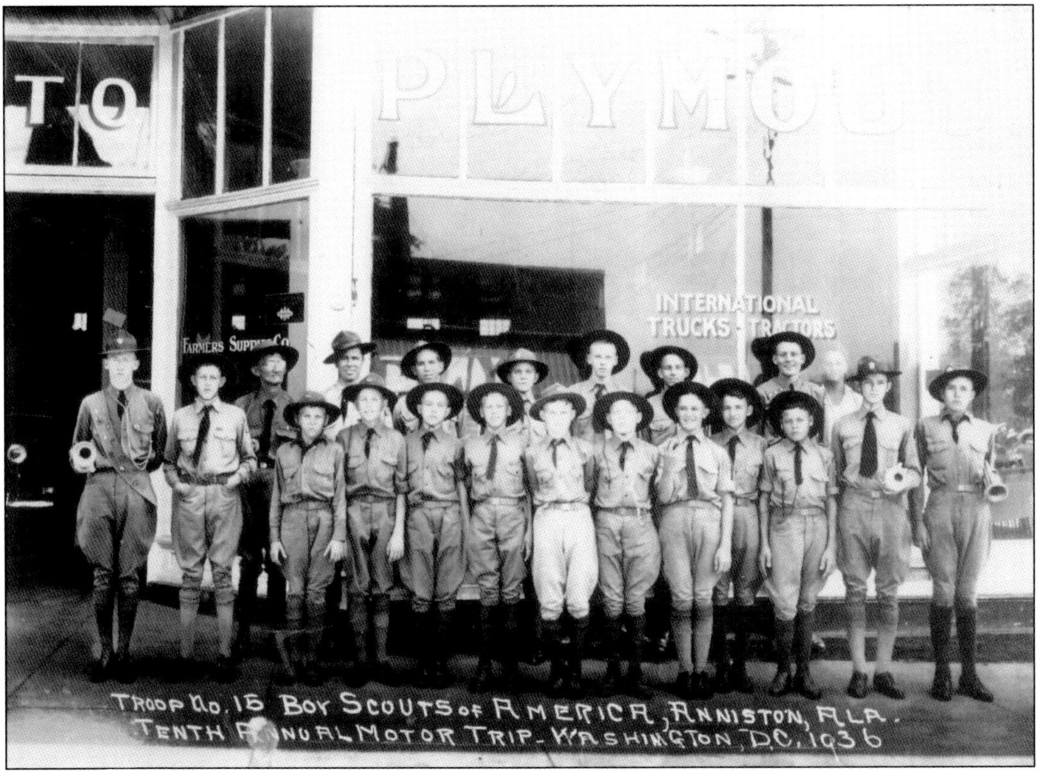

A.P. "Cap" Ezell (pictured above at far left c. 1936 and below at far right) started his tenure with Boy Scout Troop No. 15 in February 1922. Each year, the troop traveled by truck to locations throughout the United States. Even at age 64, in the late 1940s, Ezell was still actively participating in hikes and camping while instilling character in his young charges from South Anniston. He was awarded the Silver Beaver for service to the Choccolocco Council in 1932. Ezell, who was orphaned as an infant, never participated in scouting as boy, but became an exemplary scoutmaster. In June 1946, the six-acre park on South Quintard was named in honor of Ezell.

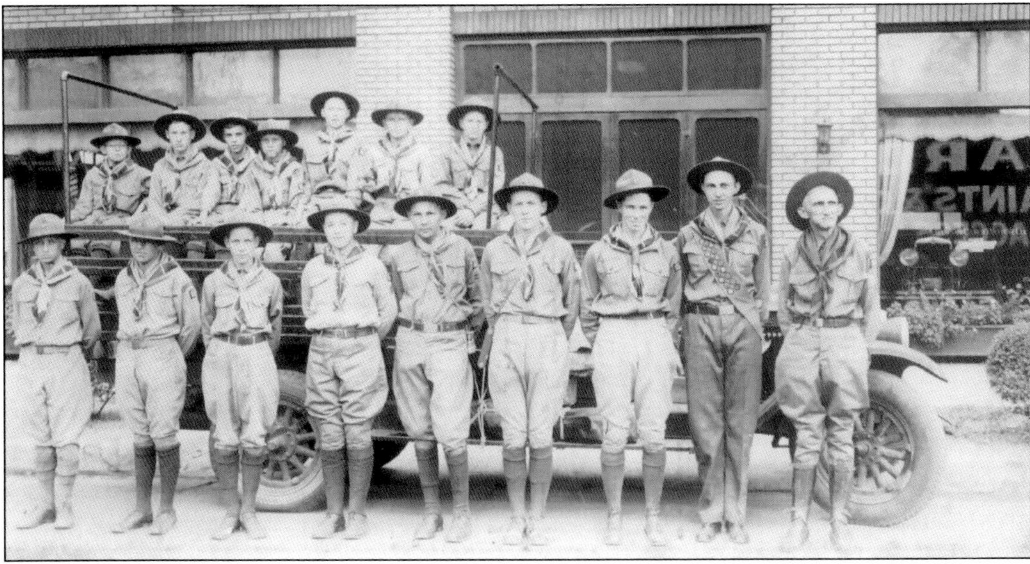

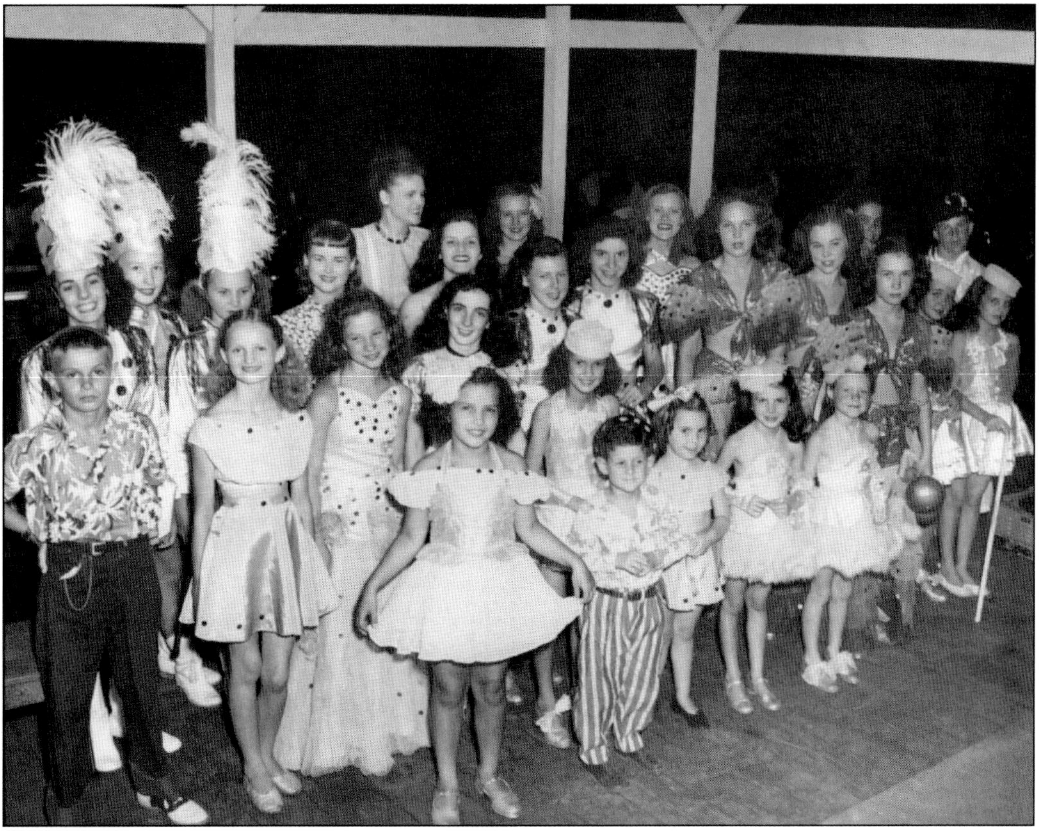

Zenobia King Hill Dancers were trained by the premier dance instructor in Anniston, Zenobia King Hill. She is seen here at rear center around 1946. Starting in 1935, Hill operated a school of dance, organized and trained the Jacksonville State University Marching Ballerinas, and produced the Miss Anniston Beauty Pageants each year. When Hill retired in 1968, one of her students, Sherry Brady, began teaching dance classes in Anniston. (PLACC-BC.)

Due to overcrowding in 1887, a new public school building for white children was constructed on Pine Avenue in West Anniston. Pine Avenue School, seen here around 1914, was the first school building in Anniston to be designed for educational use. Completed in 1888, the school was still inadequate and was ultimately replaced. Pine Avenue School closed in 1962, and the pupils were absorbed into Quintard, Woodstock, and Glen Addie Schools. (LOC.)

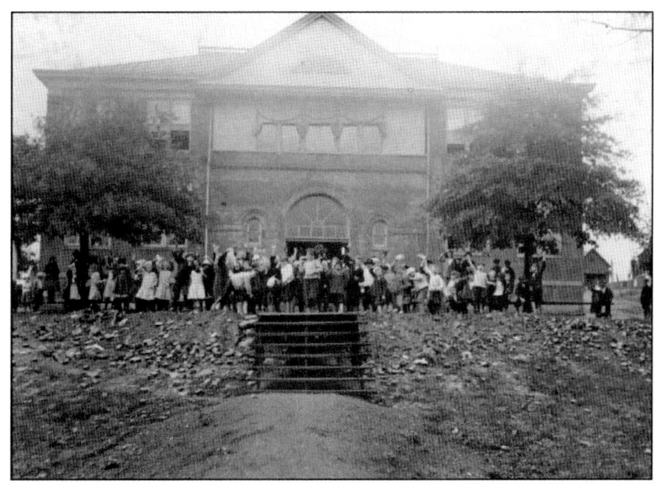

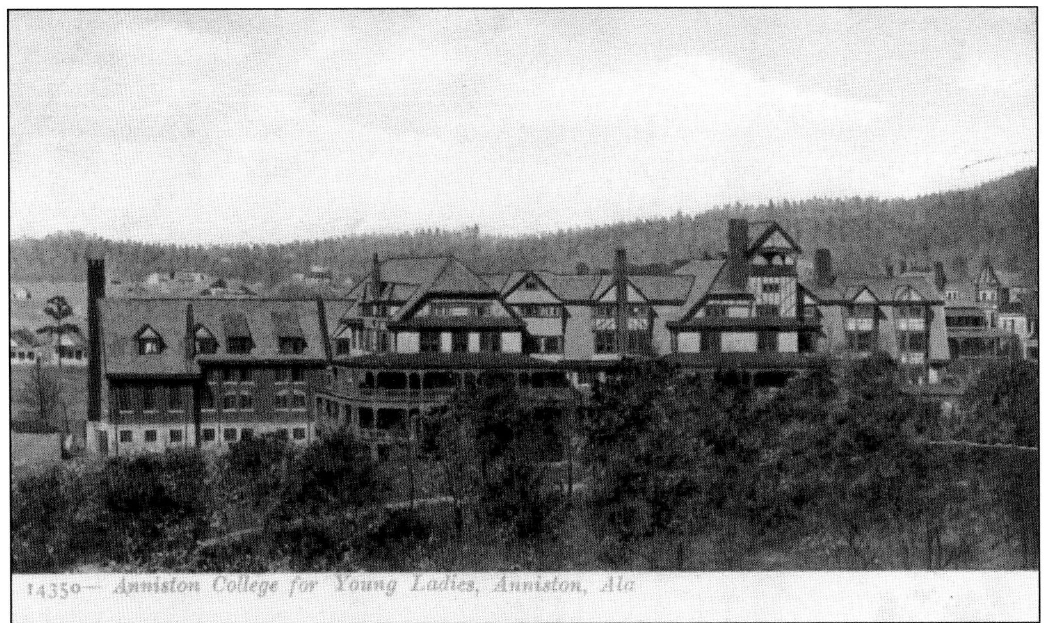

Construction on the Queen Anne–style, five-story building at Fourteenth Street and Gurnee Avenue began in October 1883. The Anniston Inn was opened to the public in April 1885, but a depression in the 1890s forced the hotel to close. The structure housed the Anniston College for Young Ladies boarding school until 1906, when it was converted to an apartment house. During World War I, the building was renovated to provide the city with a first-class hotel, but it was destroyed by fire in January 1923. (ERY.)

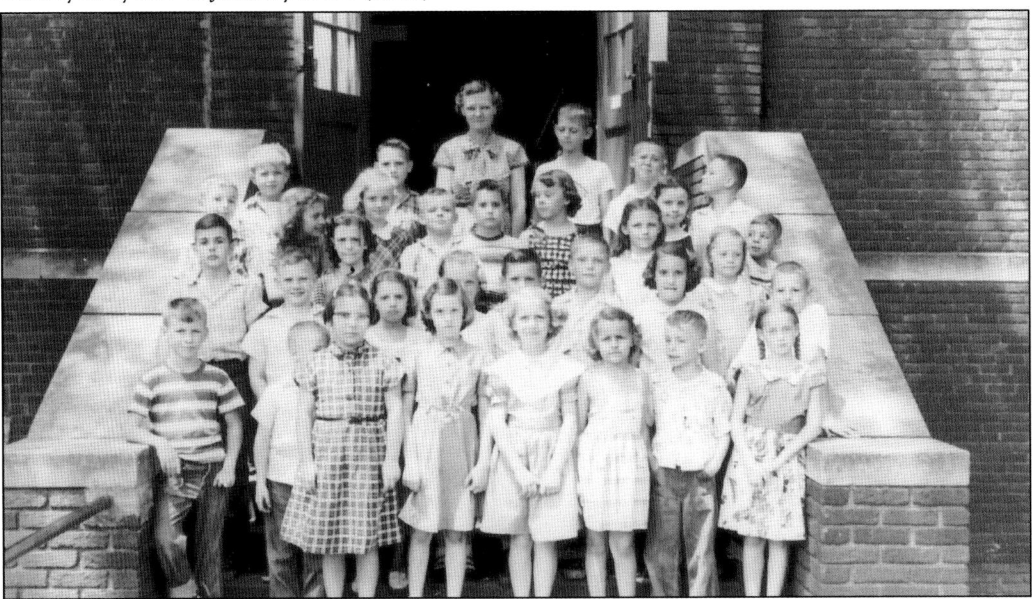

Woodstock Avenue School, located on East Tenth Street, was built in 1922 as an elementary school for children on the east side of Anniston. Here, Miss Sharp's 1954 third-grade class poses in front of the school. In 1975, the Anniston School Board closed the school, but chose to hold it in reserve for future overcrowding. By 1989, the school was renovated as mixed office space and renamed the Woodstock Professional Building. (ERY.)

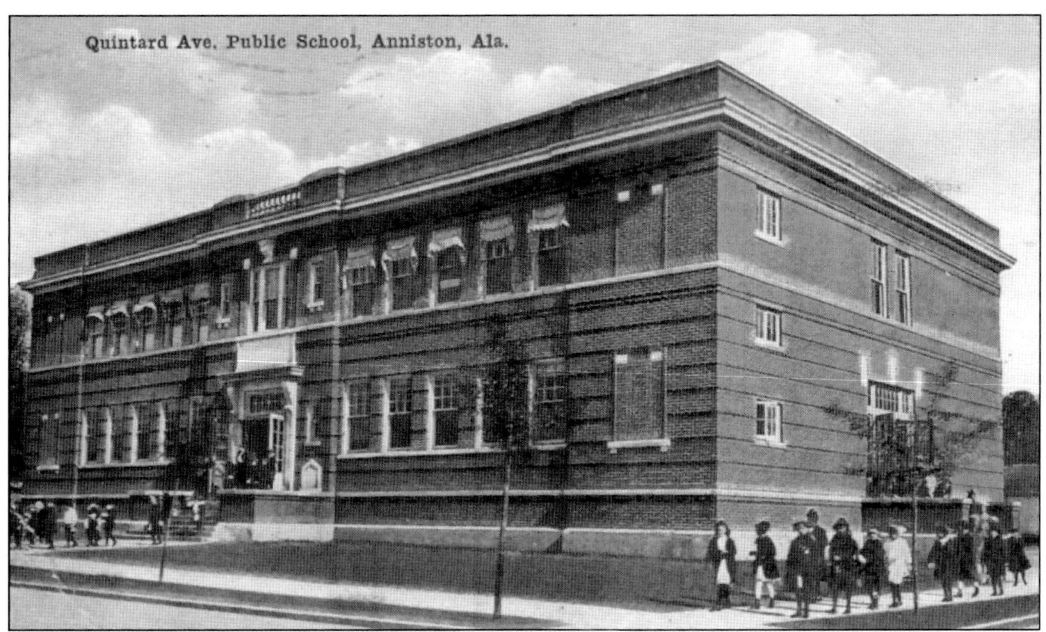

Quintard Avenue School, located at 1705 Quintard Avenue, was built in the fall of 1910 to replace the Leighton Avenue School, which was destroyed by fire the previous winter. In 1920, the city instituted the first lunchroom program at the school. From 1910 until 1927, the school was an elementary school, then converted to a junior high school to handle the overflow from neighboring Anniston High School. In the 1970s, the building was used as the offices for Vocational Rehabilitation Services. Later, the site became Centennial Memorial Park. (PLACC.)

The Northeast Civic Center, between Sixteenth and Nineteenth Streets and Rocky Hollow, was developed in the 1930s. Anniston Memorial Stadium, built in 1935 using WPA funds, was equipped with lights for nighttime events. It is seen here around 1946. From 1930 to 1944, E.D. "Chink" Lott coached the Anniston High School football team, earning a 91-22-11 record. In 1984, the stadium was named "Chink" Lott Memorial Stadium and has been used for many events, including the Turkey Bowl. In 2009, it was renamed Lott-Mosby Memorial Stadium. (PLACC-BC.)

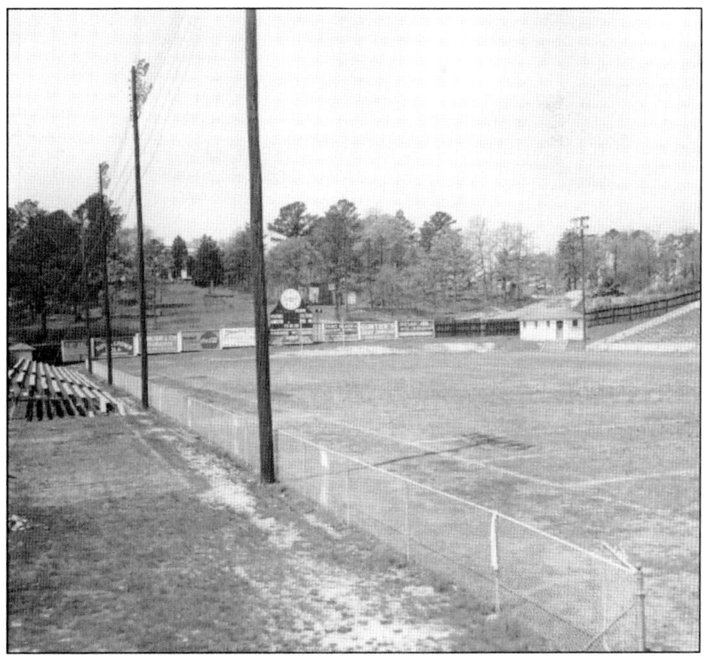

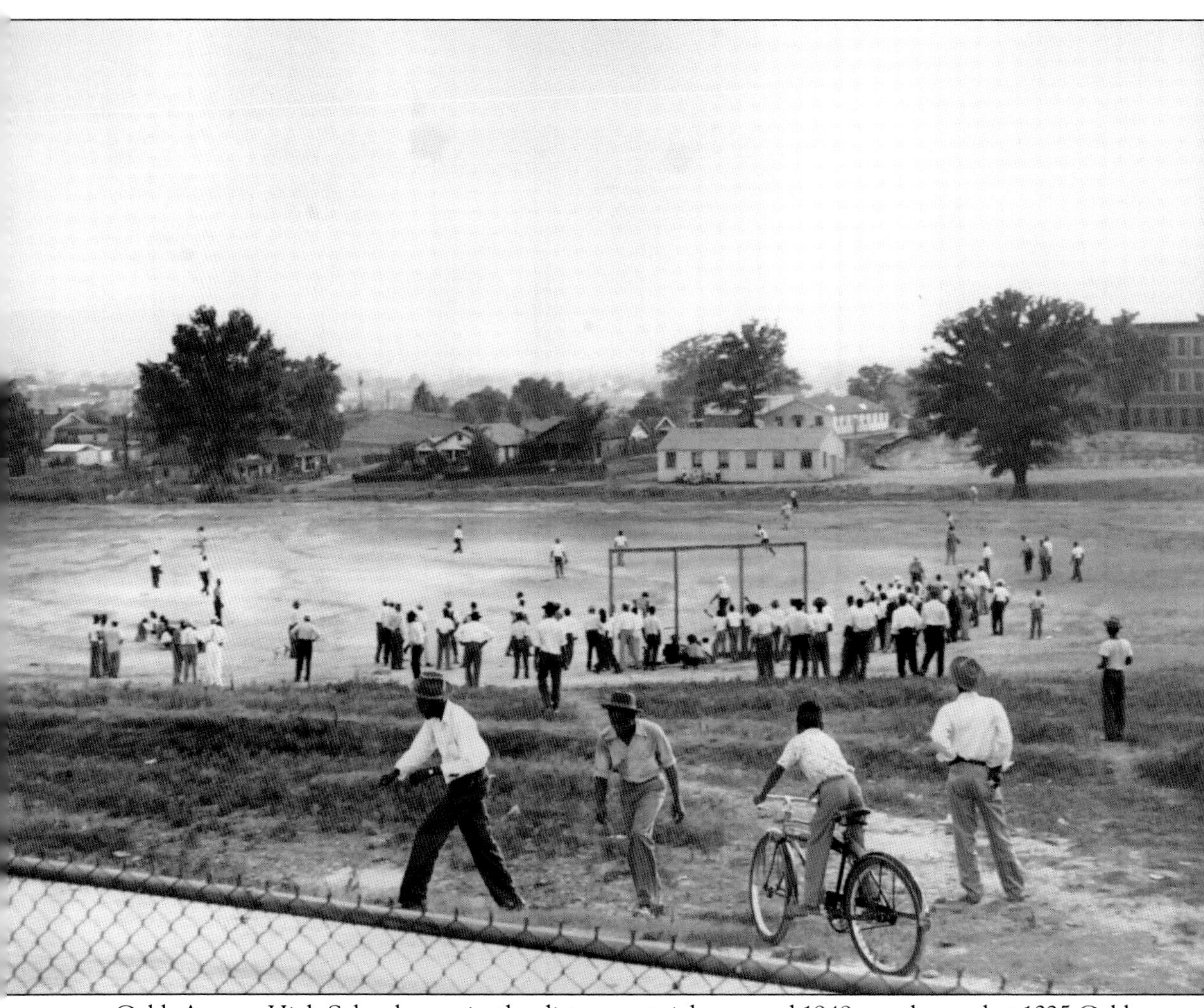

Cobb Avenue High School, seen in the distance at right around 1949, was located at 1325 Cobb Avenue. It had been constructed for black students in 1935. From 1939 to 1972, the school fielded a football team. For the 1973–1974 school year, the plan to integrate the Anniston school system called for Anniston High School to be a high school for all students in Anniston and Cobb to be a junior high school. In 1987, a new middle school was built north of town, and Cobb was converted to an elementary school. In 2015, Cobb Elementary was slated for closure due to declining enrollment. (PLACC-BC.)

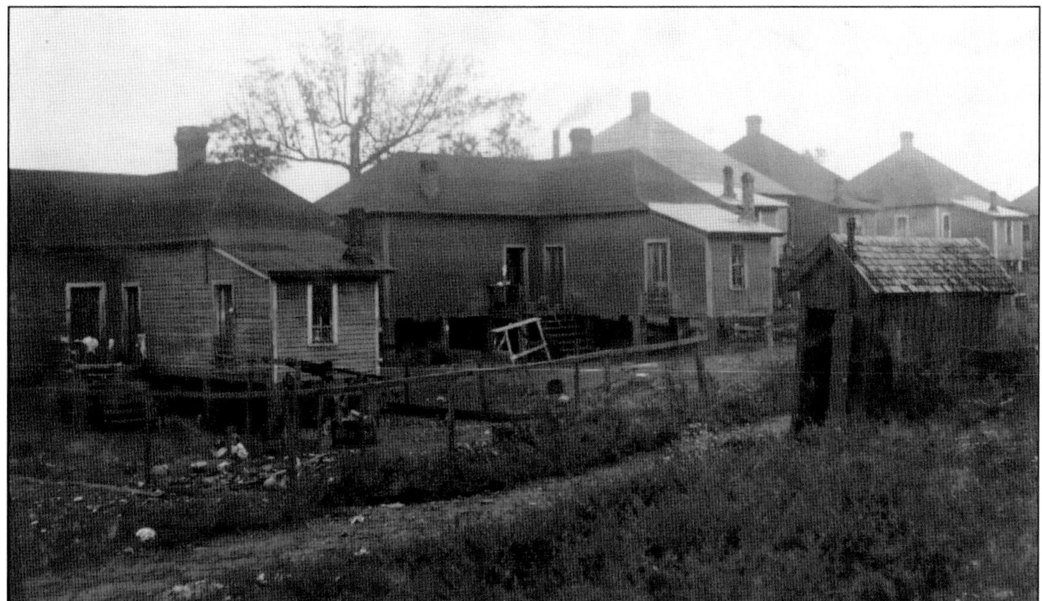

The Anniston Manufacturing Company Mill Village, seen here around 1910, was located directly behind the mill, on Pine and Mulberry Avenues. In 1879, the company constructed 30 brick tenement houses for the mill operatives. At the same time, a large amount of timber was ordered for the construction of mill houses for the additional workers. (LOC.)

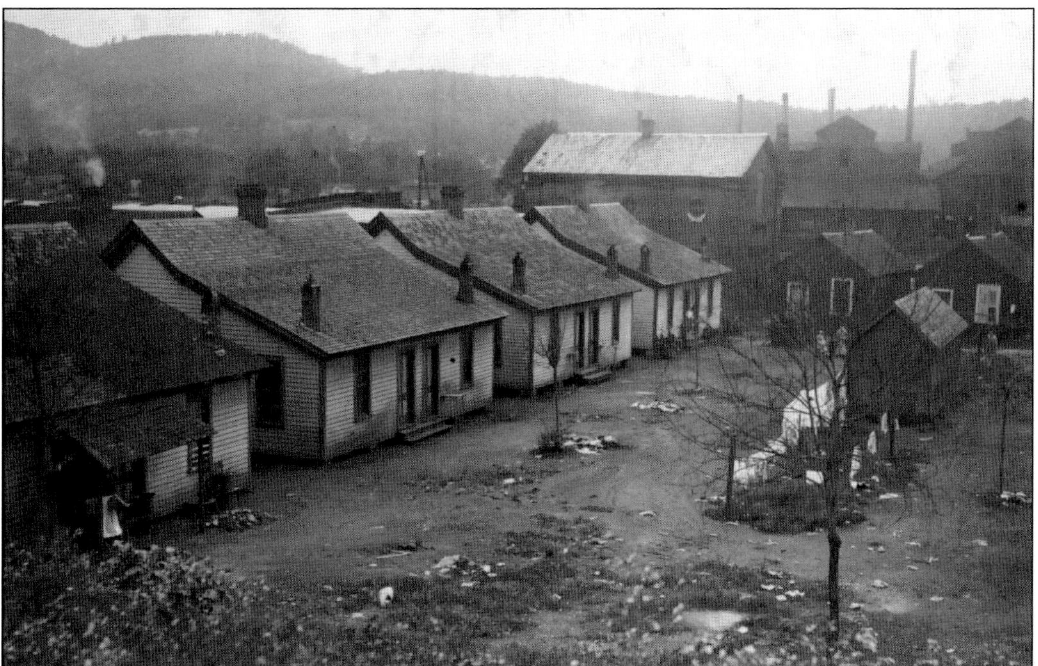

The Adelaide Mills village houses were crowded together, and sanitation was poor. In his testimony to the National Committee on Child Labor concerning the Keating-Owen Child Labor Bill in the US Senate, T. Scott Roberts, treasurer of Adelaide Mills, asked that "Congress not legislate children out of work." Since parents did not earn sufficient wages to support the family, children were forced into the mills. (LOC.)

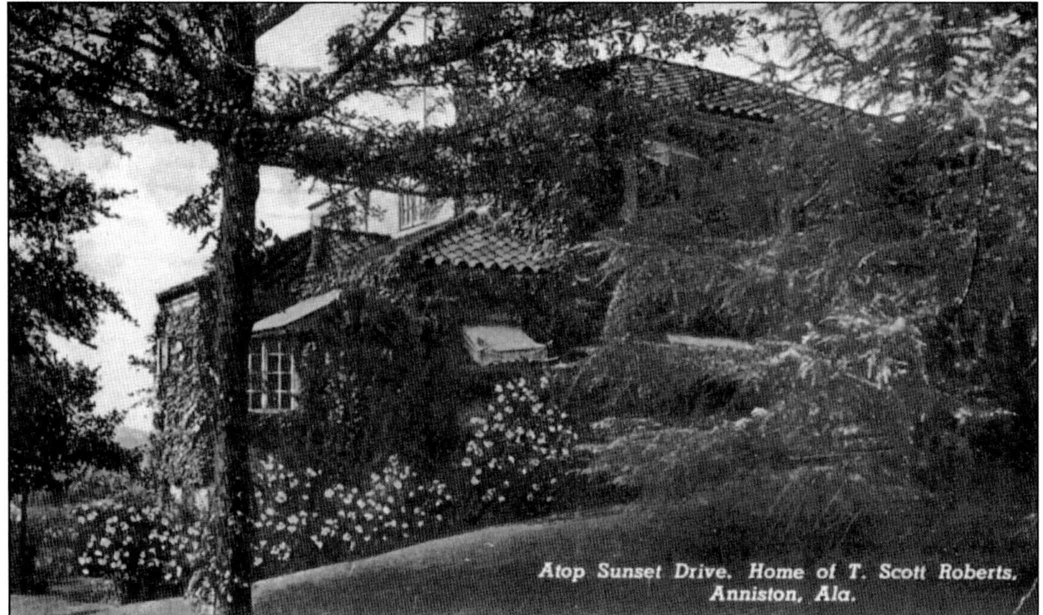

T. Scott Roberts moved from Nashville in 1905 to join Adelaide Mills and ultimately married Thomas Robinson's daughter Mary Adelaide, for whom the mill was named. Roberts joined the firm as a bookkeeper and eventually became president in 1919, when Robinson died. In 1948, Roberts was selected as chairman of the board, serving for eight years before passing away. Roberts built his home on top of Sunset Drive overlooking the city. It is seen here around 1930. (ERY.)

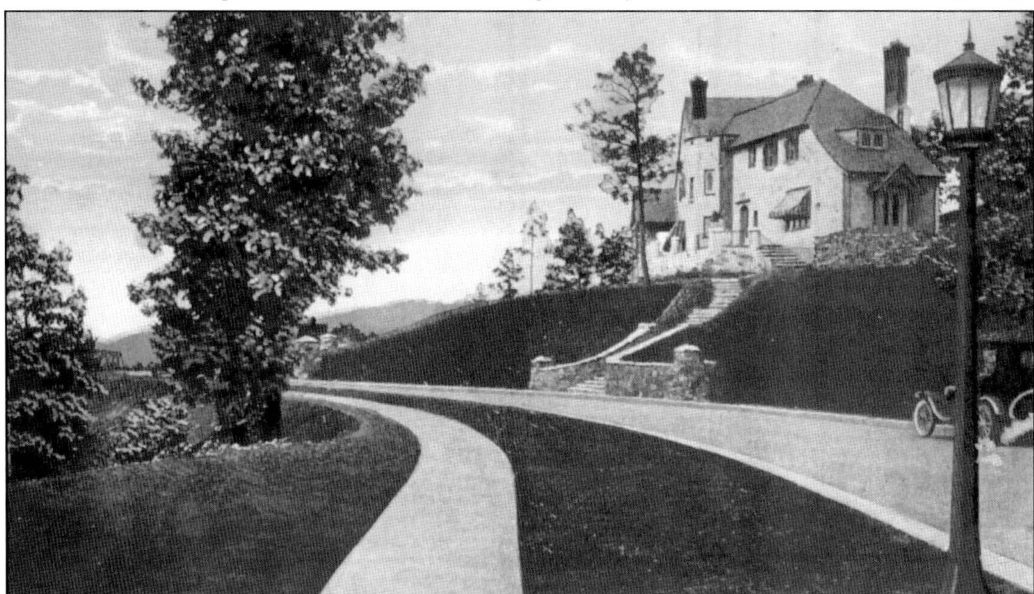

The Sunset Land Company was organized in 1921 by Hillyer Robinson and I.E. DeHart, among others. The company purchased a large tract of land on the mountain near Tenth Street to develop a residential area. By 1924, Sunset Drive was finished, with paved streets, fire protection, and all utilities installed before the homes were constructed. Between 1924 and 1930, homes were built and other streets were developed, including Cynthia Crescent, Michael Lane, Sunset Pass, and Hillyer High Road. Shown here is the home of attorney Neil Sterne. (ERY.)

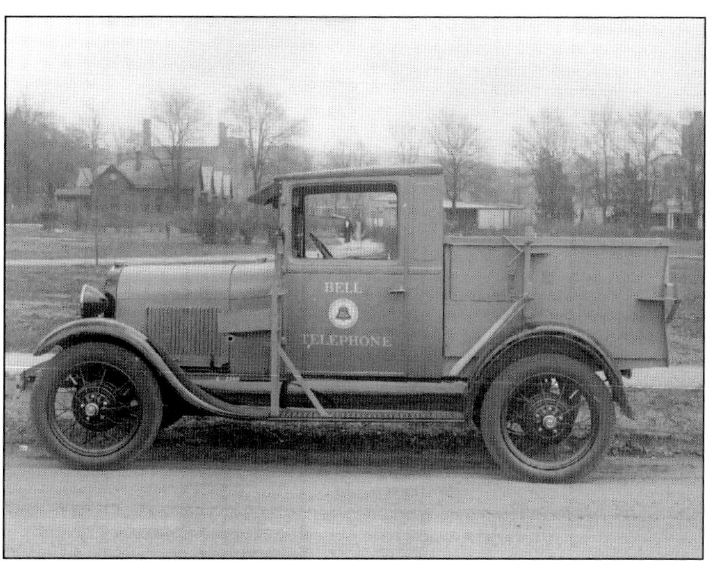

Charles Nonnenmacher, a German immigrant, moved to Anniston from Atlanta in 1883 at the invitation of Samuel Noble. Nonnenmacher built his bakery and the family residence on Eleventh Street and Gurnee Avenue. His wife, Melanie Kautz, taught German and French to the children of a local wealthy family. In 1902, Nonnenmacher built a house at 1311 Gurnee Avenue (right background) that eventually housed a law office.

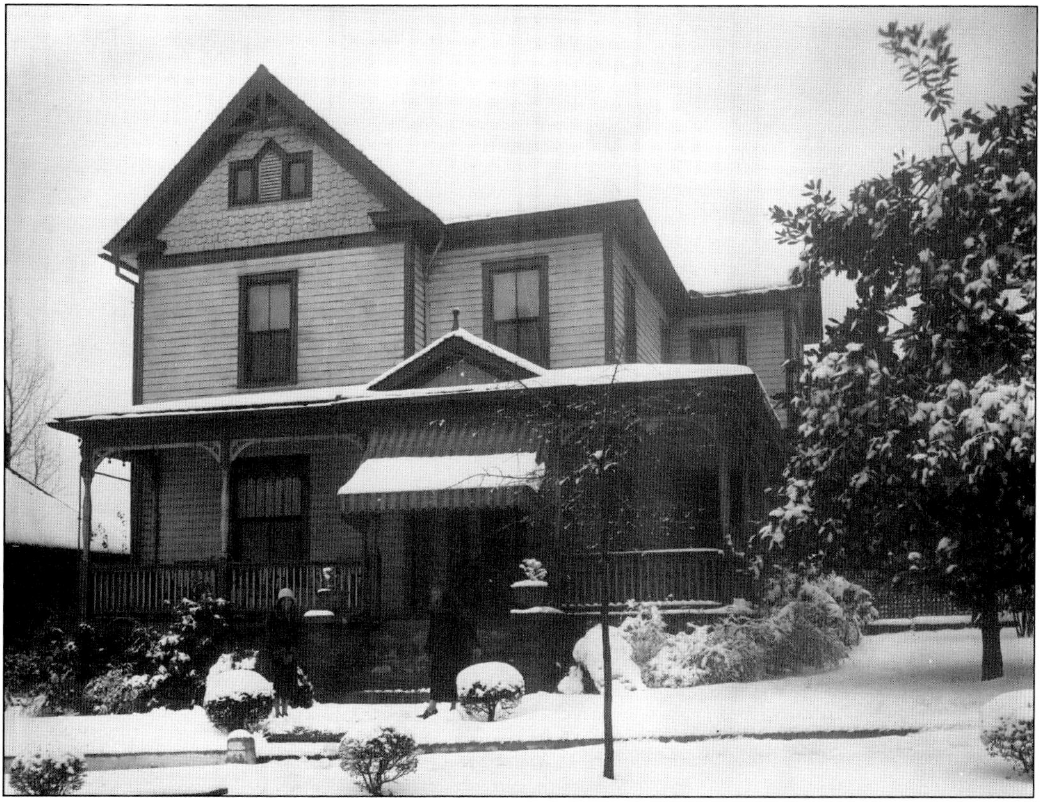

William Sherman Rivers was a prominent African American businessman in the early 20th century. He opened W.S. Rivers & Company, a grocery business at Third Street and Spruce Avenue, with his brother J.B. Rivers. From 1890 until 1950, the store was located across the street from William's home. William passed away in 1950, and his brother followed in 1963. His home is seen here around 1930. Posing in front are Mrs. Rivers and the couple's daughter Sherman.

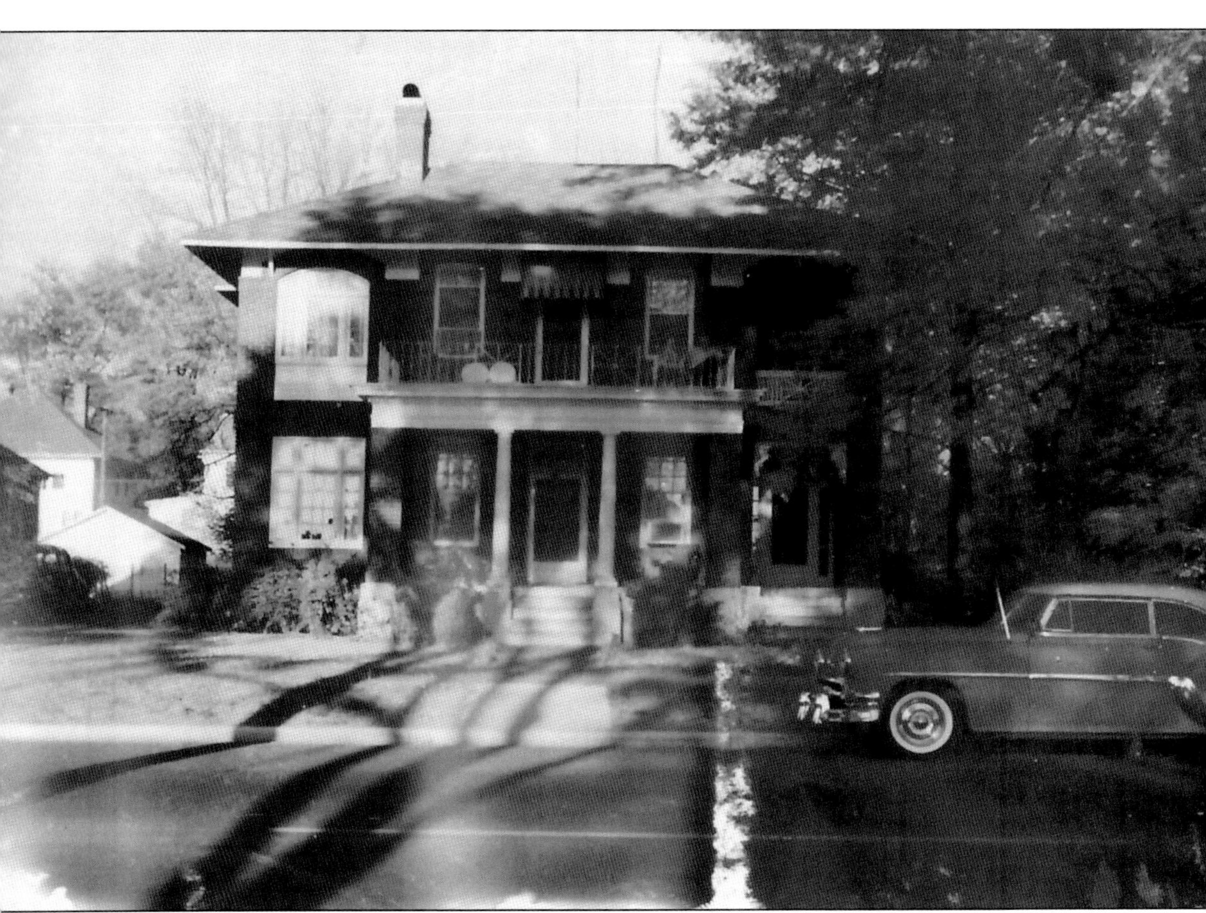

The Berman Apartments were located in the 1300 block of Quintard Avenue, next to Temple Beth-El. Etta Berman, widow of Jacob, lived in the lower floor of the home. The second floor was divided into two large apartments for tenants. When Jacob died in 1948, their son Farley returned home to run the family business. Col. Farley Berman had served in the US Army during World War II as a counterintelligence agent. He married his wife, Germaine, a French intelligence operator, during the war. The Bermans' collections were given to the city in 1992 as the foundation for the Berman Museum of World History. (ERY.)

In the 1890s, golf became a sport for the wealthy, and golf clubs emerged in America. The Anniston Country Club started around 1908 as the Highlands Golf Club. The clubhouse was located at Sixth Street and Highland Avenue in a two-room building, one of which was a Pullman kitchen. A formal opening, complete with costume ball, was held in June 1910. Eventually, the club expanded to include tennis and swimming facilities. It is seen here around 1933.

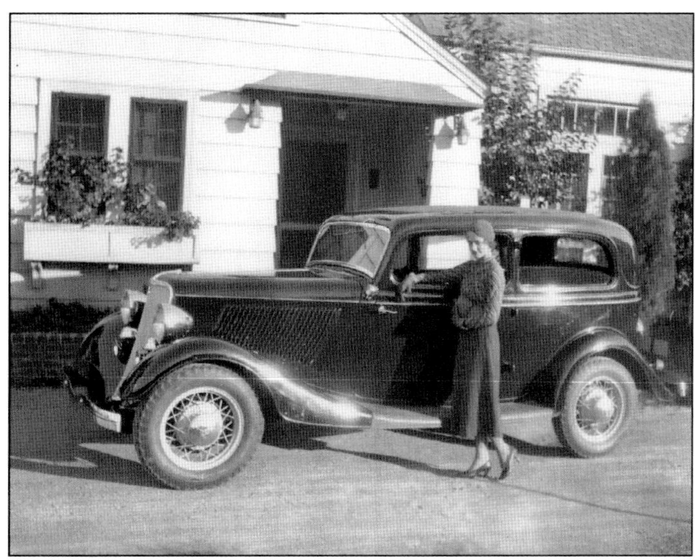

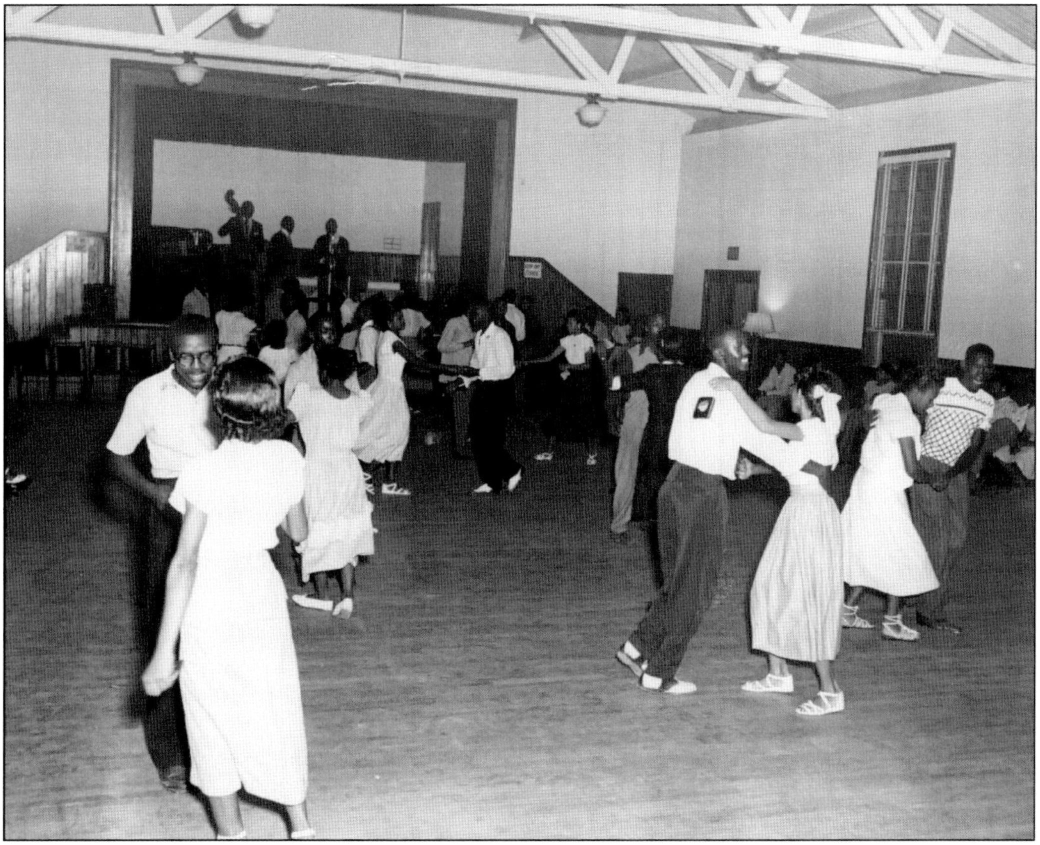

The Carver Community Center was a meeting place for the African American community. The auditorium, seen here around 1949, was used for a variety of functions, including concerts, plays, fashion shows, and dances. In the 1940s, soprano Margaret Cooper appeared with Calvin Bostic and Nathaniel Boggs in a joint recital. Dances with live music were a popular pastime from the 1940s well into the 1960s. (PLACC-BC.)

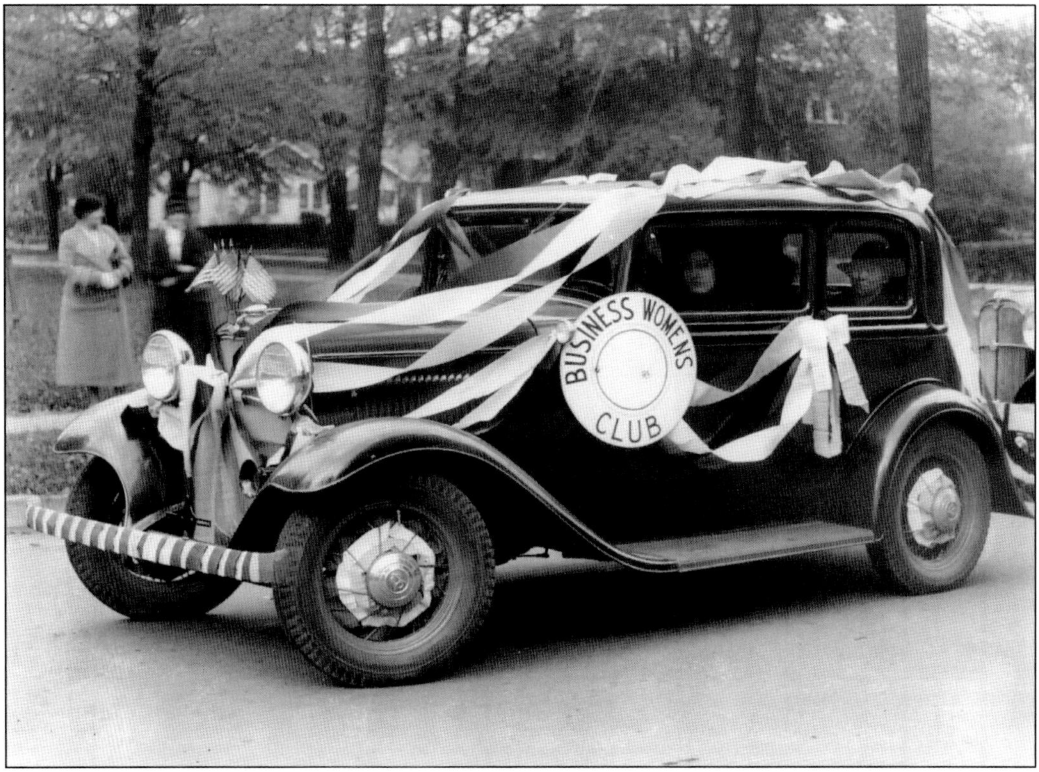

The Business and Professional Women's Club was chartered in March 1919 within the Young Women's Christian Association to provide a centralized organization for women. The club's goal was to foster cooperation with businesswomen and provide educational opportunities for young women. The group participated in all facets of community life, including the annual Armistice Parade and mentor programs for underprivileged young women in the community who wished to attend college. Seen here is the group's float for the 1932 Armistice Parade.

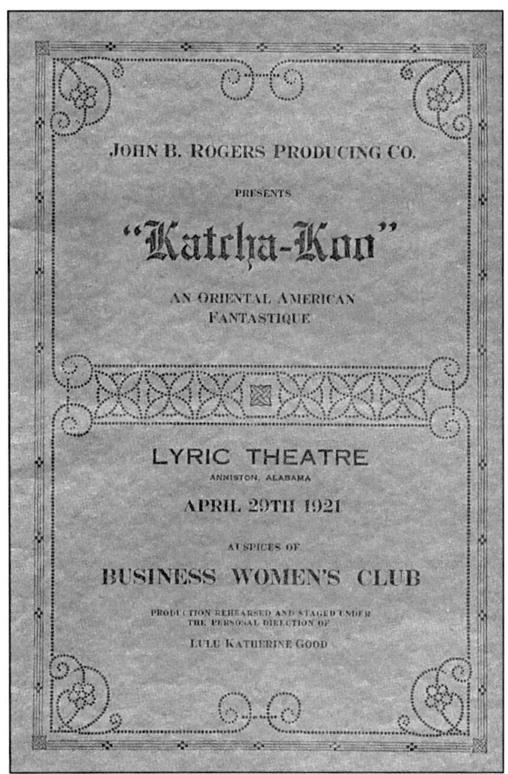

JOHN B. ROGERS PRODUCING CO.

PRESENTS

"Katcha-Koo"

AN ORIENTAL AMERICAN FANTASTIQUE

LYRIC THEATRE

ANNISTON, ALABAMA

APRIL 29TH 1921

AUSPICES OF

BUSINESS WOMEN'S CLUB

PRODUCTION REHEARSED AND STAGED UNDER THE PERSONAL DIRECTION OF

LULU KATHERINE GOOD

The Business and Professional Women's Club met every Tuesday night. The meetings consisted of presentations on topics such as national security, health and safety, international relations, and small businesses. In addition to the weekly meetings, the club sponsored cultural events such as a performance around 1921 of John B. Rogers's play *Katcha-Koo*. Shown here is the playbill for the comedy, which included Eastern dances and boasted a cast of 325. It was held at the Lyric Theatre. (ERY.)

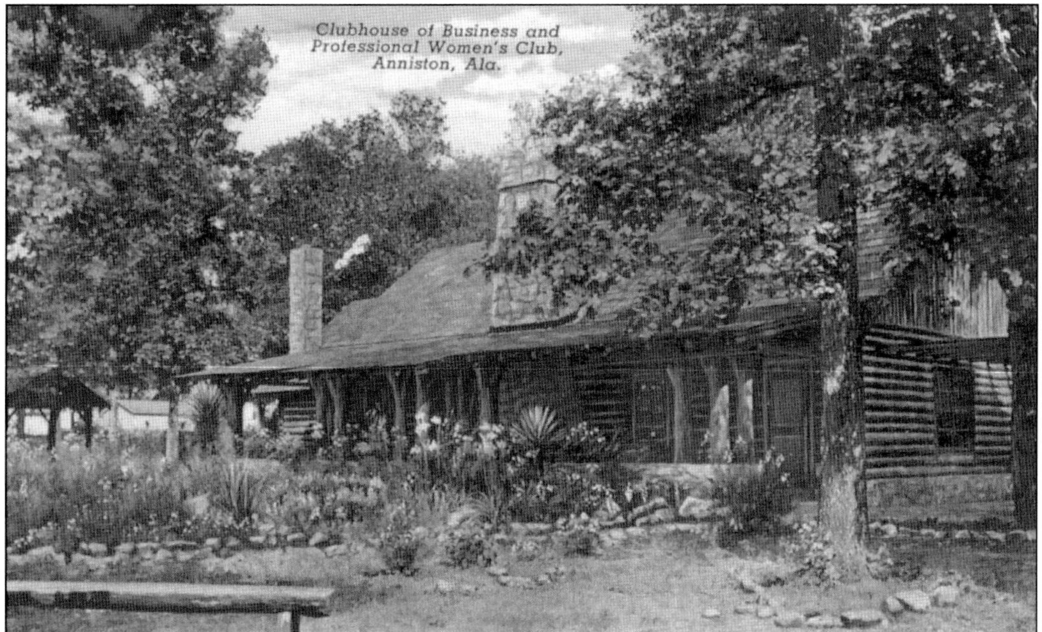

The Anniston group was the only women's club to own its clubhouse. The building, shown here around 1940, was completed in 1936 on Rocky Hollow. It was designed as a rustic log cabin with sunken gardens, walking paths, and a wishing well. The club no longer met after 1976, and the building became part of the Anniston Parks System. (ERY.)

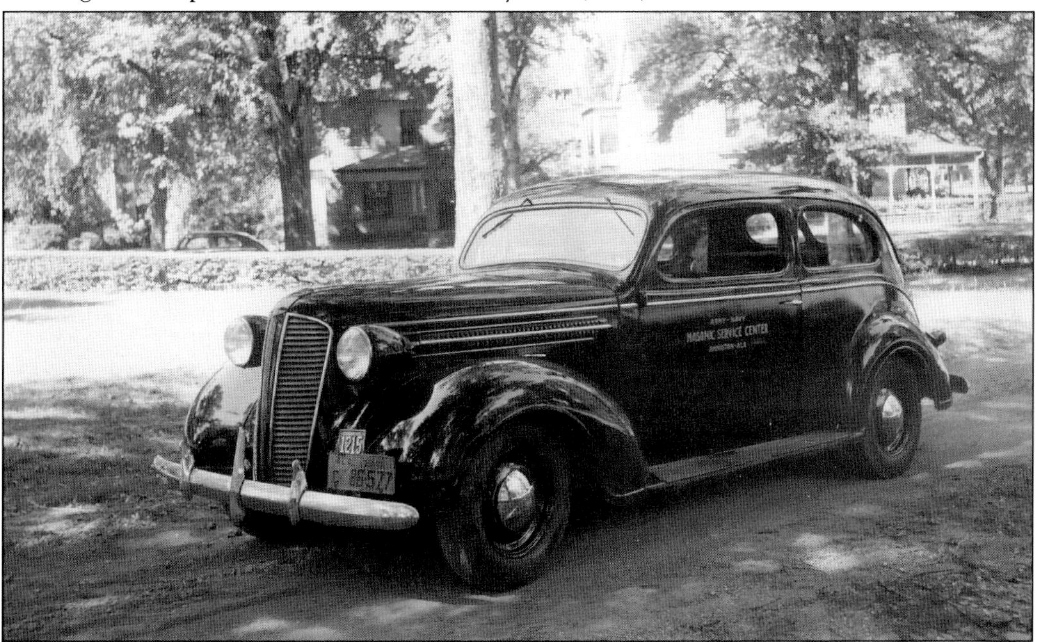

The Masonic Service Association (MSA) of North America was formed by the Freemasons in 1919 to serve Masons who were in the military, and for disaster relief. During World War II, the MSA operated Masonic Service Centers near major military facilities, supported by voluntary funds from Masonic bodies. As the war ended, the assistance was continued for veterans. Shown here on the east side of Anniston around 1943 is an Army Navy Services car.

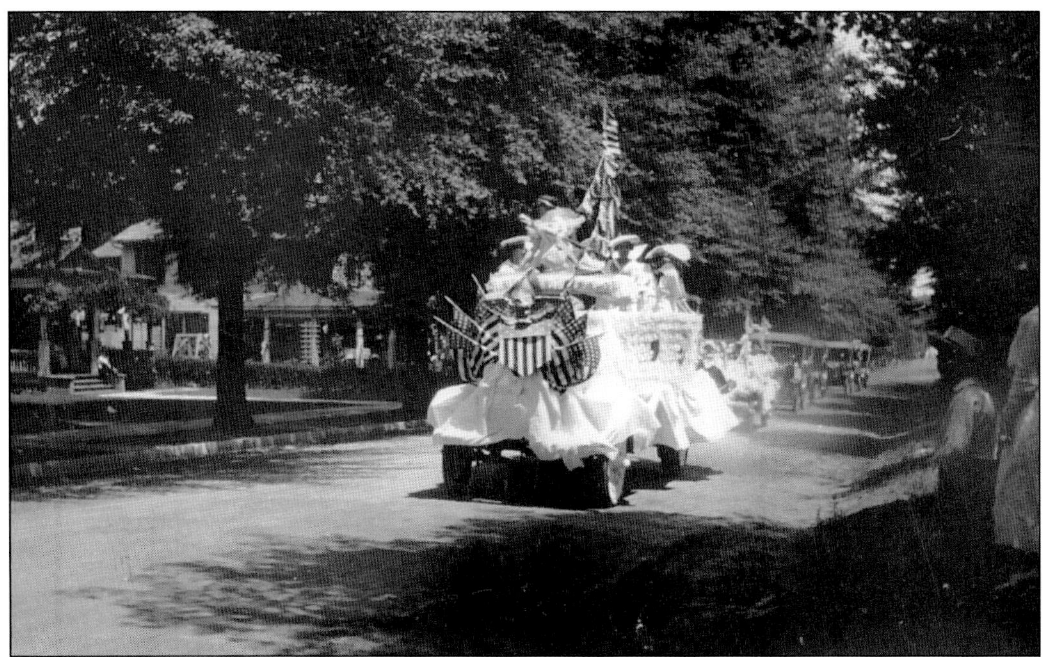

The 4th Alabama National Guard was assigned to the famed 42nd "Rainbow" Division as the 167th Infantry Regiment that fought in Europe during World War I. The regiment arrived in November 1917, fought in several major battles in France, and remained as part of the occupation force in Germany after the war. The regiment was honored with a triumphant parade when the troop train, en route to Camp Shelby, Mississippi, arrived in Anniston in May 1919.

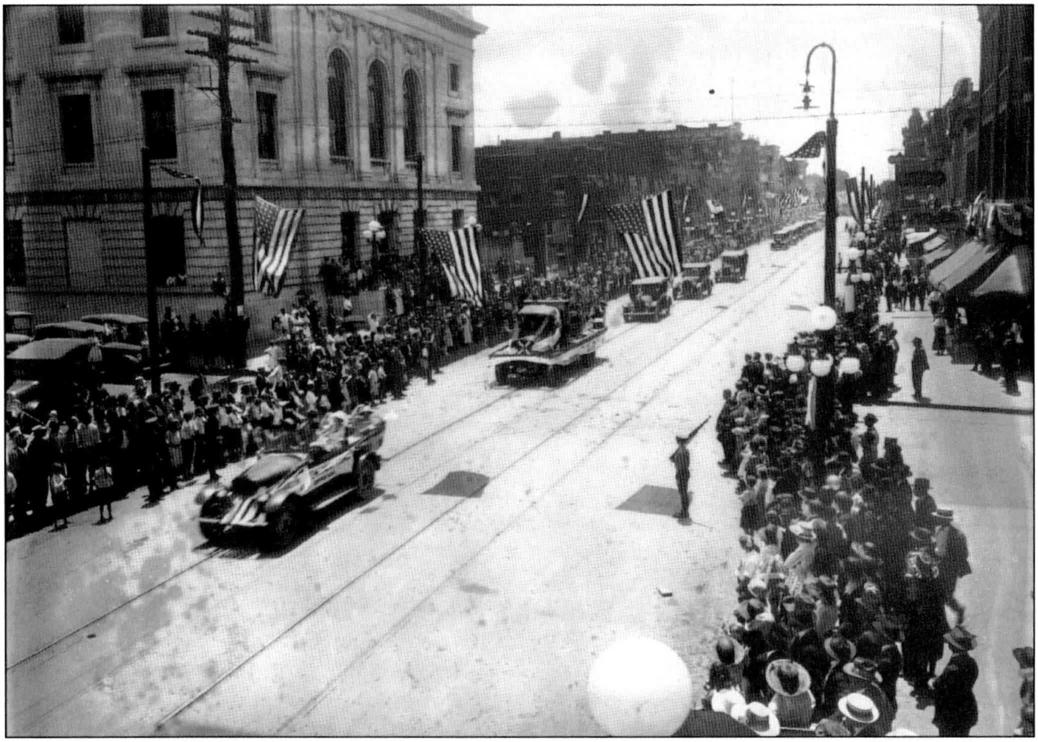

In the 1930s, Anniston's Labor Day parade became an institution, with hundreds of residents lining the streets to watch. The labor unions were included, with an estimated 3,000 to 4,000 members participating along with their floats in 1937. Seen here is the Bricklayers and Masons Union float. After a hiatus during World War II, the Anniston Labor Day parades continued into the 1950s.

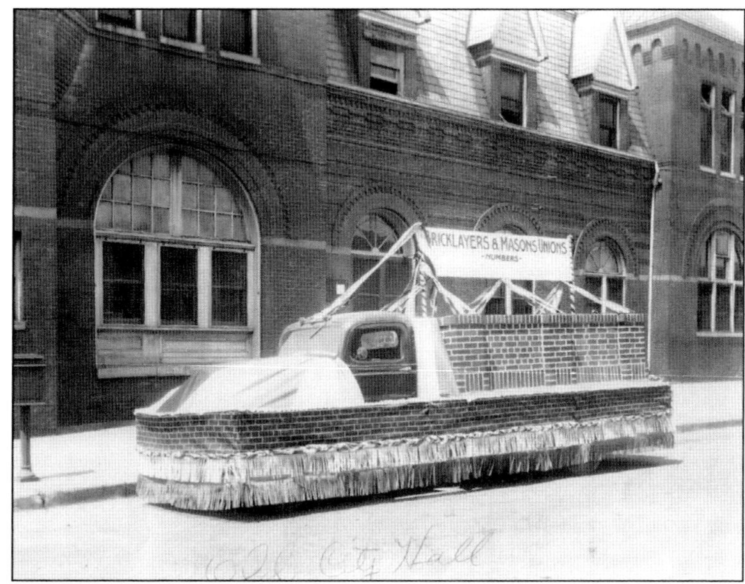

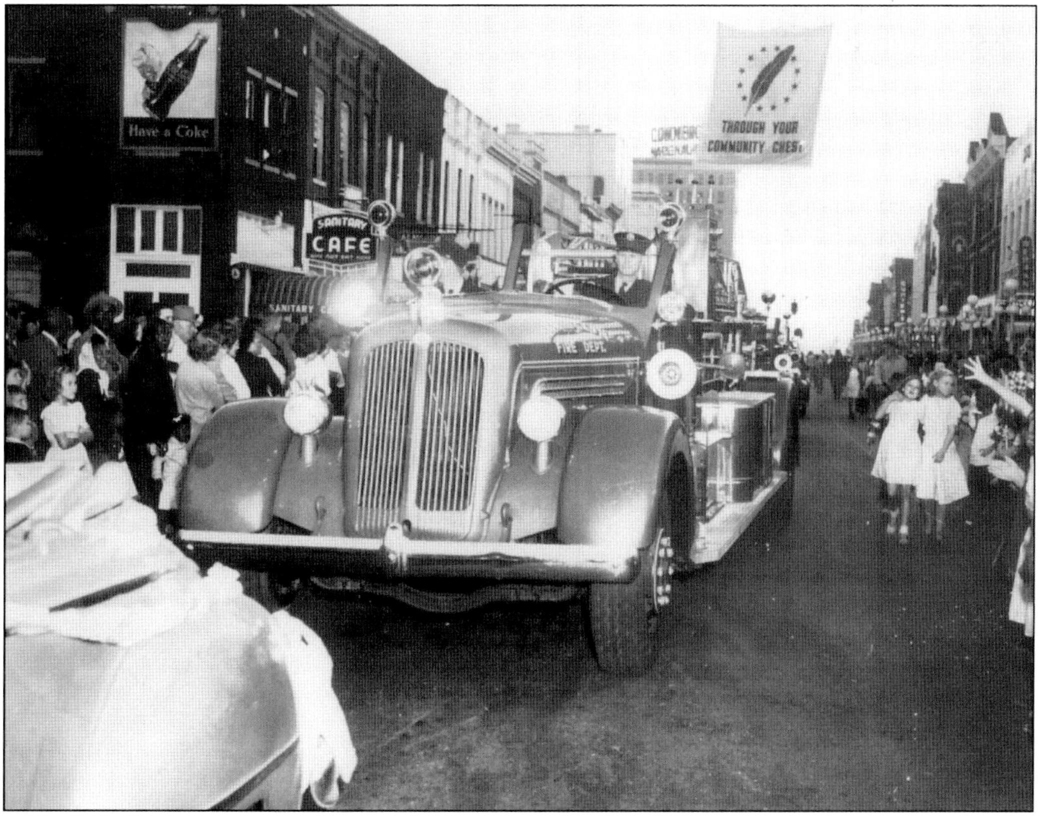

The 1949 Anniston Armistice Day Parade was one of the largest the city had ever seen. Parade committee chairman Robert E. Jones organized a 45-unit parade that included eight of the county's bands. US Army troops from the 30th Infantry and the Alabama National Guard participated. The Anniston Chamber of Commerce sponsored a dance for the visiting 30th Infantry (which had trained at Fort McClellan) at the Municipal Auditorium after the parade. (PLACC-BC.)

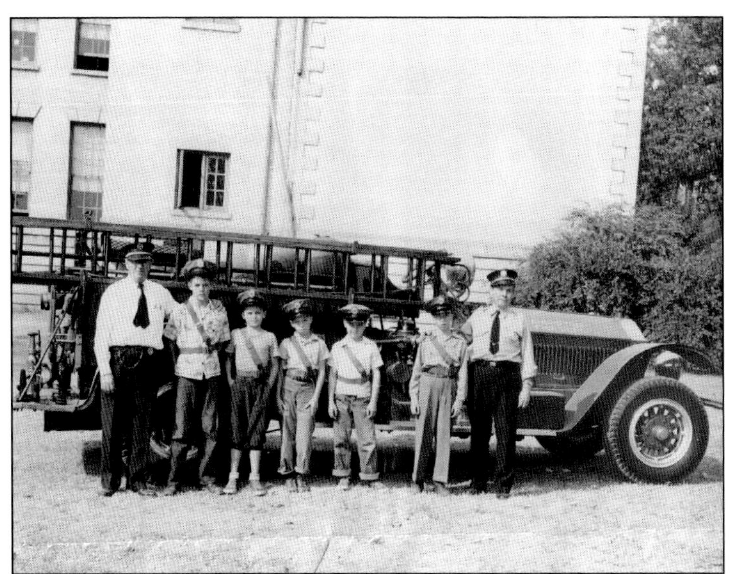

In 1946, Mayor E.D. Banks announced plans for a Junior Fire Patrol. Local schools participated in a citywide program in which young men at each school were encouraged to join. The patrol officially started in 1947, with each school selecting six junior firemen and one junior fire inspector. This program was under the direction of Chief E.E. White. Members of the Junior Fire Patrol are seen here at Wilmer School around 1948. (PLACC-BC.)

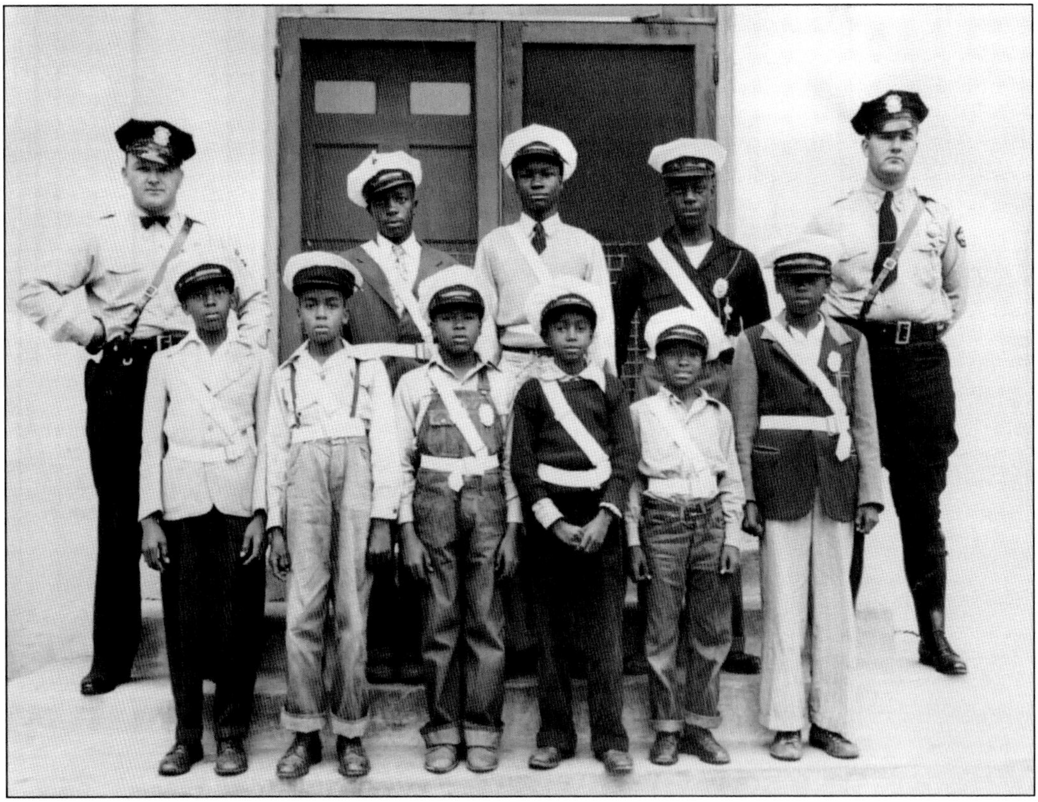

In 1946, the Junior Safety Patrol was rejuvenated by its founder, Officer Donald Dobbs. The organization was open to young men ages 6 to 13, with each school principal selecting a captain and patrolmen based on grades, leadership, and initiative. Members of the patrol were outfitted with a white cap, a belt, a whistle, and a patrol badge. The patrols were responsible for stopping cars only when children were waiting to cross the street. Motorists were reminded to obey the "stop" and "go" signs. These young patrol members pose with police officers around 1947. (PLACC-BC.)

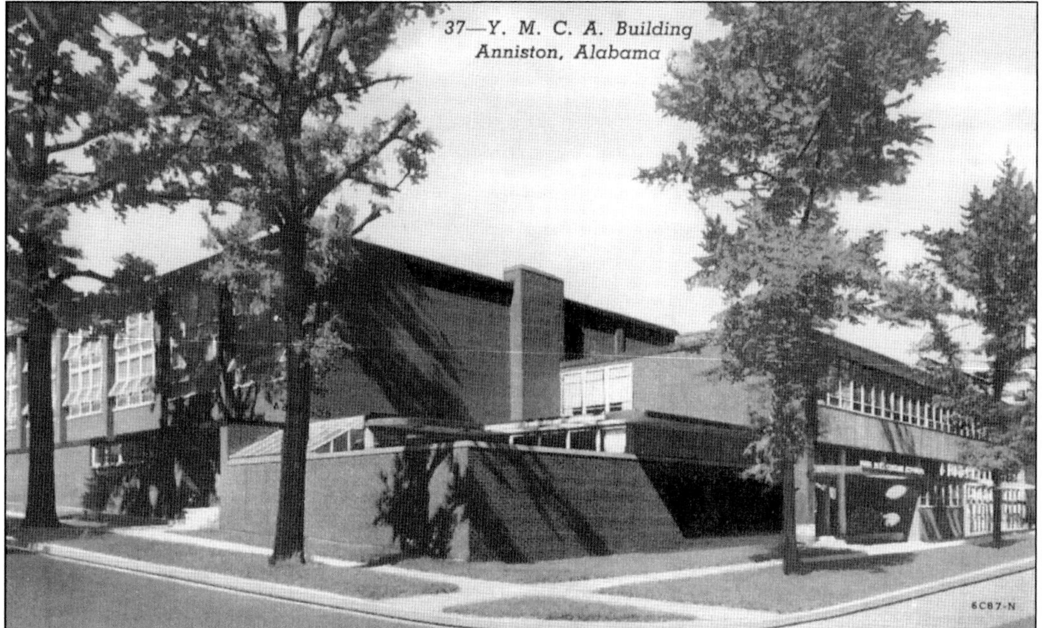

In the late 1940s, Dr. C. Hal Cleveland orchestrated a community-wide campaign to raise funds for a new YMCA facility (seen here around 1955). The building, located at Fourteenth Street and Gurnee Avenue, was opened to the public in August 1952 with a large gymnasium, meeting rooms, locker rooms, and a game lounge. The indoor swimming pool was added in 1956. In 1973–1974, the original building was remodeled to add two racquetball courts and an indoor track. Emphasis on youth programs such as Hi-Y, fitness, and aquatics was central to the mission. (ERY.)

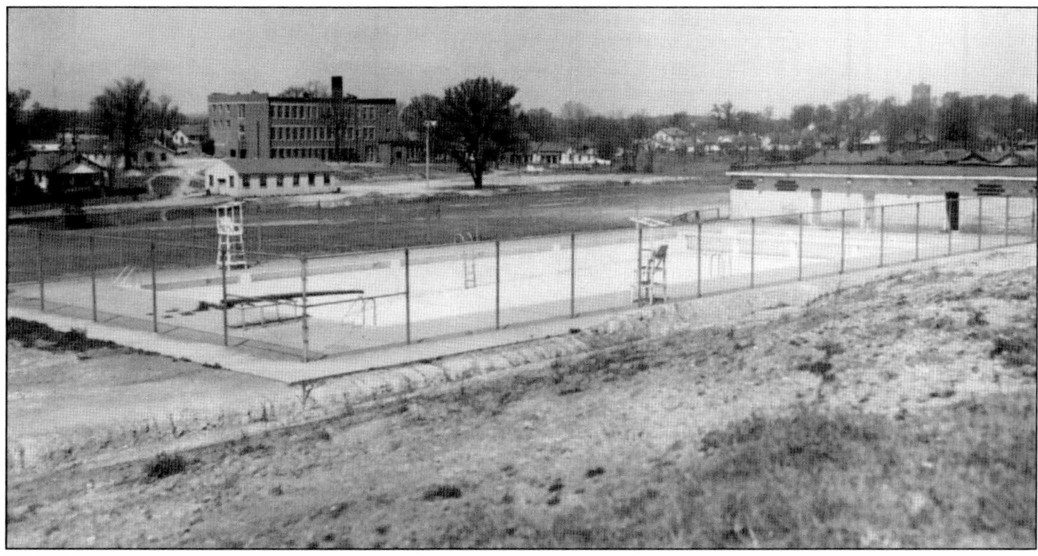

In the summer of 1947, the city operated five municipal pools: Zinn Park, Twenty-second Street, Ninth Street, Oxanna (which had lighting), and Carver. The Carver pool and bathhouses, located near the community center and Cobb High School, were for the African American community's use during segregation. The complex is seen here around 1947. The modern Carver Swim Center was located in the same area and included basketball courts, a playground, and a walking track. (PLACC-BC.)

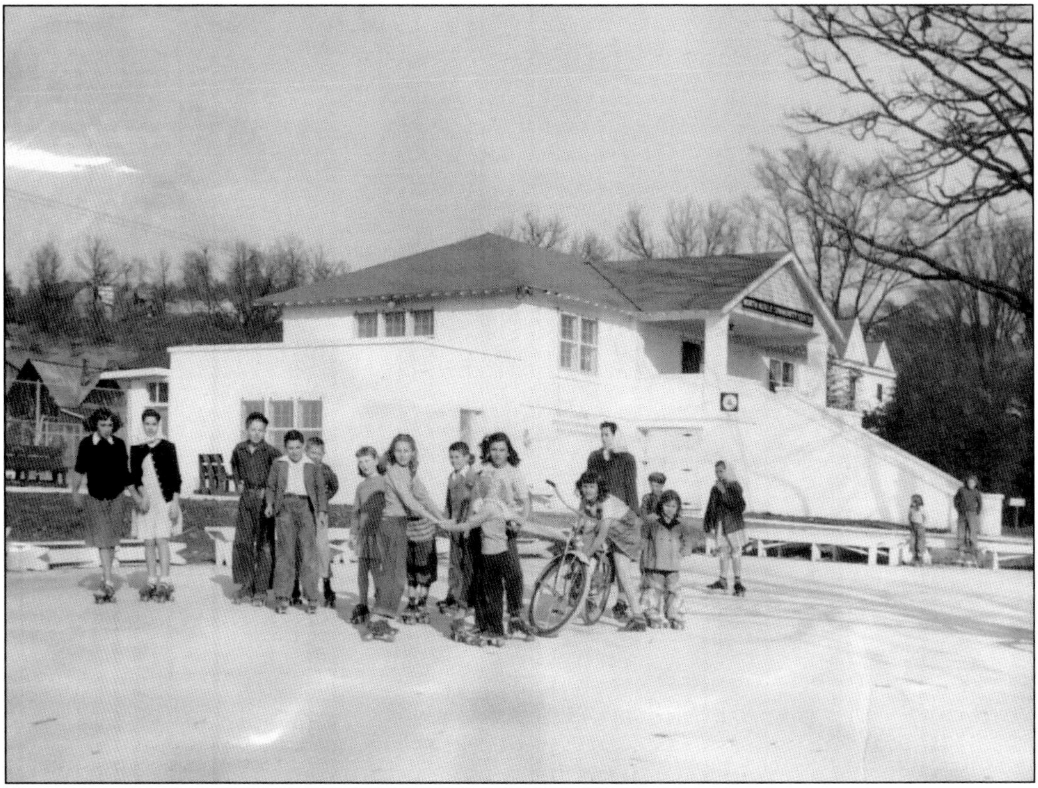

North Noble Community Center, seen here around 1950, was located at Twenty-second and Noble Streets. It was established in 1946, with a swimming pool and bathhouses. By 1947, the complex included a library on the second floor as well as meeting rooms for the Boy and Girl Scouts. Gas heat and electricity allowed the center to be used not only as a gathering place for recreation and learning, but also as a meeting space for the community. (PLACC.)

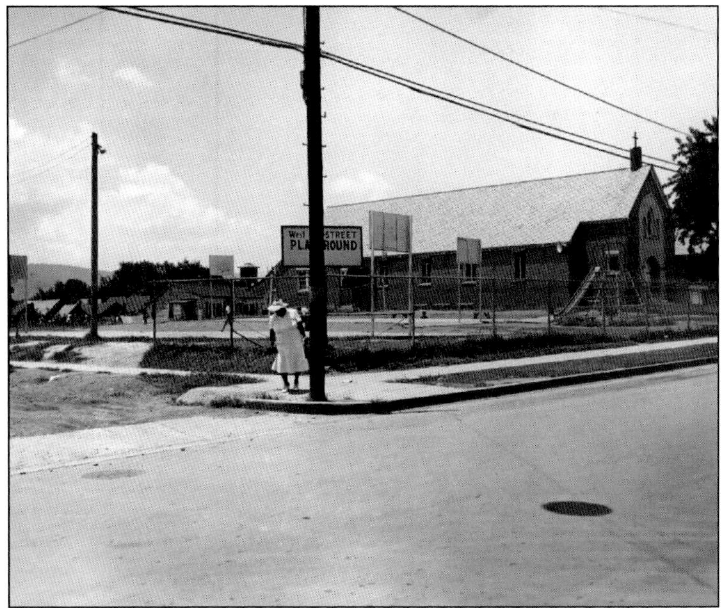

All Saints Mission was established in 1938 on West Fifteenth Street. The mission is seen here around 1946. In 1945, the Reverend Father John F. Casey solicited donations to build a playground (pictured in foreground) for the African American children in Anniston. Father Casey organized the Young Men's Development Club and the Twix Teens Girl's Club. All Saints Catholic School was built on the playground site in 1954. (PLACC-BC.)

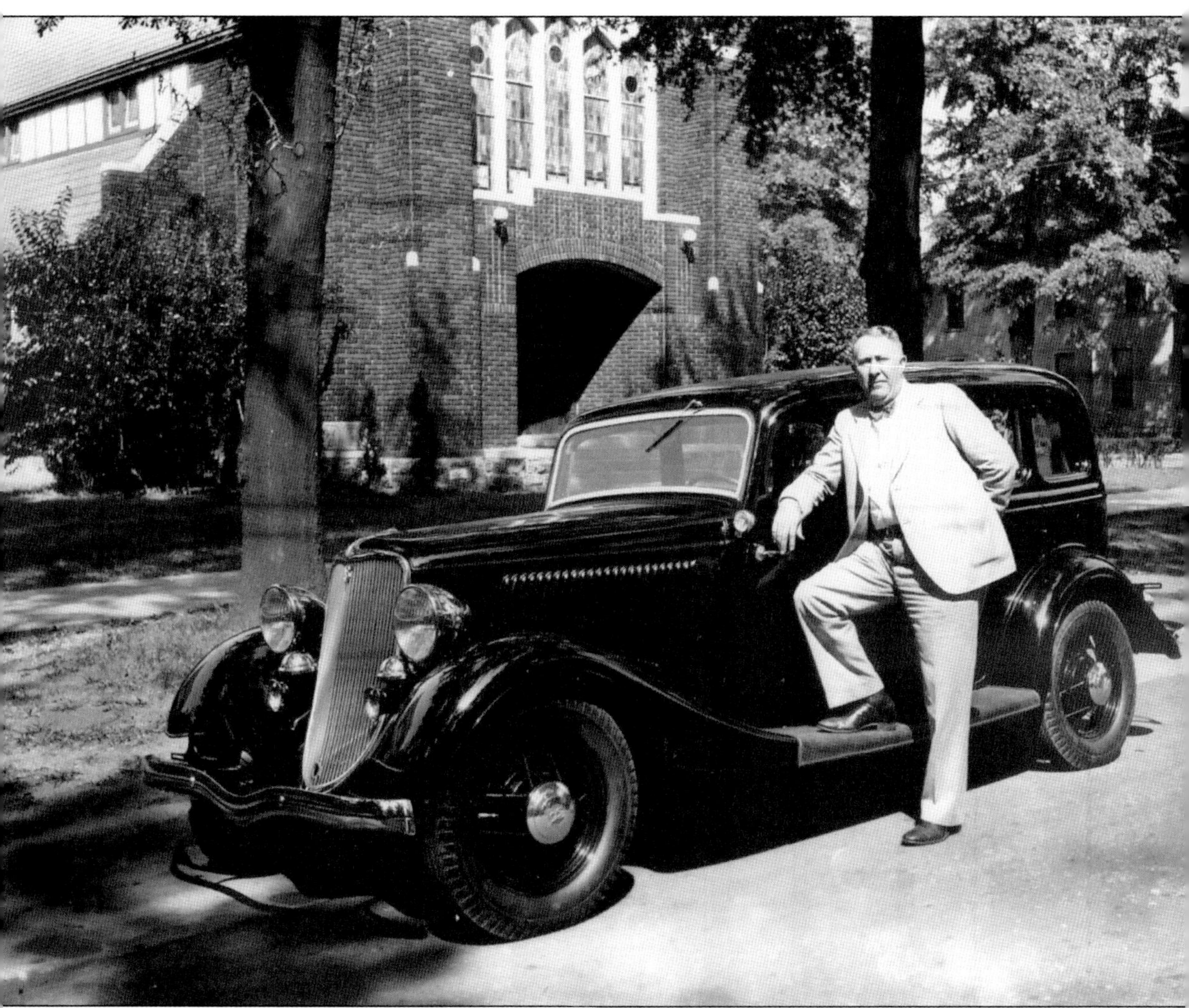

Sacred Heart Catholic Church was organized in 1884. The parish met on the second floor of Robinson Warehouse until a church was built at Third and Spruce Streets. In 1898, the parish was released from the Jesuit Fathers of Selma Mission and was allowed to build a sanctuary at Eleventh Street and Quintard Avenue. The church burned down in 1922, but was rebuilt in the same location. It is seen here around 1934. Sacred Heart Catholic School was established in 1953 on McCall Avenue. In 2000, the two local Catholic schools merged and relocated to the grounds of the former Fort McClellan School to become a K-12 school. In 1997, Sacred Heart Catholic Church sold the Quintard property to Trinity Lutheran Church and built a new parish in Golden Springs, dedicated in November 1999.

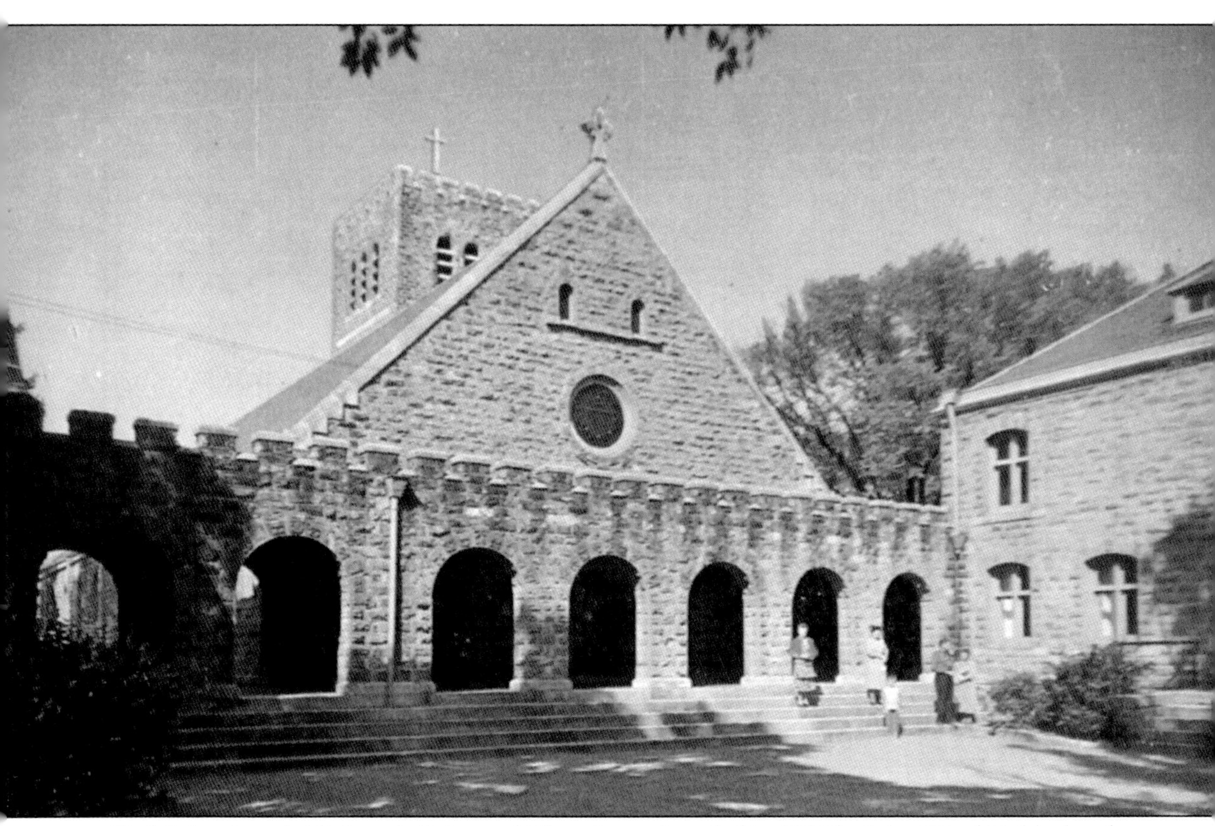

St. Michael's and All Angels Episcopal Church was founded in 1887 by John Ward Noble, brother of Samuel. The Romanesque church was consecrated on St. Michael's Day, 1890. The church contained 12 tower bells, each named for a member of the Noble family, a carrara marble altar, and the alabaster reredos with archangels Gabriel, Michael, and Raphael. A pipe organ was installed by Henry Pilcher & Sons. St. Michael's was built for the local industry workers, so it was located on 1000 West Eighteenth Street, near the workers' homes. In 1922, the Grace Church and St. Michael's ladies group opened a clinic for the welfare needs of the community that survived as the Community Services Center, a social services program. (ERY.)

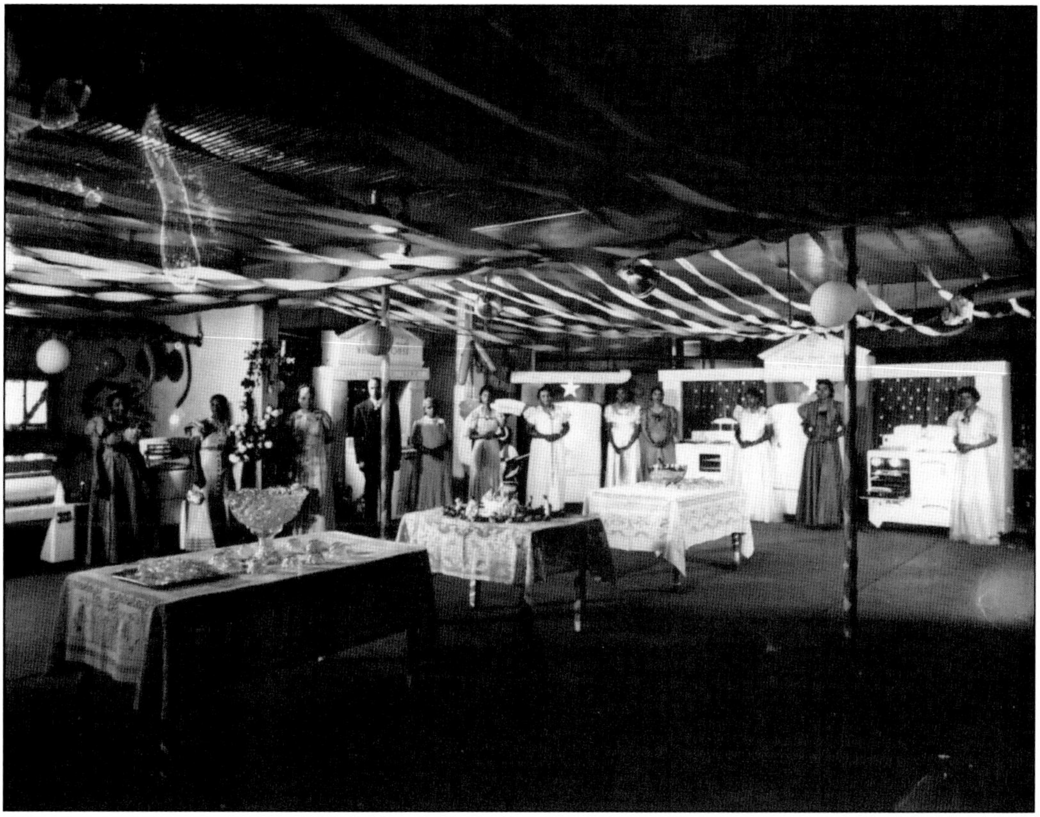

The Seventeenth Street Baptist Church traces its origins to 1880 as the Concord Baptist Church. By 1887, the church was renamed Galilee Baptist Church. Around 1900, Seventeenth Street Baptist Church moved to Cooper Avenue and Seventeenth Street. It is seen here around 1935. Dr. J.H. Eason played a huge role in the development of the church in the early years. The church, led by Rev. Nimrod Q. Reynolds for nearly 50 years, also played a role in the civil rights movement in the 1960s.

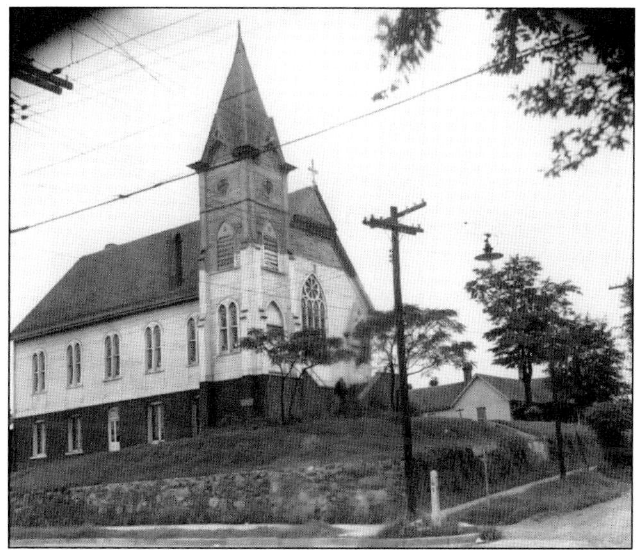

First Congregational Church, the oldest black church in Anniston, was organized in May 1875. Samuel Noble donated the land and the materials for a church, located on Fourteenth and Noble Streets. In 1885, due to increased land values, Noble exchanged the property for a lot on West Fifteenth Street and Mulberry Avenue and again paid for the church construction. The sanctuary was lost in an 1891 fire, but was quickly rebuilt with insurance funds. The site remained a church and was occupied by the First United Pentecostal Church.

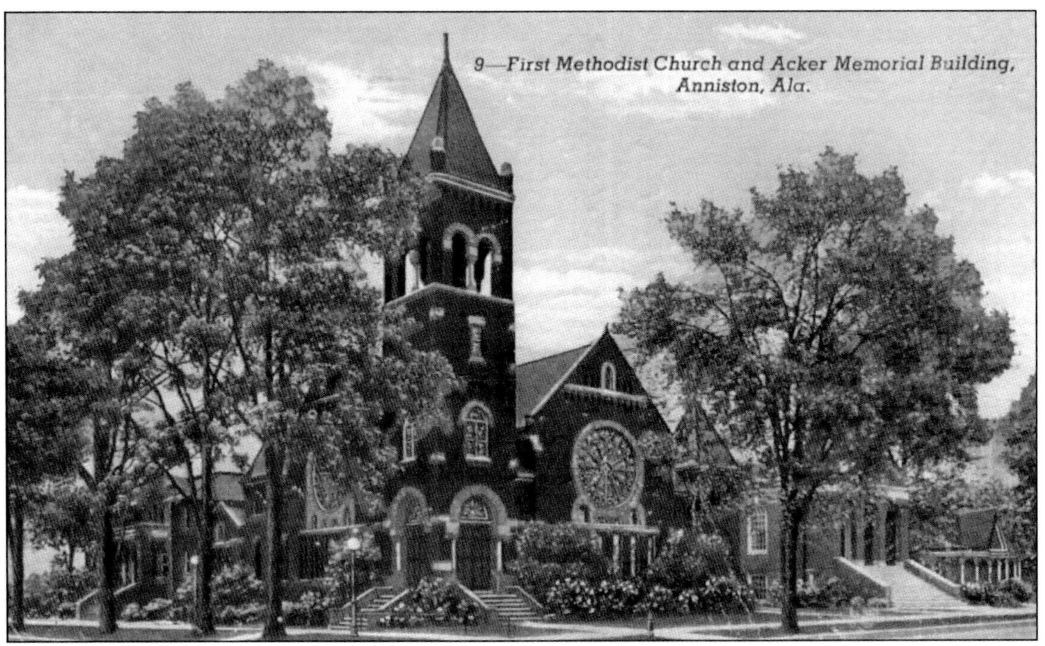
9—First Methodist Church and Acker Memorial Building, Anniston, Ala.

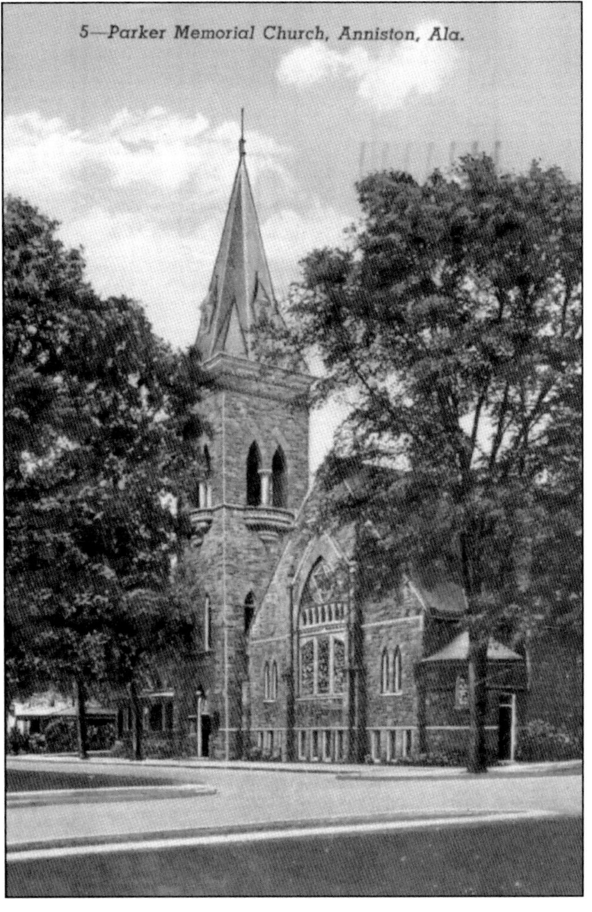
5—Parker Memorial Church, Anniston, Ala.

The Wesleyans who came to build the furnaces joined local residents to form the First Methodist Episcopal Church in 1872. Simon Jewell, a stonemason, preached under a tree until 1881, when the North Alabama Conference appointed Rev. R.A. Thompson minister for the congregation. In 1893, the Methodists built a sanctuary at Fourteenth and Noble Streets (pictured around 1938). In 1940, the Anniston church became known as First United Methodist Church. (ERY.)

The Second Baptist Church, organized in July 1887, changed its name to Twelfth Street Baptist Church after purchasing a lot at Twelfth Street and Quintard Avenue. During construction, prominent Annistonian Duncan T. Parker lost his wife and son to pneumonia, so he donated money to pay for the main auditorium in their memory. Over the years, Parker Memorial Baptist Church has expanded to occupy the entire 1200 block of Quintard and the Dearmanville Campus. (ERY.)

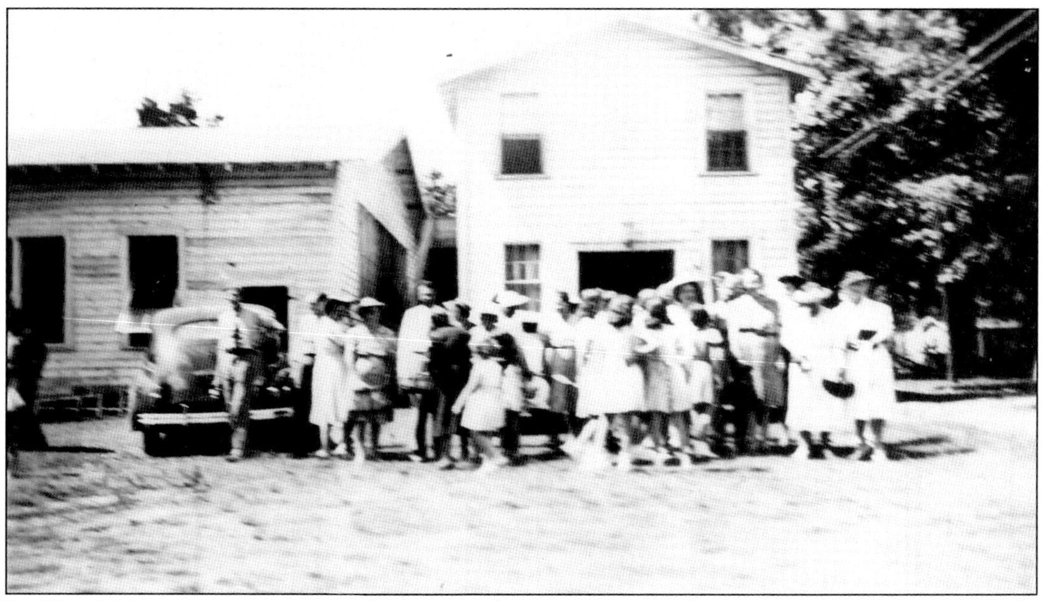

By World War II, Anniston's population was about 25,000, and the city was expanding, especially to the north. Many people did not have transportation to attend worship services far from home, so a church within walking distance was beneficial. Many smaller churches, primarily Baptist and Methodist, were founded in the communities. Seen here around 1935 is Noble Street Baptist Church at 1923 Noble Street. (NSBC.)

The First Baptist Church was organized in 1882, with Rev. E.T. Smith leading the congregation. A permanent sanctuary was built in 1904 at Fourteenth Street and Pine Avenue (pictured around 1920). The congregation worshipped here until a 1948 fire destroyed the building. Some of the members rebuilt on the same site, then moved to Twenty-second Street Baptist Church. The remaining congregation built a sanctuary on Marvin Hill. The Pine Avenue site was ultimately sold to AME Zion Church. (ERY.)

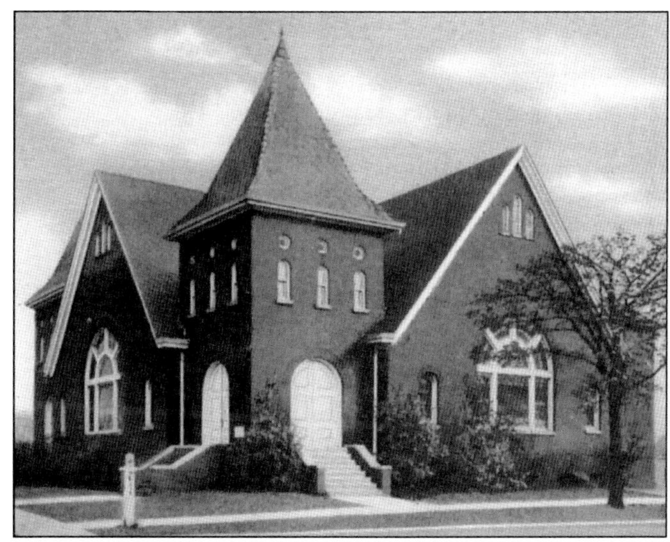

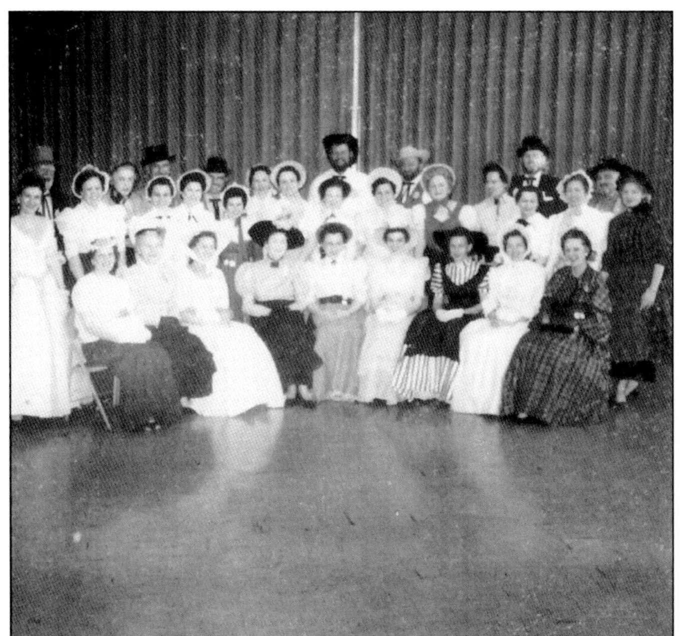

In May 1958, the city of Anniston celebrated her diamond jubilee, commemorating 75 years since the town was opened to the public. The jubilee included a huge parade, with Jubilee Belles and Brothers of Brush chapters dressing the parts of 1880s townspeople. The Alabama Power chapter is shown here. All the industries, churches, and community organizations participated in the celebration, which culminated with the presentation of *The Wondrous Years*, an outdoor play performed nightly during Jubilee Week at Memorial Stadium. (ERY.)

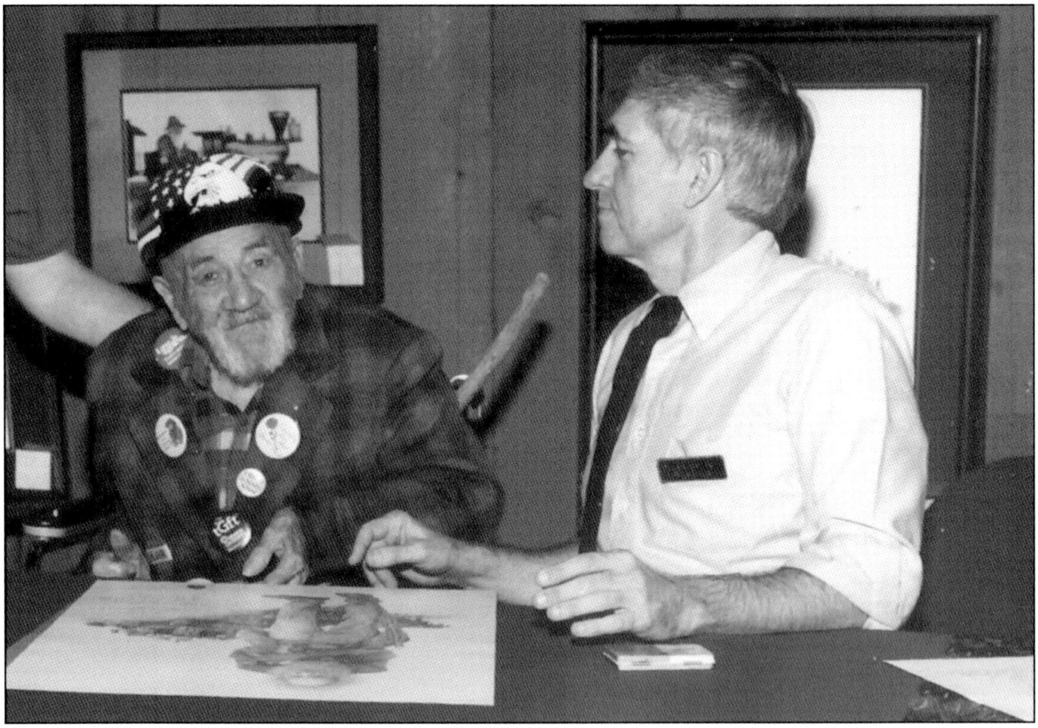

"The Goatman," a colorful Southern folk character, traveled throughout the Southeast with his herd of goats, sometimes as many as 30, pulling his wobbly iron wagon. Born Charles "Ches" McCartney in Iowa around 1901, he made a living selling various items off his cart and postcards of himself with the goats. Anniston artist Larry Martin made several sketches of McCartney, who died in a Georgia nursing home in 1998. McCartney is pictured here at left around 1990 with Martin. (ERY.)

Four

Outside the City Limits

Many communities outside the city limits played an important role in providing a workforce and a consumer base for Anniston, the largest city. Many of these communities still exist in Calhoun County.

Joseph Saks, a German immigrant, settled in Anniston in the 1880s and established The Famous, later called Saks Clothing Company, which he operated for over 40 years. He also owned an 800-acre farm just north of the city. The Saks Community, which was named in his honor, received tracts of land to build a school and community center on the old farm.

Blue Mountain, an area just north of Anniston, was home to the Linen Thread Company, which purchased the Blue Mountain Mill in 1916. The population consisted mostly of employees from the mill. The mill was an integral part of social, civic, educational, and recreational pursuits. In the early 1950s, the mayor was the plant manager, and mill executives and employees made up the town council.

Alexandria, originally named Houston's Store, then Coffeeville, was settled around 1834 by prominent citizens, including Matthew Houston and Dr. Atkinson Pelham, father of Maj. John Pelham. The community had a post office on the L&N Railroad line.

Wellington, named for O.M. Alexander's hometown in Ohio, was a small community founded in 1904 near Tallasseehatchee Creek where the L&N and Seaboard Air Line Railroad lines crossed. The stores, depot, and post office were built to accommodate train passengers. The passenger trains ended service in the mid-1960s, and the freight offices were closed a few years later. By the mid-1980s, only the post office, Heathcock Grocery, and a few homes remained, surrounded by pastureland.

The US military saw the area outside Anniston as a prime site for a training facility. Blue Mountain had housed Camp Shipp during the Spanish-American War and for National Guard Training in the summer of 1912. The US Army decided to acquire land in 1917 and build a military training post, Camp McClellan. By the 1930s, the post had earned fort status and remained a vital part of the community until it was closed in 1999.

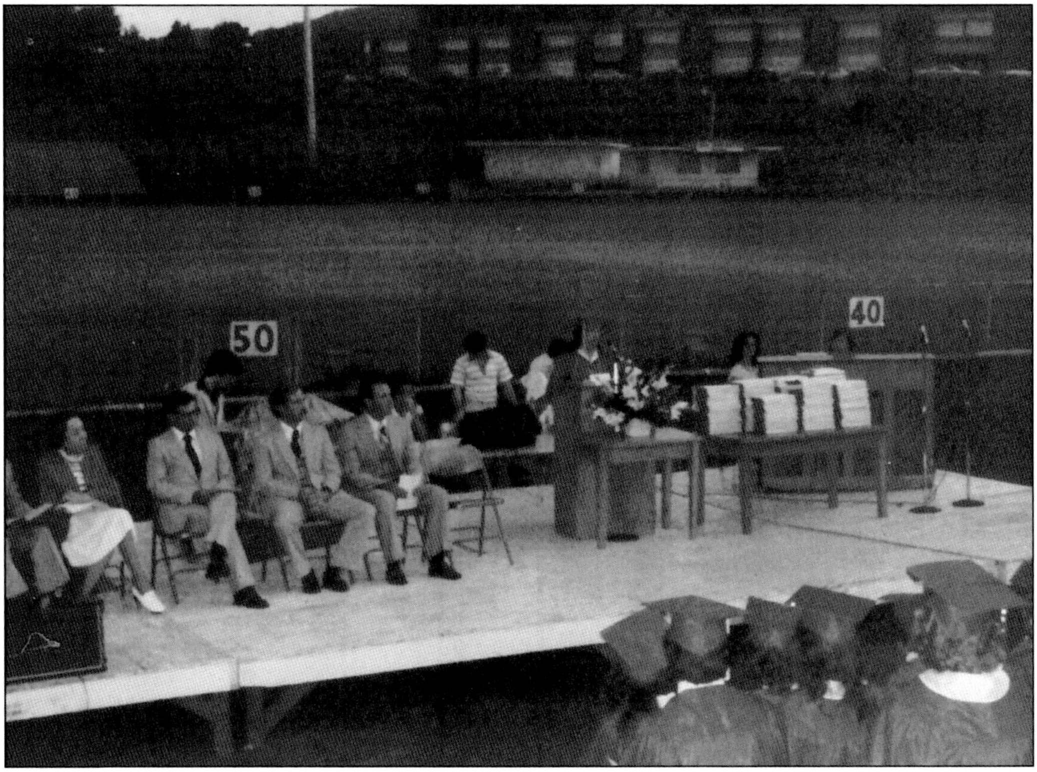

In the 1920s, Joseph Saks donated land, money, and materials for a school for the families that lived on his farm. The school originally accommodated students through ninth grade. By the 1950s, the school had expanded to include three brick buildings to house students through the 12th grade. The school's athletic complex consisted of two gyms and multiple sports fields, including a large football field (seen here in 1980). The educational and sports complex occupied a site between Saks Road and Highway 431 and between Forty-third and Forty-fifth Streets. (CRK.)

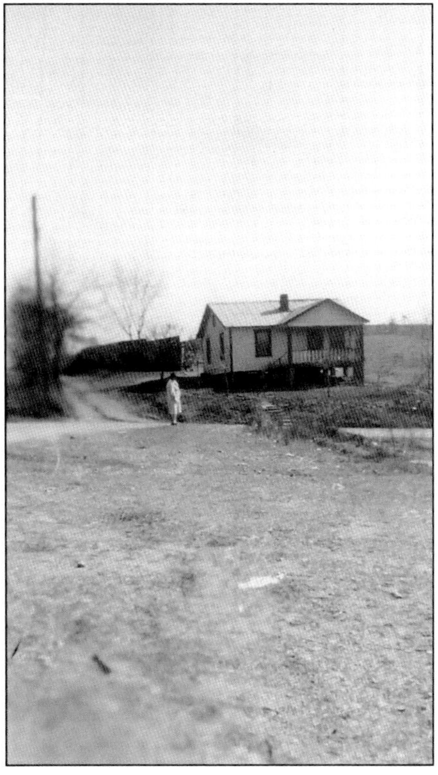

R.H. Cobb was part of Corning Land Company and organized Anniston Lime & Coal Company, which packed up to 500 barrels of lime daily for use in Louisiana's sugar-refining plants. He settled approximately three miles from downtown, in an unincorporated area that bordered Anniston to the east and the south. The area became known as West End–Cobb Town. The community ran from Morrisville Road through Eulaton, and south of the Birmingham Highway. Shown here is Carter Street around 1945. (ERY.)

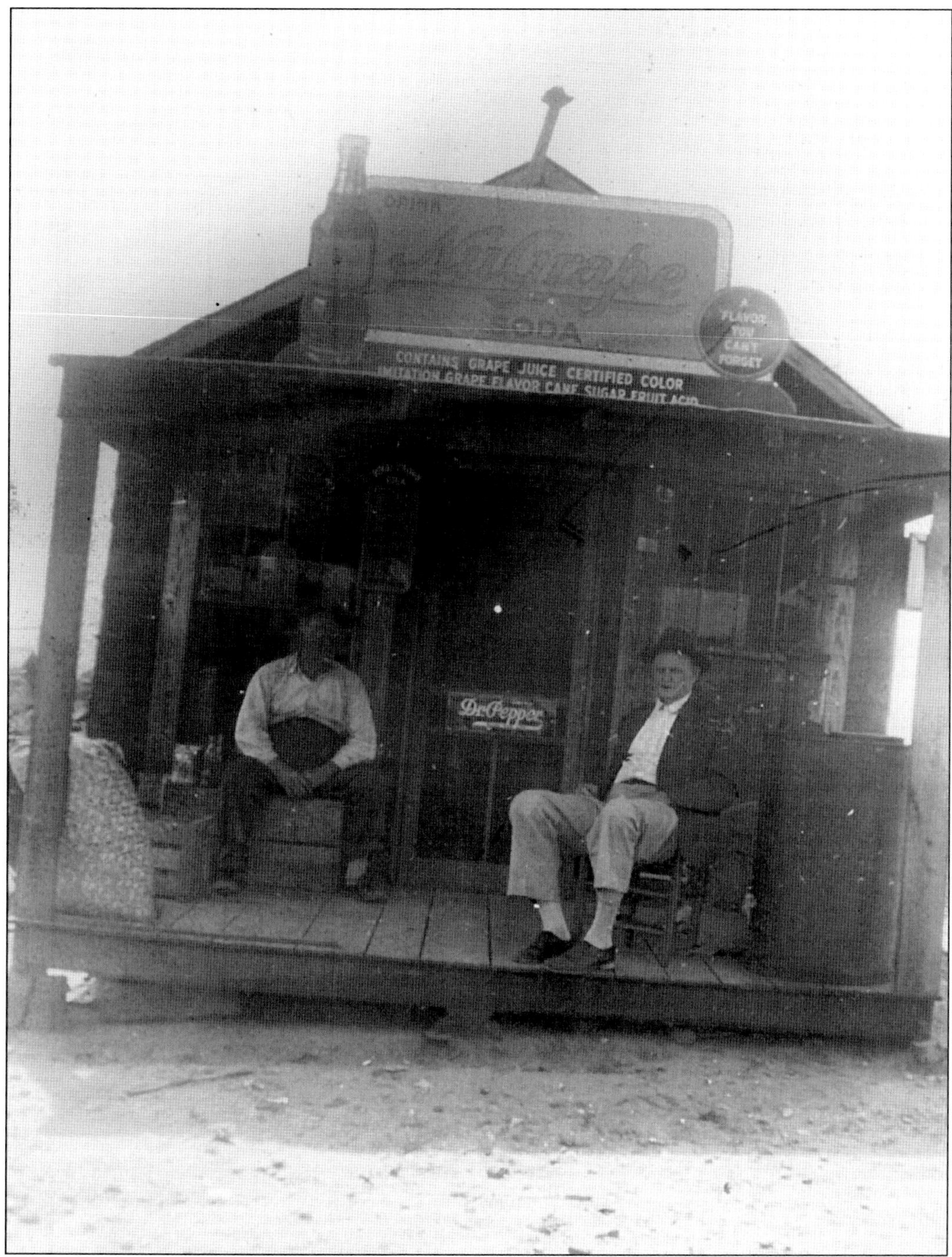

Due to the distance from town and a lack of reliable transportation, many neighborhoods had a grocer. Patrons could purchase laundry detergent, soft drinks, candy, and cooking oil nearby rather than having to walk into town. Burgess Grocery (pictured around 1945) was operated by Charlie W. Burgess (left) at the corner of West Eleventh and Carter Streets in West End–Cobb Town. When Burgess died in 1960, his widow, Minnie, continued to operate the store until the early 1970s. The man at right is not identified. (ERY.)

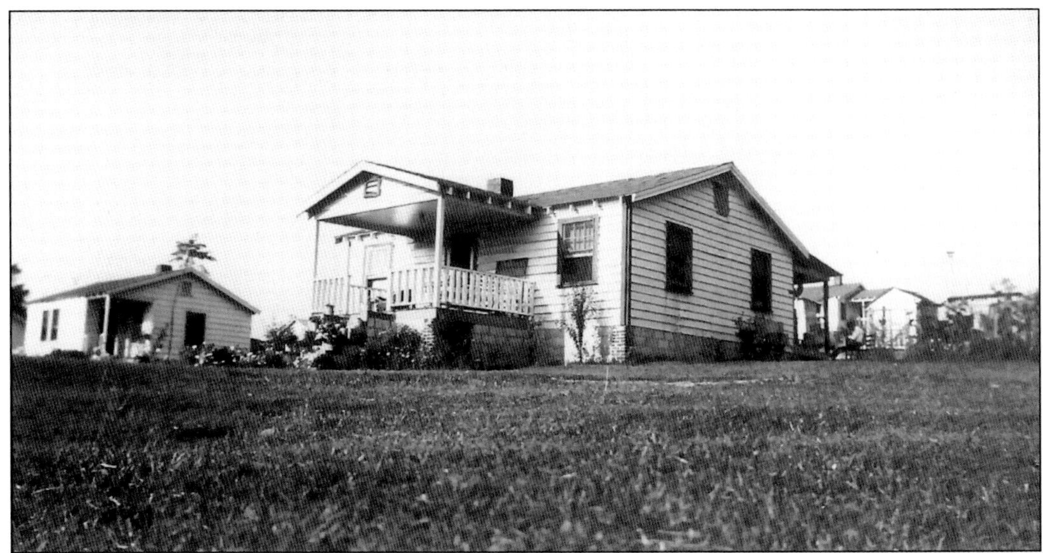

Blue Mountain grew during the 1940s to include new house construction. Shown here is Rice Avenue around 1945. Most people who lived in the town worked at the Blue Mountain Mill, which closed in 2000. In 2003, part of Blue Mountain was annexed into Anniston, while the remaining portion stayed an unincorporated part of Calhoun County. (ERY.)

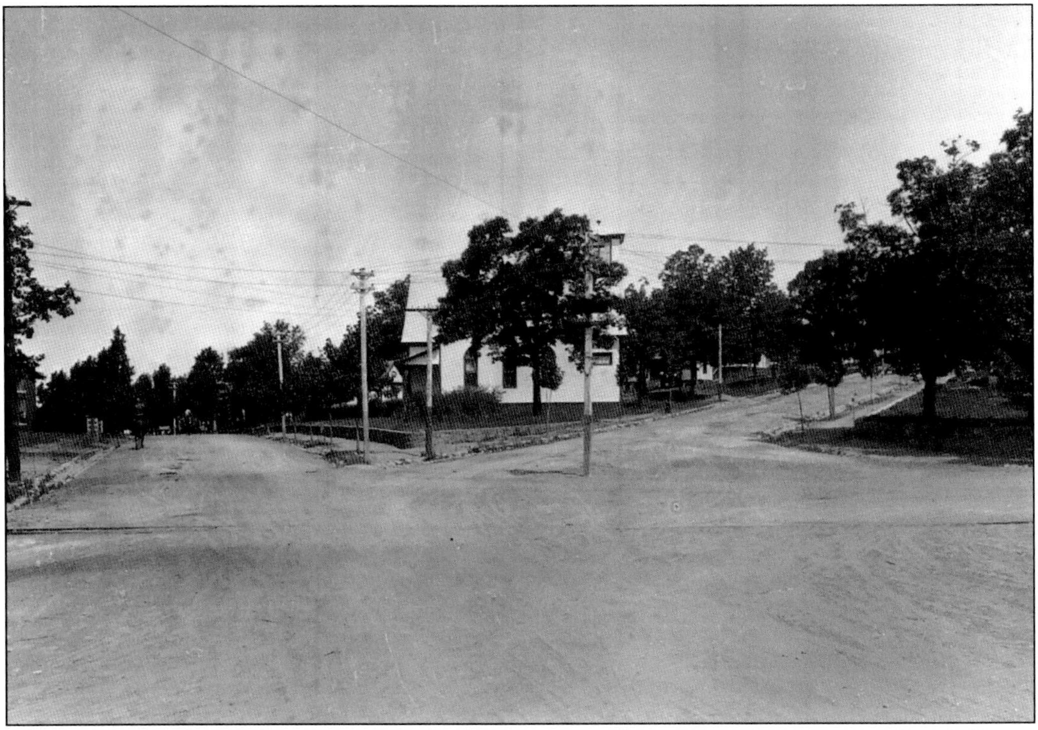

The Blue Mountain Mill (entrance at far left) was organized in 1897 as the American Net & Twine Company with one building and 100 workers producing cotton threads and twines. By 1928, the mill was operated as the Linen Thread Company, making threads, rope, and commercial fish and sports netting. The Blue Mountain Baptist Church (center), located across the street from the mill, was founded in 1903.

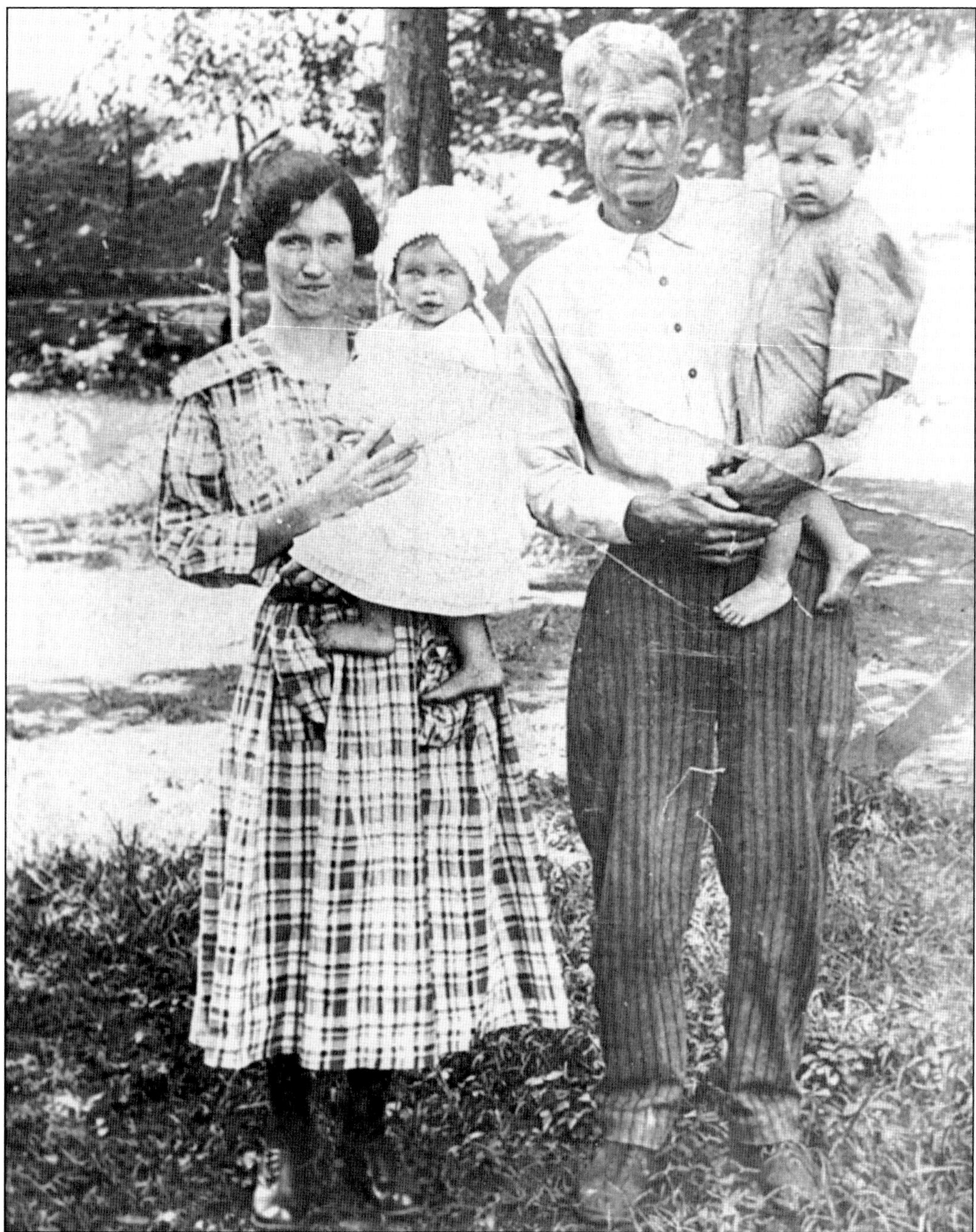

The Leatherwood Community, named for Zachariah Leatherwood, was an area northwest of Anniston. In the late 1890s, the area was called Fergusonville when the post office was established. The post office no longer existed after 1899, and the area reverted back to its original name when it began developing in the 1920s. By 1926, Leatherwood had a Baptist church, J.H. McQueen's store, and a blacksmith shop. Many of the inhabitants, like the Jake Miller family (shown around 1919), worked their farms for food and in the many textile mills and foundries in Anniston and Blue Mountain for income. The area grew when the Anniston Army Depot was built a few miles away during World War II. (ERY.)

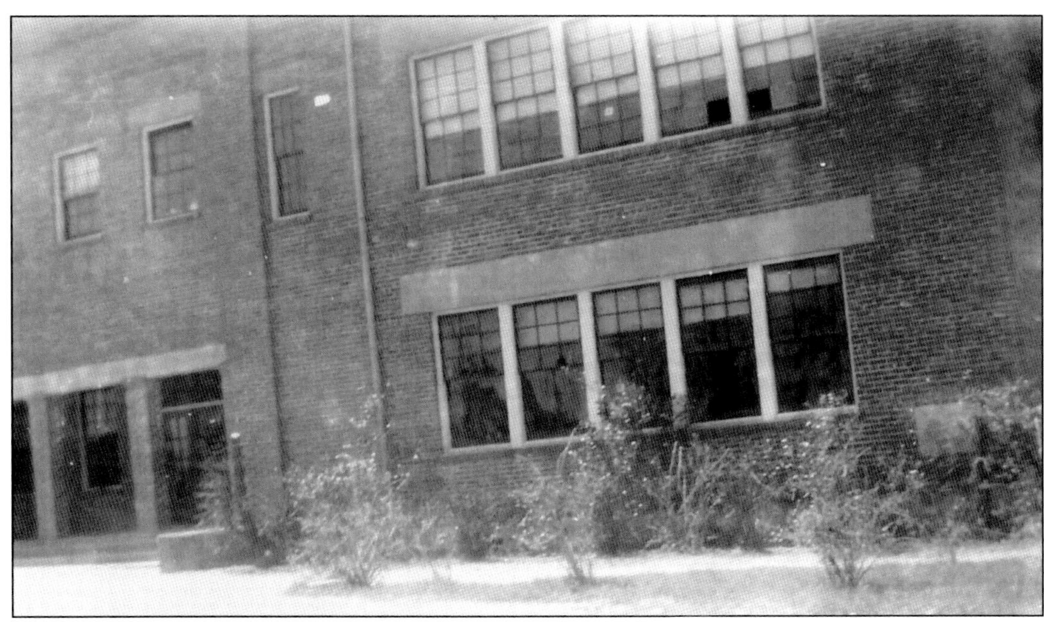

Alexandria had several private academies, but in May 1919, plans for a high school building began when D.P. Haynes and Miller Herrin donated five acres of land. To raise funds for construction, the community held plays, wrestling matches, and barbeques. In 1917, a three-mil ad valorem tax was also added. Rapid construction on the two-story brick building allowed classes to meet in August 1920, with students transported from Blue Mountain. Within three years, the school was overcrowded, so additional land was secured from W.L. McCullars to build more classrooms. A vocational education and home economics facility (shown below around 1945), with six classrooms and two offices, was added in 1928 and replaced in 1962. The original two-story brick high school (shown above around 1945) was demolished in 1966 to make way for a modern facility. (Both, ERY.)

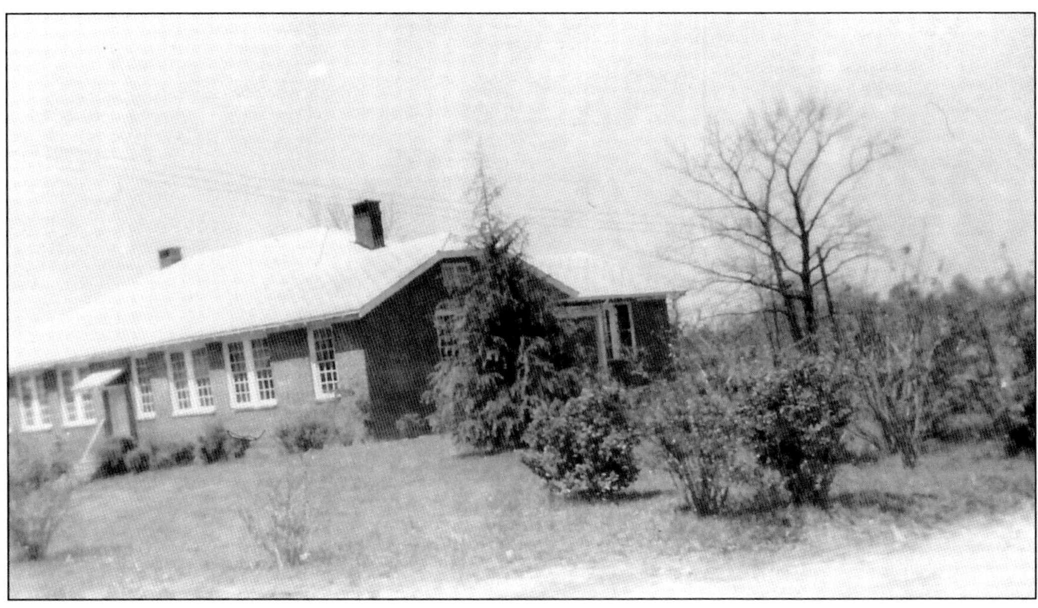

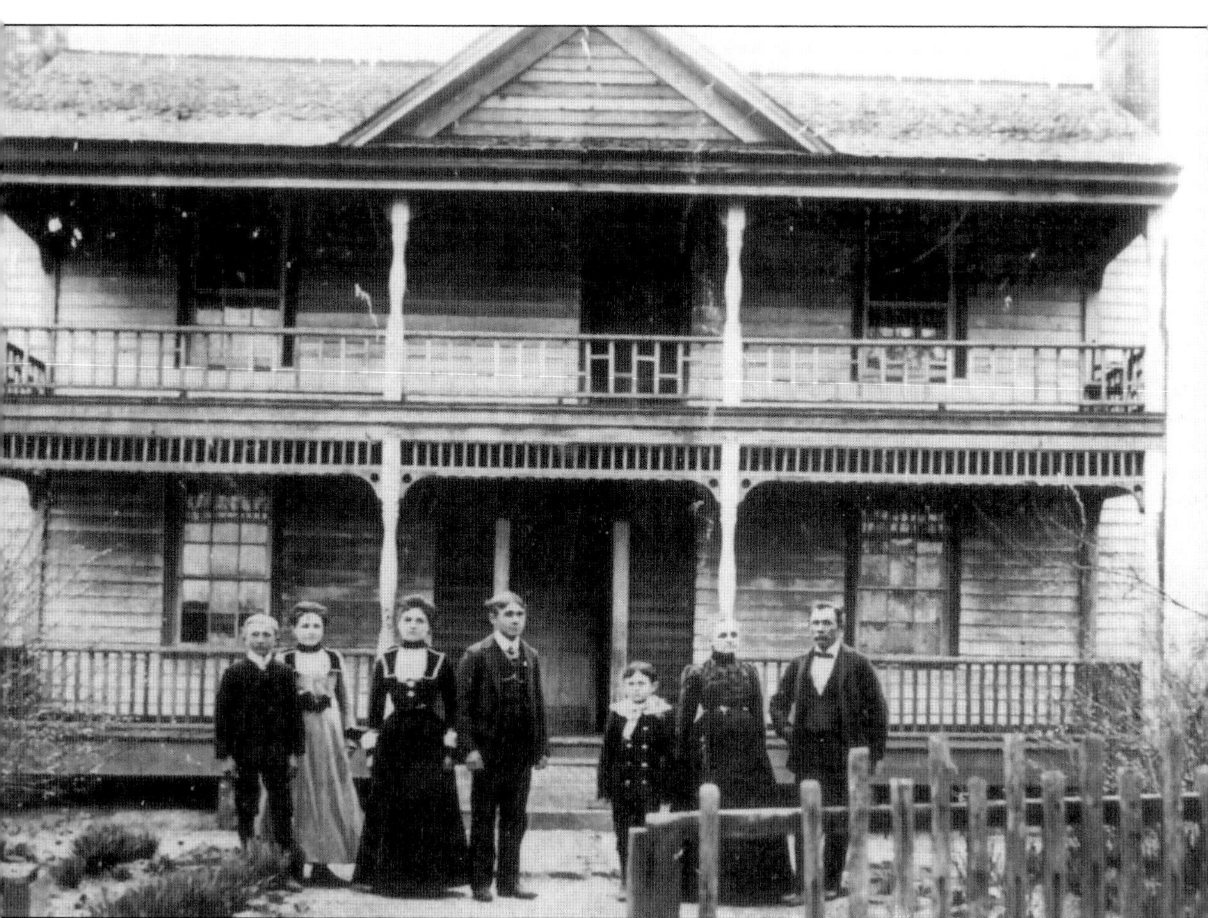

Silas Woodruff, a native of Spartanburg, South Carolina, moved to the Wellington area in the 1820s and built a two-story clapboard house. In the late 1800s, Robert W. Dickie purchased the home. In 1904, Dickie sold the house to the Ariail family. Some of the Dickie family remained in Wellington, including Mollie (second from left), who married W.G. Pearson. Dr. Emmett H. Dickie (fourth from left) became a prominent physician and member of the Murray County (Georgia) Memorial Hospital board of directors. From left to right are Bob, Mollie, Willie, Emmett, Shelley, Lou, and R.W. Dickie. (RPT.)

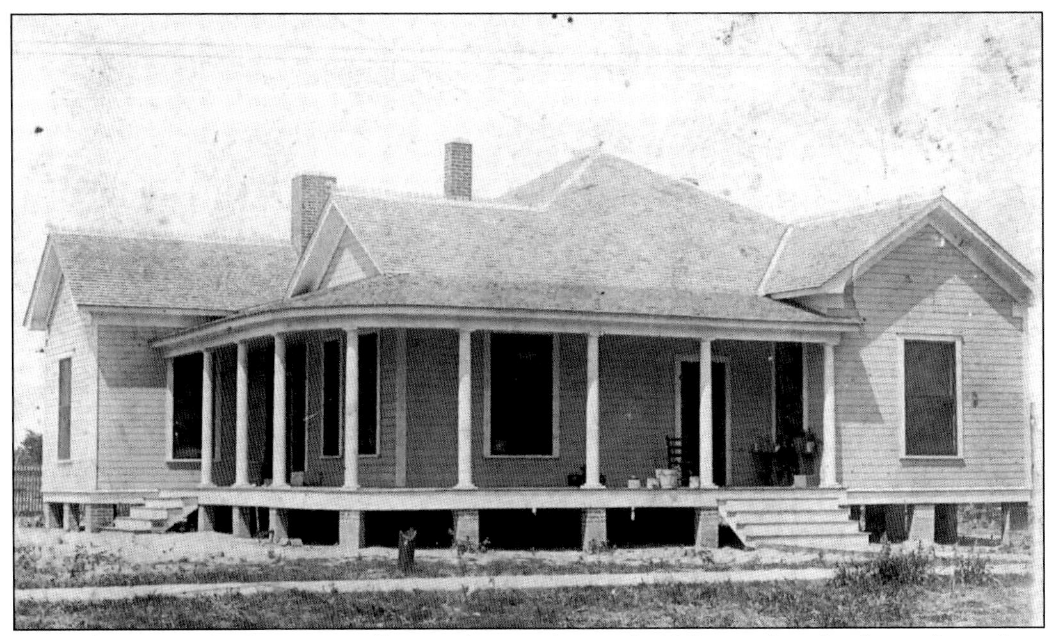

The Robert W. Dickie home in Wellington (pictured around 1905) was a boardinghouse for workers on both the L&N and Seaboard Air Line Railroads. Much of the Wellington community was affected when a tornado tore through the area in December 1954. The storm injured 12 people and destroyed the post office, stores, and many houses, including the boardinghouse. Wellington endured another powerful tornado in April 2011, which killed several people and damaged many homes. (RPT.)

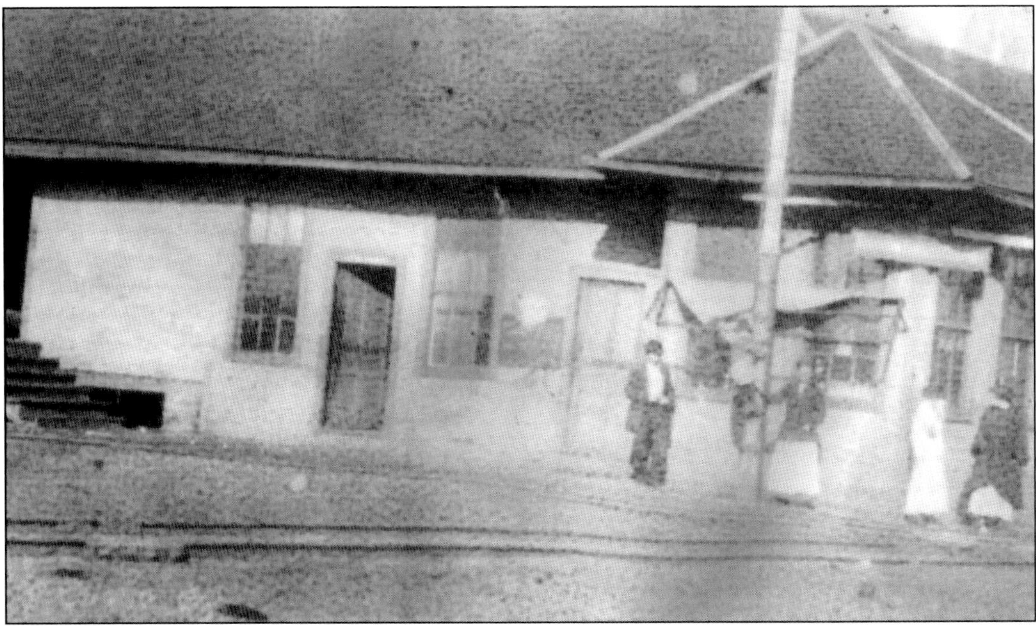

At Wellington, the Seaboard Air Line ran east to west and crossed the L&N mineral tracks. The L&N rail line ran north and south between Gadsden and Anniston. The train depot (pictured around 1908) survived the 1954 tornado, only to be torn down around 1966 when passenger and freight service ended. (RPT.)

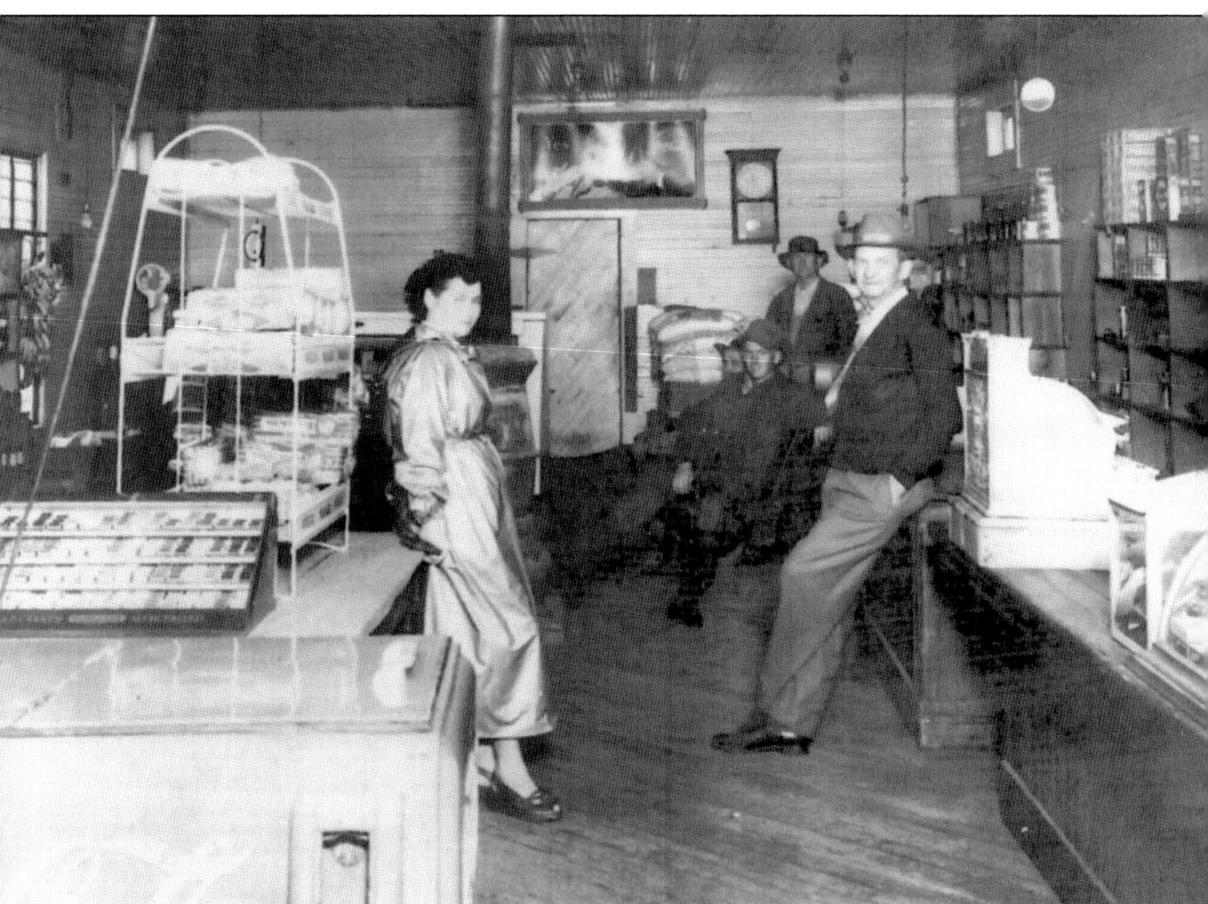

W.G. "Pop" Pearson (right) operated Pop Pearson's Store at the corner of Washington Avenue and Wellington Drive from 1945 until 1963. He is seen here in his store around 1945. The store served as a meeting place and was central to the community. In 1938, Pearson founded Pearson's Barbeque, later Pop's Barbeque, at 622 Leighton Avenue in Anniston. Pearson sold the business to Carl Thagard, who operated the restaurant from around 1951 until 1973. (RPT.)

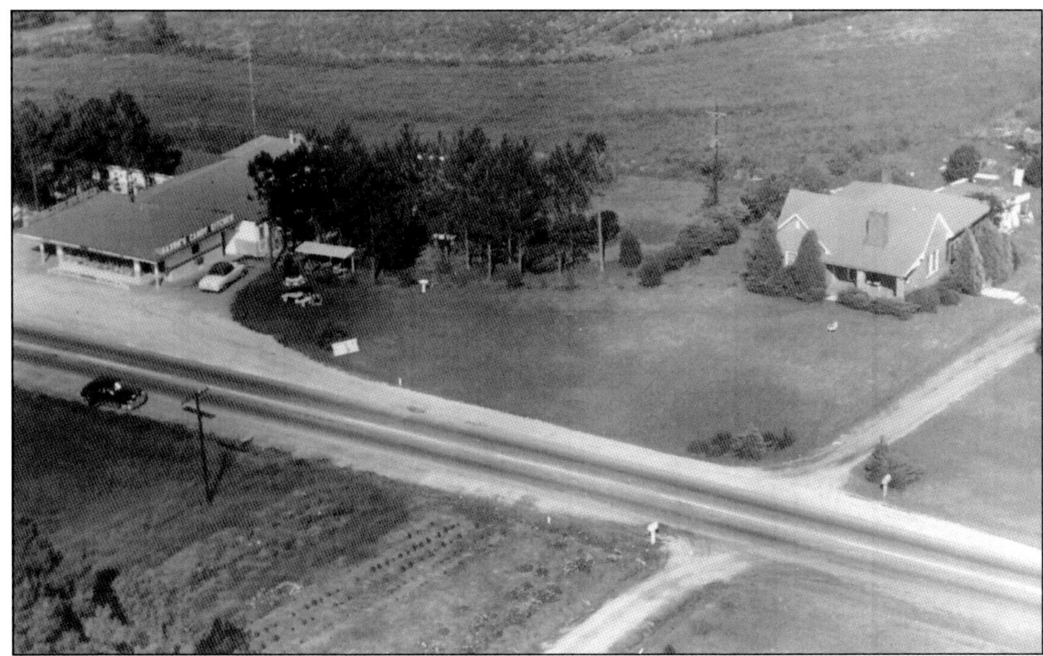

In 1939, Henry E. "H.E." Saxon and his wife, Cora, started Saxon's Candies, using recipes sold to them by Pop Kavenaugh. Throughout World War II the business was small, due to rationing of key ingredients such as sugar. The Saxons expanded the business to create the first roadside store, Saxon's Candy Box, in 1947. They built a larger store and home at Wellington on US 241, a highly traveled route to Florida. The store and home are seen above around 1950. As the candy gained popularity, Saxon's expanded into a series of chain stores in 1953 that included a souvenir shop and restaurant. In 1960, Saxon's opened a store at 1117 Noble Street, and the Wellington location became the home office and manufacturing plant. The creation of US 431 meant the route would go through the original Saxon's store, so a new manufacturing plant was built in 1966 off Highway 431. It is seen below during a snowstorm. In 1968, Henry was killed in an automobile crash. Cora continued to operate the store locations until the mid-1970s, when the business operated solely as a mail-order company. It ceased operation in 1988. (Both, SAX.)

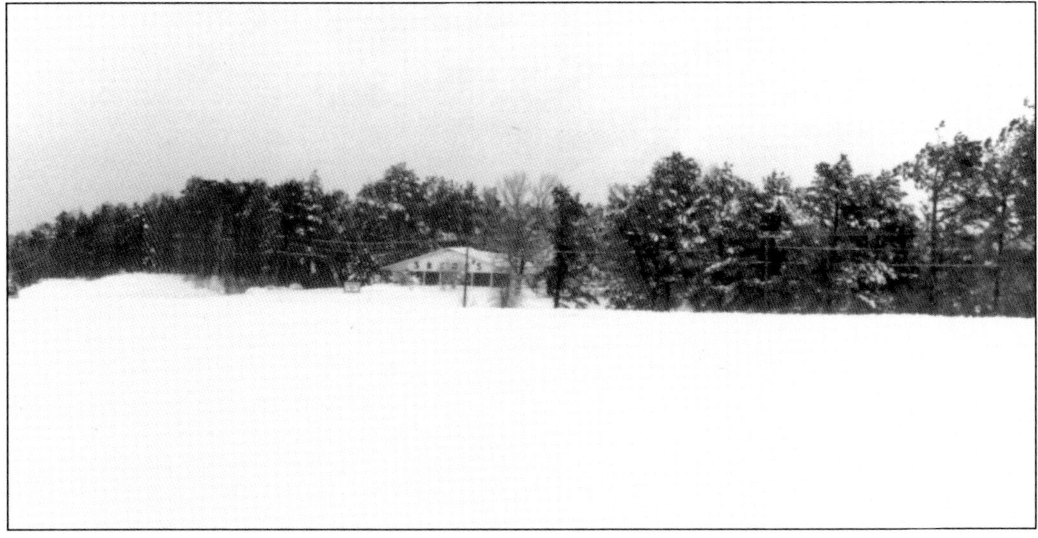

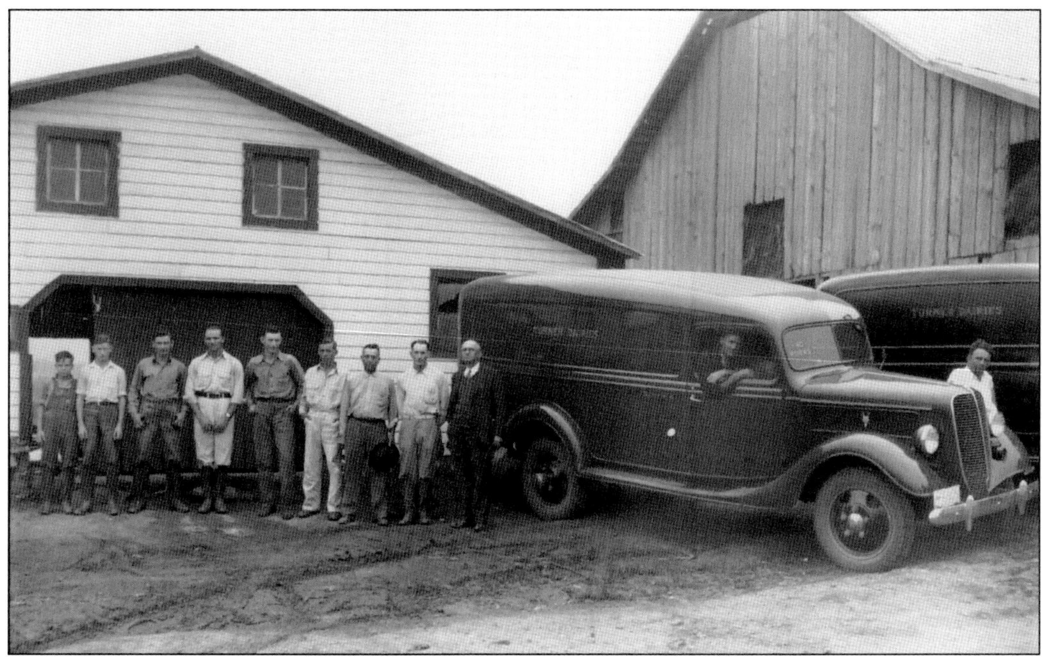

Turner Dairies was located at 591 Coldwater Road, near the Anniston airport. E.L. Turner and his family incorporated the dairy in March 1947 with $60,000 in capital. By 1951, the dairy operated as a Mello Dairy. The dairy maintained an office in the National Bank Building at 1101 Noble Street during the 1950s. Milk products made at the dairy were available for home delivery and at local grocery stores until the dairy ceased operations by 1977.

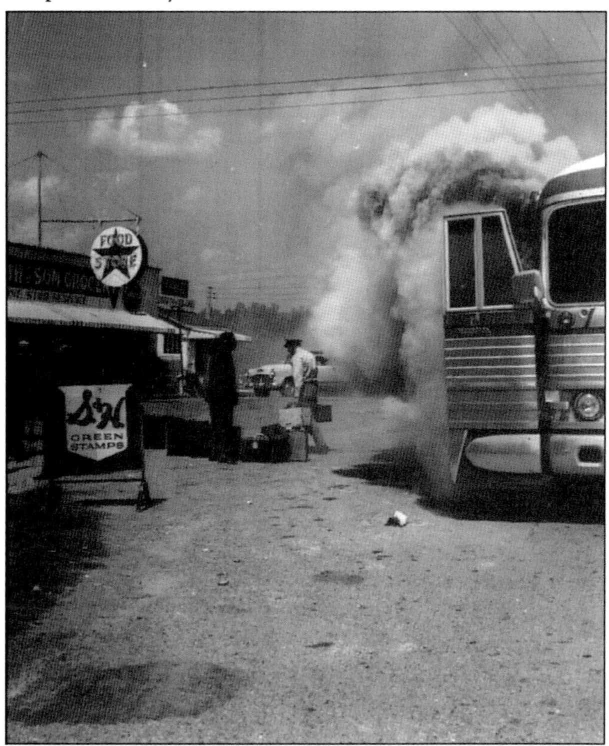

Forsyth & Son Grocery and service station, owned by Richard Edward Forsyth Sr. from 1932 to 1974, was located on the Birmingham Highway, approximately five miles from town. In May 1961, Freedom Riders attempting to integrate the interstate transportation system were forced off the road at Forsyth's, due to flat tires on the Greyhound bus. A mob surrounded the bus and tossed a bundle of flaming rags through the vehicle's broken window. After escaping the burning bus, several of the Freedom Riders were beaten by the mob. A federal grand jury in Birmingham indicted nine men for the crime, but none were ever convicted. (PLACC.)

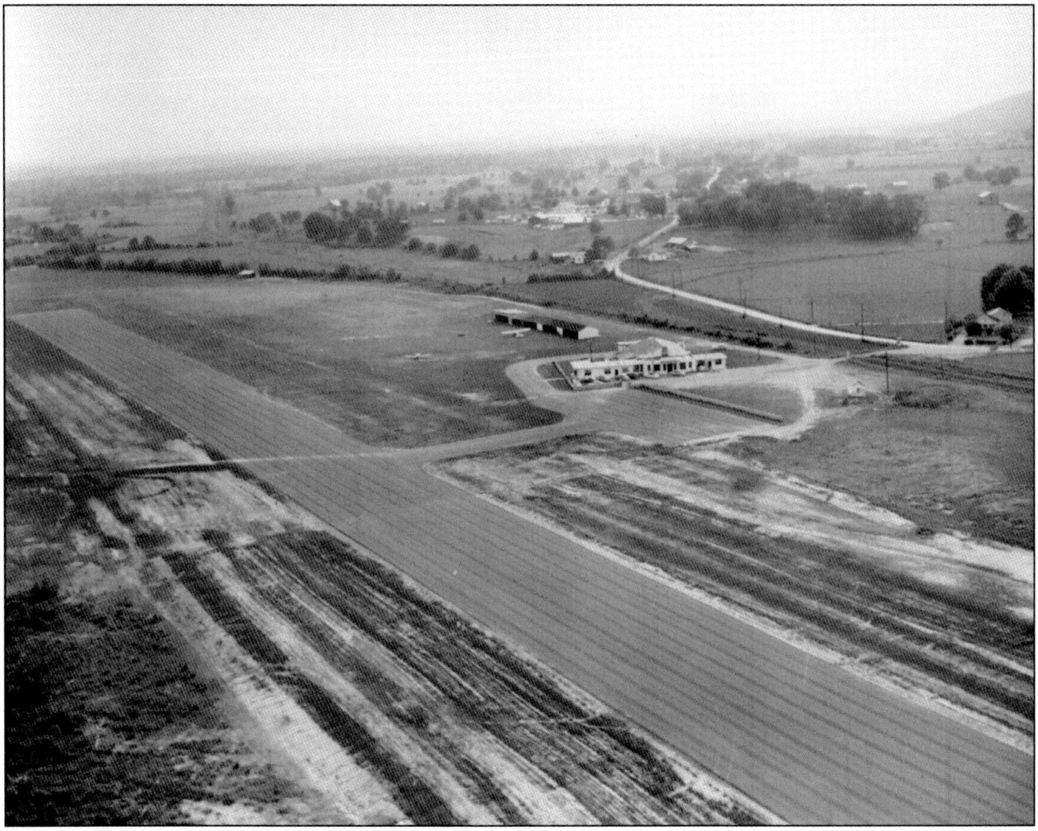

The Anniston Regional Airport, located within the Oxford City limits, was created in 1921 by the Anniston Exchange Club. In 1928, the airport operated as an emergency landing field. Using WPA funds, the Anniston Airport Board expanded and upgraded the field (pictured around 1940). The terminal, built in 1966, was used for commuter service until 1996, when the airport was maintained as an uncontrolled field. The facilities accommodated pilots with fuel, hangar space, and workstations, as well as runways capable of landing a C-5.

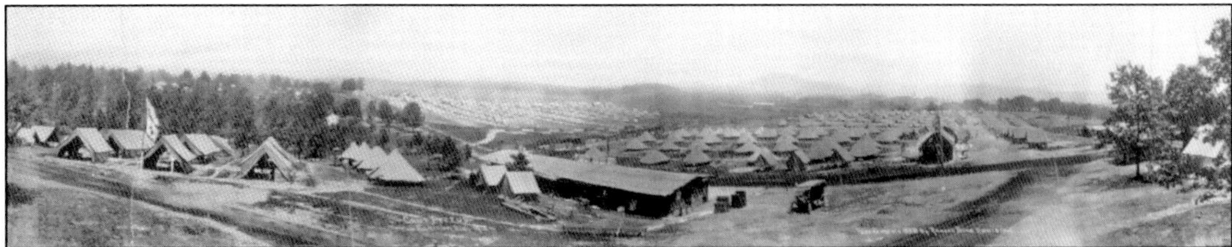

Camp Pettus, under the command of Col. John T. VanOrsdale, was established approximately two miles from Anniston to serve as the training area for the Southern States Maneuvers. From July 6 to August 4, 1912, National Guardsmen from Alabama, South Carolina, North Carolina, Tennessee, Florida, Georgia, and Kentucky arrived for mock battles and drills. The 17th Infantry Regiment and 11th Cavalry stayed the entire month, but the militias were only required to spend 10 days in the "tent city." (LOC.)

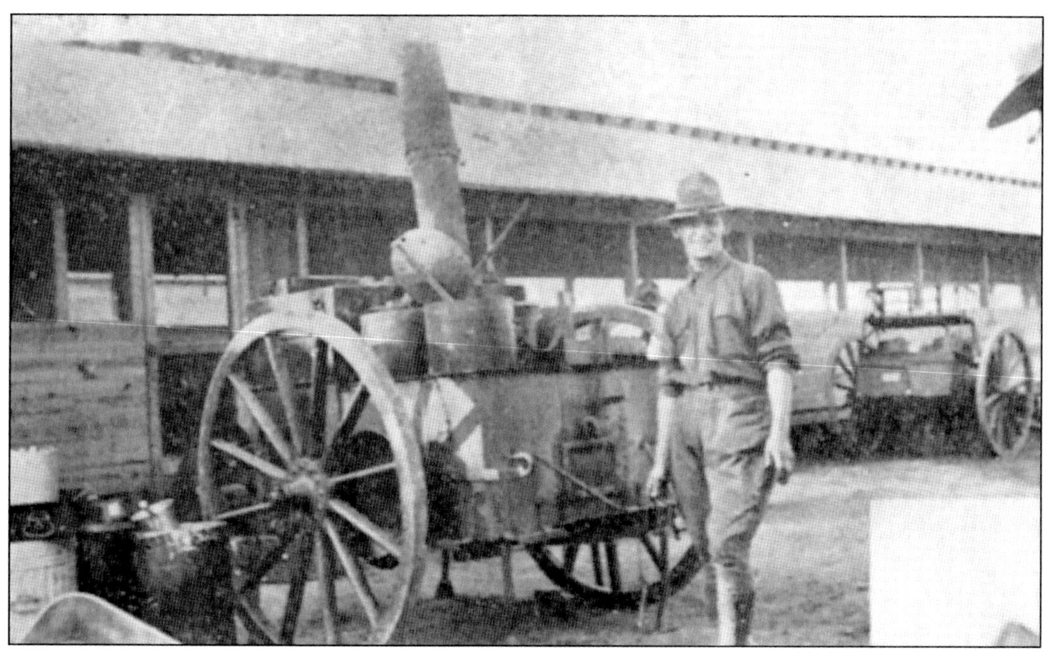

Camp McClellan, named for Gen. George B. McClellan, was designated a World War I mobilization camp. Construction started in July 1917, and by the end of the war, the camp boasted 1,551 wooden structures. In the summer, soldiers were housed in both wooden structures and tents. Field kitchens, such as those shown in the above photograph around 1917, were equipped to feed 500 men each. Shown below, temporary field hospitals were among the wooden structures constructed on post. (Both, PLACC.)

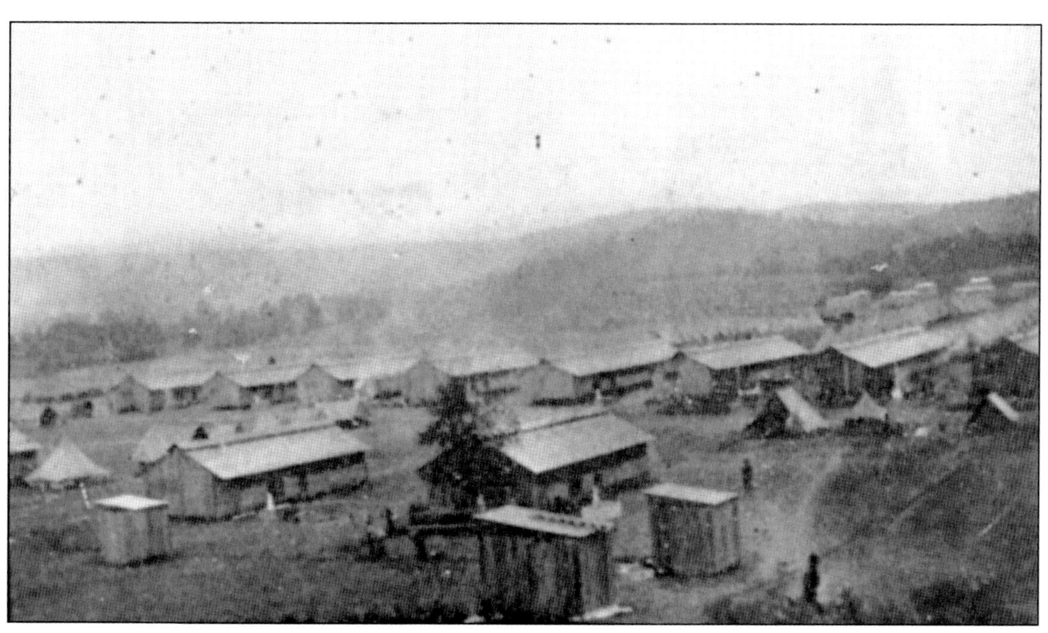

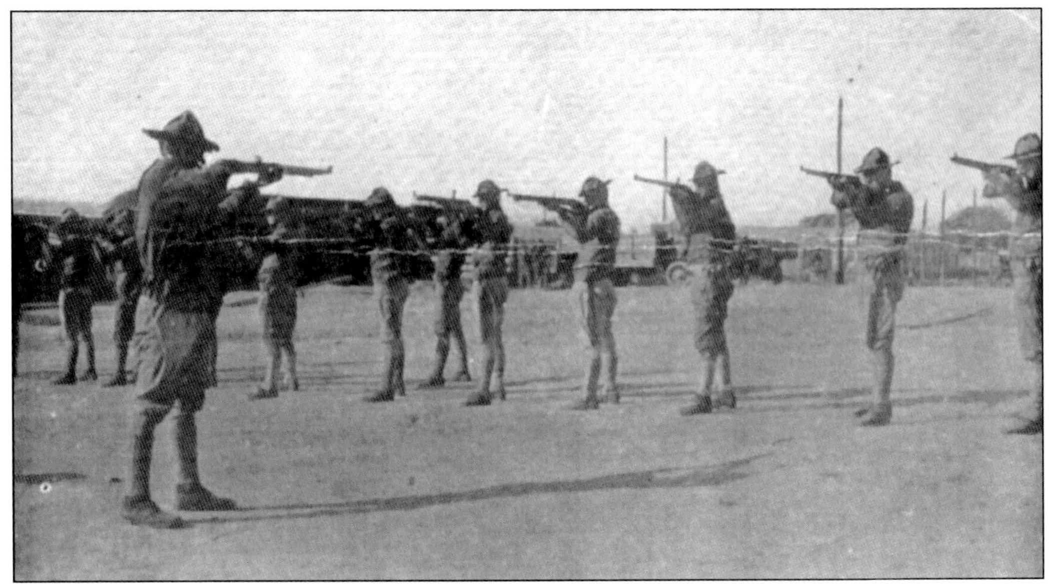

The 29th National Guard Division from the Mid-Atlantic states arrived in mid-1917. A short time later, other troops arrived at the camp, including the 6th Division, 157th Depot Brigade, 11th and 12th Training Battalions, and 1st, 2nd, and 3rd Development Regiments, as well as the Maryland 1st Separate Negro Company. The camp boasted an aviation field, machine-gun and rifle ranges (pictured around 1917), remount depot, sewage plant, and machine-gun camp. (RPT.)

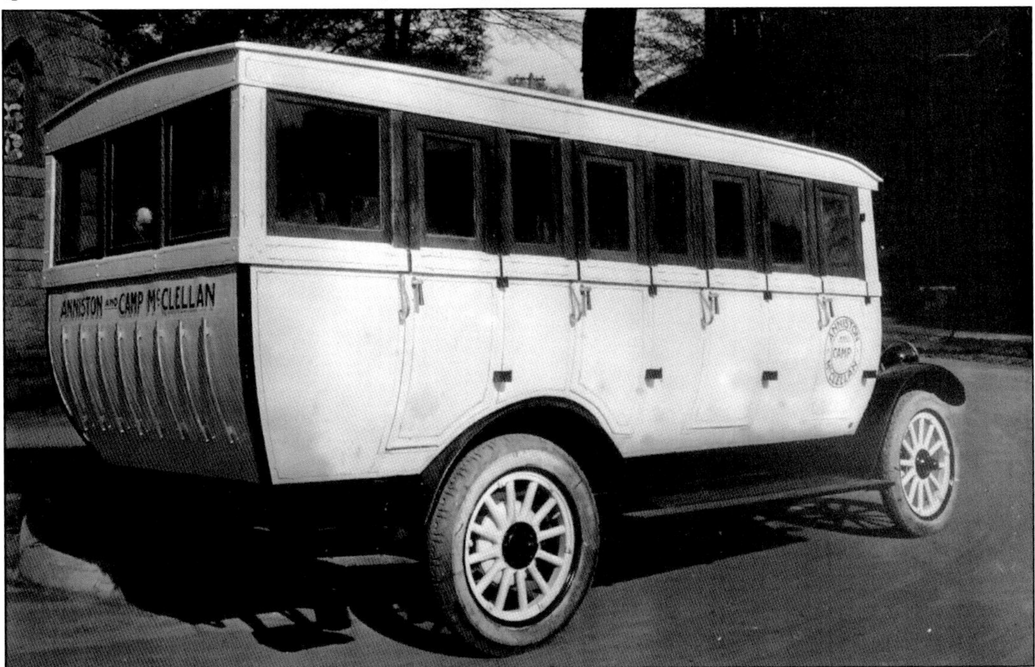

Anniston's support of the military had been evident from the start. In June 1917, when the government needed the property immediately, farmers had to vacate the land and lose their crops. When the US Congress failed to react quickly, Anniston underwrote the cost of the farmers' crops. Anniston believed business would be generated by the camp, including locally made buses, such as this one, shown around 1920 at Twelfth Street and Quintard Avenue.

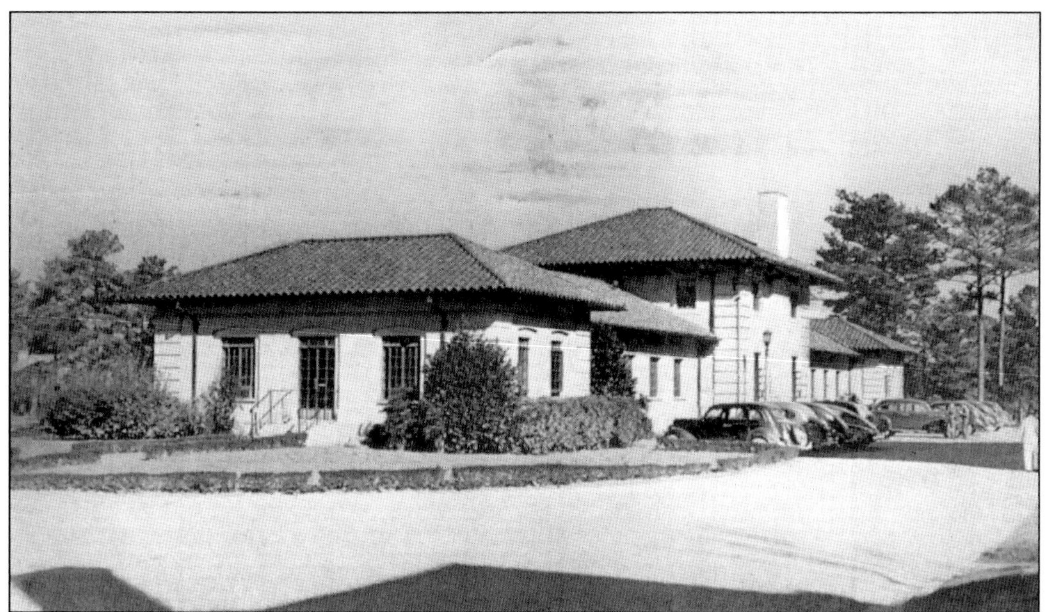

In 1929, McClellan was designated a permanent Regular Army post, which led to new construction and growth on the base. The fort was designed for an infantry regiment, with a standard layout for a civilian training summer camp. The post headquarters area, known as "The Hill," was constructed in the Spanish Colonial Revival style, with a combination of administrative and residential functions. Buckner Hall (pictured around 1939), located at 61 Buckner Circle and completed in 1934, served as the main post headquarters. (ERY.)

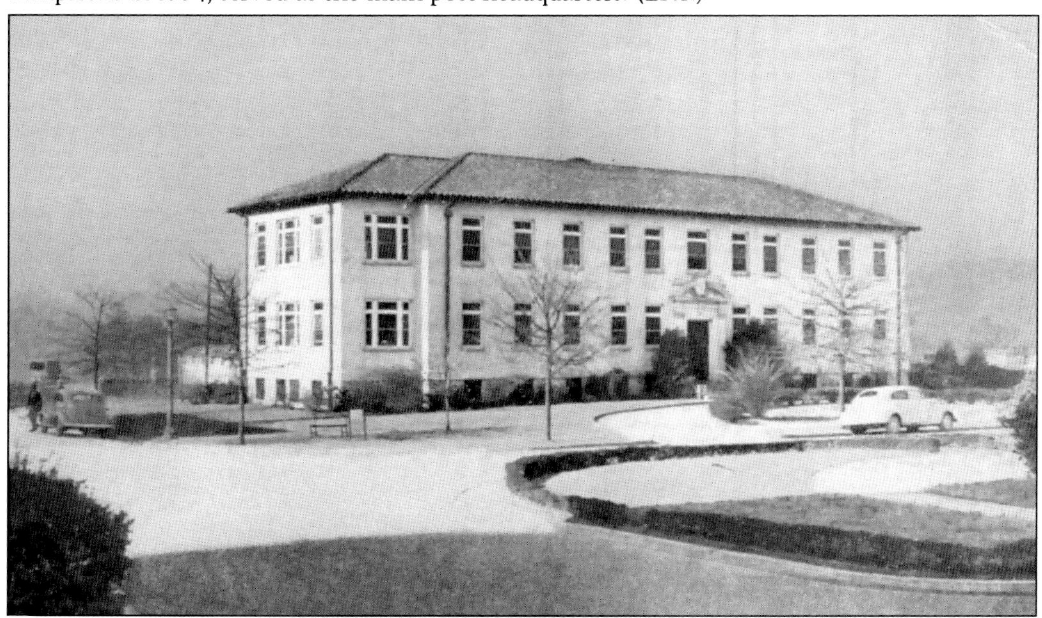

The Patton Building, constructed in 1931 on Buckner Circle, served as the base hospital. It is shown here around 1935. During World War II, hospital wards were built in another area, so the building housed a Special Army Treatment Center and a morgue until 1955. In 1985, the provost marshal and military police office occupied the building, and a jail was added. Since 1999, the building has served as multiuse office space. (ERY.)

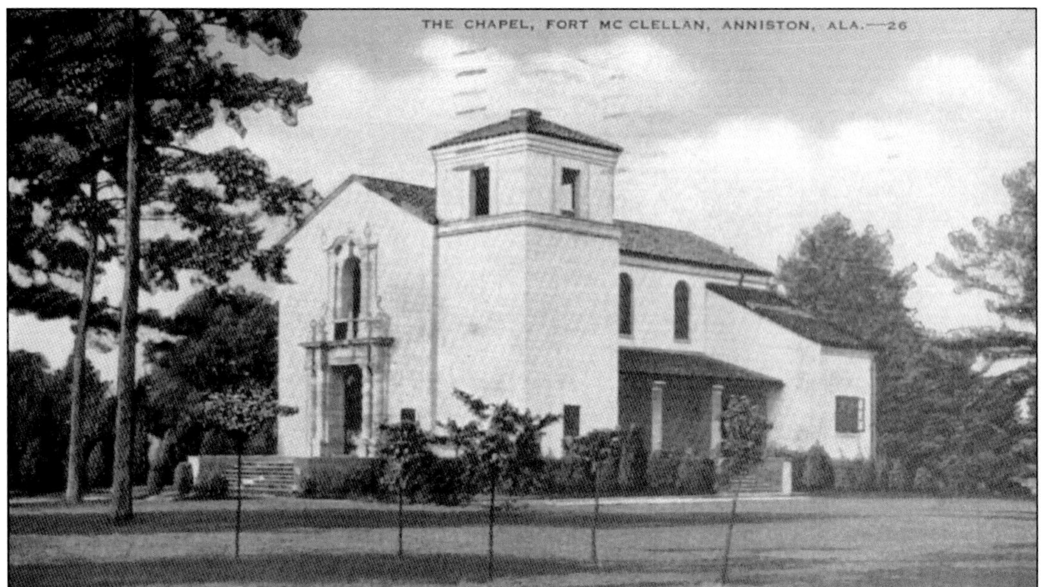

Churches were built throughout the post. During World War II, some of the chapels, such as Piney Woods, were built to be temporary houses of worship in the training areas. Permanent chapels were also built, including the Soldier's Chapel near Galloway Gate, the Centurion Chapel near Summerall Gate, and the Silver Chapel (pictured around 1936) on Buckner Circle. (ERY.)

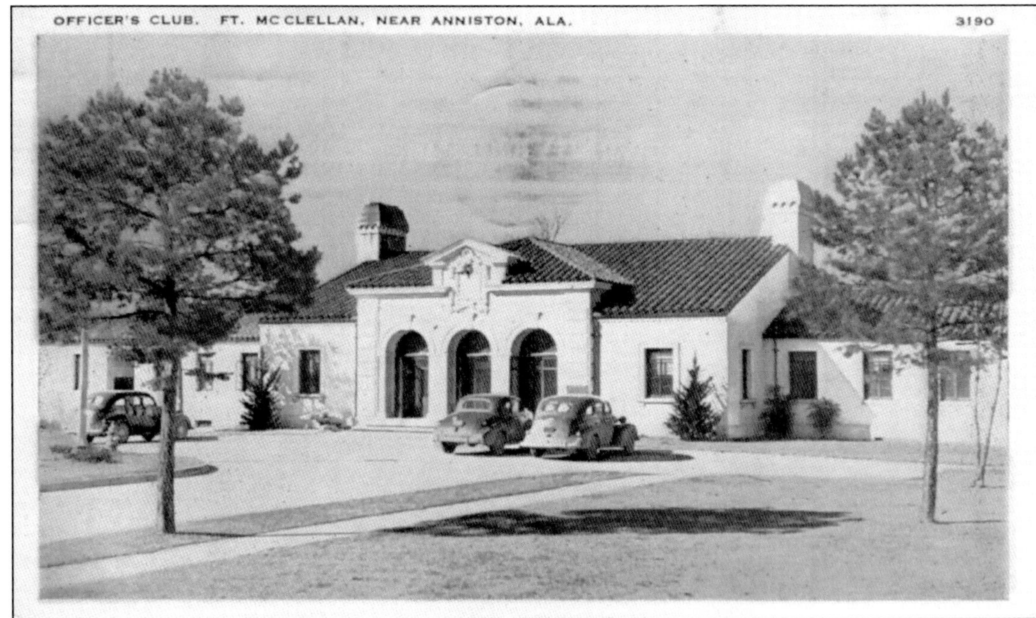

Remington Hall Officer's Club was constructed on Buckner Circle in 1936 using WPA funds. The building housed the bachelor officers' quarters and later served as the Officer's Open Mess. The 22nd Infantry Regiment named the Officer's Club in honor of Second Lt. Philip Remington, who was credited with killing Philippine rebel leader Datu Ali in 1905. During World War II, the building was renovated and the German prisoners of war housed at Fort McClellan were credited with carving the bar and painting murals in the lounge area. Since 1999, the building has remained closed except for a brief period when it served as a restaurant. (ERY.)

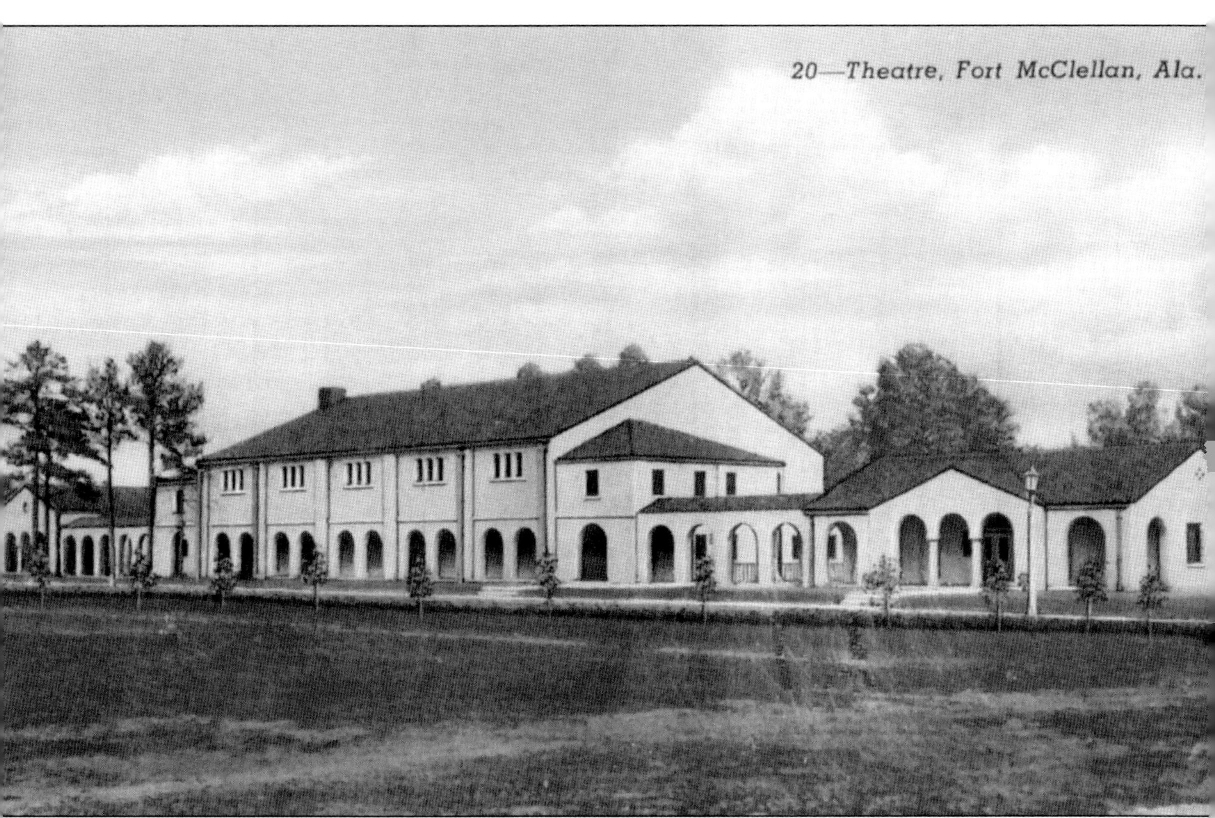

Built in 1936, the Recreation Center was constructed using WPA funds dedicated to making improvements at Fort McClellan. The complex consisted of three buildings connected by a colonnade. Seen here around 1936, the structures are, from left to right, a movie theater, gymnasium, and the enlisted men's service club. After the fort closed, the buildings were renovated to serve as a theater, exhibit hall, and meeting space. (ERY.)

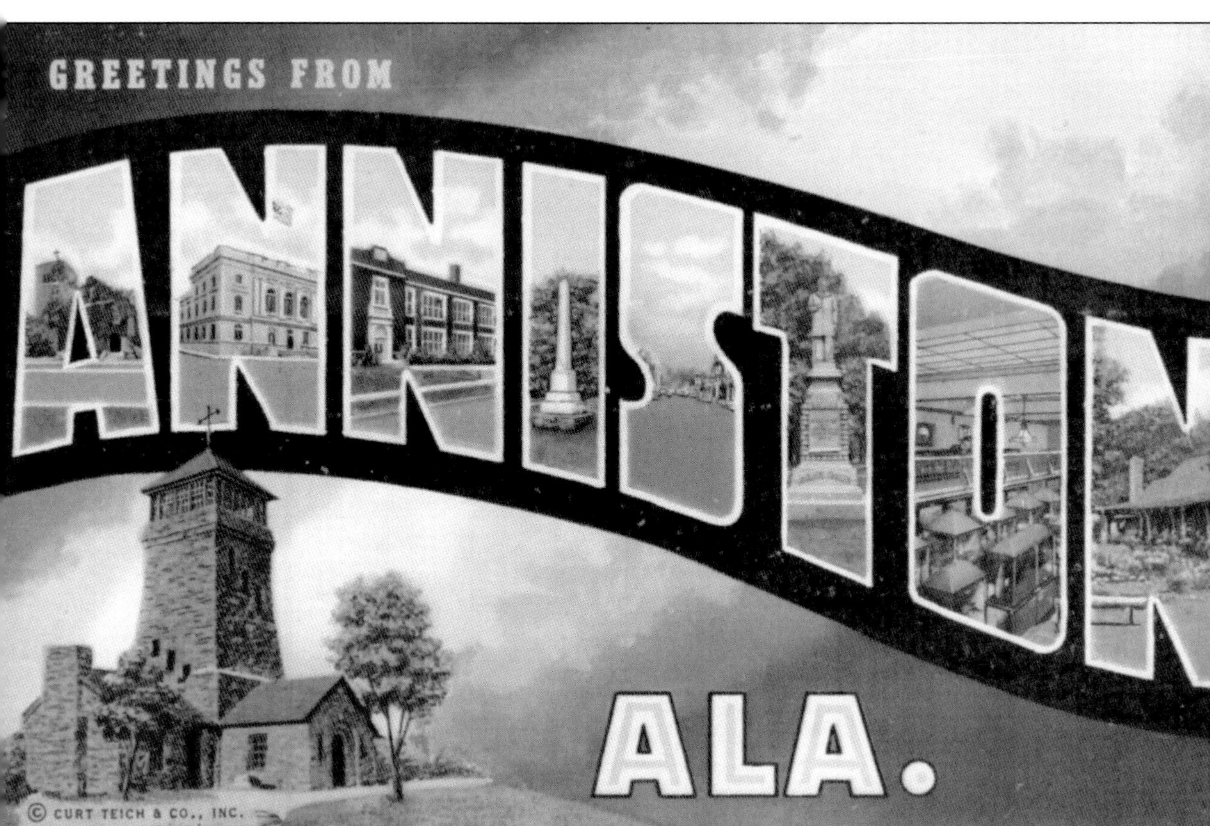

In 2015, Anniston faces an uncertain future. The city has lost many of its early buildings to fire, neglect, and destruction. There has been limited restoration of the remaining historic buildings. Since 1999, the city's population has steadily declined. The economy has suffered due to the loss of jobs and business from Fort McClellan as well as the 2008 recession. With completion of the Eastern Bypass, traffic from I-20 will be routed around the city to US 431. It is unknown if Anniston will return to "The Model City" it was at her apex. (ERY.)

Bibliography

Anniston City Directory. Anniston, AL: 1887–1903.

Anniston City Directory. Birmingham, AL: R.L. Polk & Co., 1904–2014.

Anniston Diamond Jubilee, Inc. *Anniston Diamond Jubilee, Commemorating Seventy-Five Years of Progress*. Anniston, AL: Higginbotham and Sawyer, 1958.

Anniston Files. Alabama Room, Calhoun County Public Library.

Anniston Star. 1900–2015.

Anniston Star 75th Anniversary Edition. November 20, 1957.

Entire, Robert, ed. *Anniston, Alabama Centennial 1883–1983, Commemorative Book and Centennial Program*. Anniston, AL: Higginbotham's Inc., 1983.

Reed, Mary Beth, Charles E. Cantley, and J.W. Joseph. *Fort McClellan: A Popular History*. Stone Mountain, GA: New South Associates, 1996.

Consistent with our mission to preserve history on a local level, this book was printed in South Carolina on American-made paper and manufactured entirely in the United States. Products carrying the accredited Forest Stewardship Council (FSC) label are printed on 100 percent FSC-certified paper.

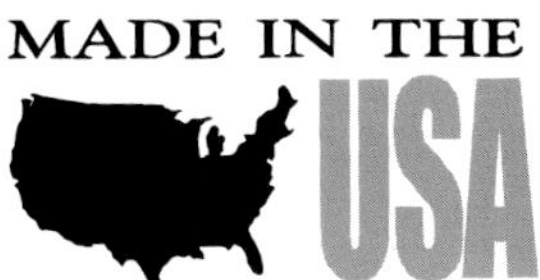